# The JOYS of ENTERTAINING

BEVERLY REESE CHURCH AND BETHANY EWALD BULTMAN

# *The* JOYS *of* ENTERTAINING

ABBEVILLE PRESS · PUBLISHERS · NEW YORK

Library of Congress
Cataloging-in-Publication Data
Bultman, Bethany Ewald.

    The joys of entertaining.
    Bibliography: p.
    Includes index.
    1. Entertaining.   I. Church,
Beverly Reese. II. Title.
GV1471.B965      1987
793.2        87-1146
ISBN 0-89659-752-0


Frontispiece photograph: HIMMEL
Photograph this page: JEFFERY

Editor: Regina Kahney
Copyeditor: Virginia Croft
Production manager: Dana Cole
Illustrator: Philippe Weisbecker
Designer: James Wageman

To our husbands, who have been supportive and understanding.

To our sons, who have survived and thrived in spite of it.

To our fathers, who taught us joy.

To our mothers, who showed us how to entertain with grace and style.

# CONTENTS

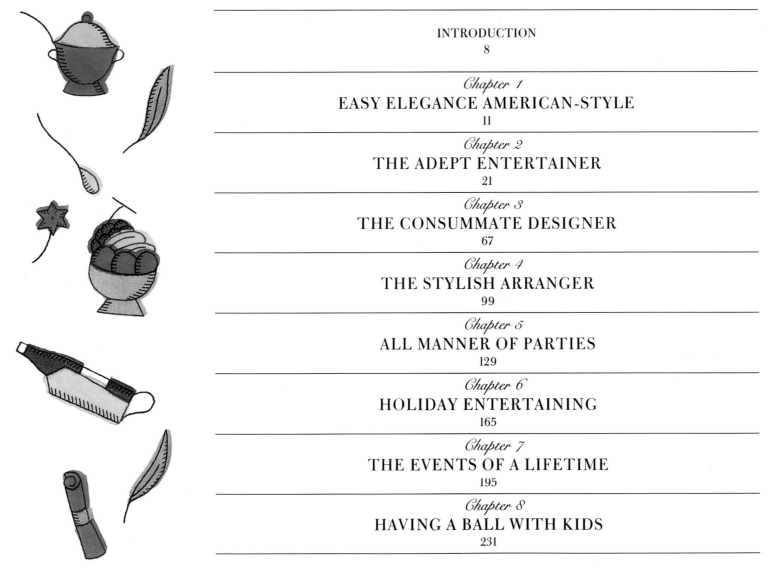

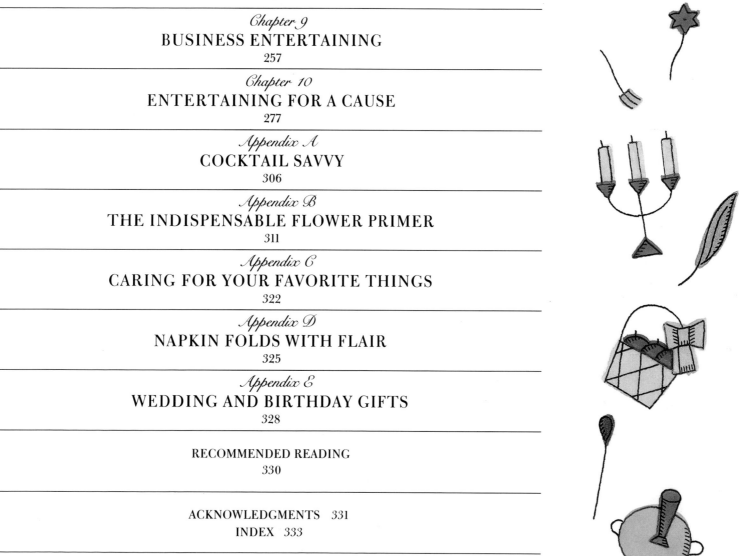

# INTRODUCTION

You may wonder why two busy women with diverse interests, and from completely different fields, would want to team up to write a reference book on entertaining. The answer is very simple: We wanted to write the book that we needed ourselves to help us deal with the numerous entertaining dilemmas that always faced us—and that may yet materialize! By pooling our widely varying experiences and imaginations, we came to realize that there was more than one solution to any problem. What emerged from our conversations and research was this book full of information, ideas, solutions, and realism.

Despite our different points of view, we share the same concept: The greatest gift you can give your friends is being yourself. The ability to share your personality with others, like the ability to appreciate fine art, is not an inborn talent. Rather, it is learned from sharing life's experiences. A ready ear, a keen eye for detail, a willingness to please, careful attention to the comforts of guests, and an ability to laugh at life's mischief are the components of successful entertaining.

Three years of research and more than two hundred interviews with people all over America have combined to create a book about style and elegance tempered with a strong dose of reality. We've interviewed many a successful hostess who can drive a car-pool at five and preside over a multimillion-dollar fund-raiser at six that lands her in the "Eye" column of *W*. Along the way we spent hours talking with people who entertain confidently, people we sat next to on planes or met in the checkout line at the grocery store, old school chums, magazine editors, party planners, floral designers, renowned decorators, and movie stars. The oldest person we interviewed was ninety-six, the youngest was four. There was one well-known hostess who told us that giving parties was like having babies: "Nature helps you forget everything but the happy part."

We have isolated several American party-giving styles that characterize the way in which those we interviewed like to entertain. These are the nuts and bolts that help you imagine and make real the style you love best. Pick the one which is closest to the way you like (or would like) to entertain, and keep it uppermost in your mind as you read this book. The result will be an enhancement of your own personal entertaining style. It is *your* taste that is the crucial factor for your success.

All those we interviewed had at least one party disaster to share with us. We created "The Adept Entertainer" to forewarn and guide the host through every facet and pitfall of party-giving.

Style and finesse should be a breeze after reading "The Consummate Designer" and "The Stylish Arranger." Here we show you the styling tips used in magazines, but we tell you how to do them by utilizing all of the resources you may have forgotten you had.

"All Manner of Parties," "Holiday Entertaining," and "The Events of a Lifetime" are primarily for those who are tired of giving the same old party. As lifestyles have changed so have the ways in which people approach entertaining for traditional events.

We both have a ball with our children and

their pals, so for this section of the book we interviewed many children. Several pediatricians, parents, teachers, and child psychologists participated in helping us solve the real-life problems that occur when big people try to create fun for little- and middle-sized people. There isn't an idea in the chapter, however, that we didn't "kid test" before including.

The chapter on corporate entertaining was gleaned from many a corporate chief who told us of his or her uncertain progress on the path to self-assurance and success. Imagine having to plan a party for strangers that could make or break a big deal! This is a reality to many professionals today; it need not be traumatic.

By the time you get to the fund-raising chapter, you should be ready to tackle any large-scale project. Friends all over America have shared their fund-raising expertise with us, so novice and pro alike will find at least a few tips to add a bit of sparkle to the occasional party or the social event of the year. There's a wealth of inspiration on every level of gracious living.

The appendixes are a compendium of the information that you might be able to find in other books—but which ones? Well, it's all here for you in the ultimate source book for entertaining—all of the information you need to know to set up the bar, order the flowers, buy the gifts, and clean your linens afterward. Have fun, be yourself, and don't worry—your next party will be a raging success!

—*Bethany and Beverly*

# *Chapter 1*
# EASY ELEGANCE AMERICAN-STYLE

*T*oday's American entertaining style was born of practicality mixed with finesse, decorum tempered by originality, and old world tradition mixed with a bit of wit. More than ever, successful parties express the energy, individuality, and confidence of the giver rather than the ability to conform to rules. It does not matter whether the party takes place in a studio apartment, on a grand estate, or under the shade of a tree. ❧ Just

 because many of us do not have the time or the help to iron, shine, polish, cook, and clean does not mean that we have forsaken gracious entertaining. What we lack in resources we make up for in style. Those who have converted their dining rooms into home offices or even exercise areas have discovered that they can entertain just as elegantly on the lawn or around the fireplace in the living room. All it takes is imagination and some advance preparation. Events can be streamlined so that the host can have as much fun as the guest. ◈ Our lifestyles are ever changing. We have moved from a strictly couples-oriented society to one that enjoys the company of single, divorced, and widowed friends, both as party guests and party givers. Entertaining—the way in which we share ourselves with other people—can be done by anyone, on any budget. Whether you have just moved into your first house or a tiny apartment in a new city, the essence of you—yourself, your imagination, your interest in others—in short, your hospitality—is the same.

*Why serve tea indoors on a beautiful day? Instead, enjoy the company of good friends in a casual garden setting.*
SCHLVZ

The American spirit of individuality and ingenuity can be seen in the many and varied ways in which we choose to entertain. From that first American party in 1621, when Plymouth Colony's governor William Bradford invited Wampanoag Indian chief Nassasoit to dinner and the chief showed up with ninety extra braves, five deer, and some popcorn slathered in maple syrup, to the current vogue for exuberant charity galas, American party givers have developed a host of entertaining formats to reflect their myriad personalities.

## The Impromptu Celebrant
Driving past a gorgeous display of produce at a vegetable stand, a Connecticut man is compelled to stop. On impulse, he buys baskets of several varieties of apples. As he munches on a crisp, tart McCoun, he is so dazzled by the taste that he decides his pleasure must be shared. Before returning home, he adds several bottles of wine and a hunk of good, sharp Cheddar to his purchases.

At home, he lights a roaring fire, pours a glass of wine, and gets on the telephone. Half an hour later, several friends have joined him. Some are in the kitchen making baked apples, pies, and fritters, while the others make a meal of apples and cheese in front of the fire. No one notices that the floor is still strewn with Sunday's newspapers or that the bed is only half made. The party is an unexpected treat for all.

## Au Courant
Being a busy executive does nothing to deter this Chicago hostess from entertaining. What she can't spend in time she makes up for in effects. Every party becomes a showcase for her style and imagination. Even when she entertains in a restaurant, she adds a few personal touches—her own Pakistani napkins tied in a special knot, a sculpture as centerpiece, a little tagged gift instead of a place card for each guest.

At home she first decides on the mood she wants to create, then coordinates her collection of napkins, china, and music to go with it. Her favorite at-home food is an assortment of take-out appetizers from Thai, Korean, Japanese, and Chinese restaurants, which she serves with such elegance on her unusual ceramics that no one ever suspects—or cares—that she didn't make them in her own kitchen.

Arriving guests are greeted by the fragrance of potpourri and baskets full of blooming plants placed around the floor. Guests take off their shoes and settle on down pillows around an oversized coffee table for drinks and the hors d'oeuvres. Long ago she gave up entertaining in her dining room, which has been converted to another use. Dessert is apt to be Chinese ginger ice cream and chocolate cognac cake surrounded by chocolate truffles. An unforgettable evening!

## Classic Simplicity
A widowed Virginia lady who has recently moved from her old family home to a seaside bungalow on Long Island loves the quiet solitude interrupted only by the occasional muted clang of a bell buoy. She has made a new group of friends in all age groups and from varied backgrounds.

*Cozy clutter (right) can provide a comfortable environment for entertaining. Nineteenth-century Dutch still life; American mirror, circa 1820; French still life, 1876; and Daumier cartoon from Lucullus. HIMMEL*

*Flowers don't have to be a necessity, nor does expensive china. Exert your personality and style. A few live fish and matching china (right) add pizzazz to take-out Peking duck served with San Francisco artist/chef Carol Pulitzer's own homemade coriander crepes. Music adds an extra touch to make the evening special. BEADLE*

Pretty pillows made from lace hand-
kerchiefs, hand towels, dresser scarves,
and napkins add charm to plain
surroundings. The windows
and skirted tables are draped with
quilts, embroidered sheets, and lace
tablecloths. Fine pieces of lace can be
used on tabletops if protected by a layer
of glass. HIMMEL

Mathilde Leary, Dathel Coleman,
and their husbands plan the trips on
their boats with total efficiency.
They bring all the food aboard in
labeled containers so that perishable
food is eaten first. From California
Cooking by the Los Angeles County
Musuem of Art (NY: Clarkson N.
Potter, 1986). SKOTT

15

*Nothing happens by accident when this clever hostess entertains. No flower arrangement, tablecloth, or entertainment is ever repeated, yet each new scheme is designed to wow.* HARDIN

Her favorite party is Sunday tea, after which everyone goes to a movie or takes a long walk on the beach. She has recycled all her fine family linens, and now guests sit cozily among lacy pillows made from embroidered napkins and enjoy a view framed by curtains made from damask tablecloths.

Her house is filled with the aroma of baking bread (from a frozen food package) and fresh brioche (from a bakery). For the pièce de résistance, she makes her famous Charlotte Russe with flaming cherries jubilee. Guests serve themselves right from the kitchen and sit at tables set up all through the cottage. It's a warm and friendly gathering, and friends even help straighten up—something she never would have dreamed of twenty years ago.

## Dedicated Executives

This Mill Valley couple is so busy traveling for their separate careers that the two are rarely in the same city during the week, but on the weekends they rent a boat, a condominium, or a cottage wherever their jobs have taken one of them. Sometimes they invite another couple; other times they prefer only each other's company. They have two cardinal rules: work doesn't come with them and there are no phones.

Each is responsible for one day's meals. After a week of expense-account eating, they prefer healthy, fresh food—plenty of broiled fish, fresh fruit, and vegetables. They run, swim, play tennis or racquetball, ski, or sail by day and read at night. Their guests always leave with a feeling of having done something truly special for themselves.

## The Elegant Organizer

By early spring this hostess is busy planning parties for the summer at her country house. Her desk is littered with notes on what she has served to whom in the past and who she has invited with whom. She even has a picture card file of table settings so that nothing is ever repeated.

Each of her dinner parties will have four tables of eight. It will be country formal—ladies in long dresses and men in sport coats. The food will come from the most fashionable caterer; the flowers will have definite flair. At her first party she will have a mime troupe perform while guests are having cocktails; at her second party there will be a steel band for dancing after dinner. Along with her husband's business associates, guests will include a literary figure, someone from a current news story, a bit of old guard society, a rising young executive, and someone from out of town no one knows. Her party will be perfect down to the last detail and she will seem to do it all effortlessly.

## Premier Perfectionists

The cocktail buffet is the perfect choice for this lively Palm Beach couple. At the beginning of the season they host three large parties on three consecutive nights. For each party there is a different menu planned around variations on the same marvelous decorations, and tents are set up in the back garden for dancing. There might be a Moroccan night with gold lamé palm trees, belly dancers, and waiters carrying flaming kebabs, or the theme might be a Versailles party hosted by Louis XIV.

Their secret to success is that they use only the best party planners and give them an unlimited budget. Everyone who is anyone is invited, and they eagerly anticipate the parties each year. As additional "insurance," important people from all walks of life are invited, and there are always a few famous actors and new stars. The parties glitter to such an extent that the hosts need not entertain for the rest of the season and their friends knock themselves out to entertain them with equal regality.

## Feast of Friendship

This busy young Pittsburgh couple plans parties around exquisite food and their ability to assemble a group of fascinating conversationalists in an easy, relaxed setting. The food takes days to prepare: homemade pasta with pesto made from their own garden-fresh basil and a "Lord, I have met my redeemer" dessert served with espresso made from home-roasted coffee beans.

Guests may wear whatever they like, from bare feet and Indian pajamas to a new evening dress crying out to be shown off. They are greeted by the sounds of contemporary jazz from Miles Davis to Kenny G. The rustic pine table is bare save for the food served on old family silver, crystal, and china. The party usually begins at seven on a weeknight, yet hours later one or two guests will still be at the table talking, oblivious that the others have left and one of their hosts has already turned in. The parties at this house are a memorable feast of friendship where "My home is your home" is a reality, not a cliché.

*Two hours before party time, the party designers begin to put the last of the table decorations in place (left), and the catering staff starts to check each table to make certain that each piece of silver is polished to perfection and there is not the slightest chip in one of the wine glasses.* JEFFERY

*After dinner on the porch (right), the children play outside until they drop fully clothed into a sound sleep, and the adults relax on the porch swing, where they relive tales of the past and dream of the future.* HIMMEL

*Create a table setting around the food being served. Green onions and three gerbera daisies are banked around the saucer of a tureen filled with chilled vichyssoise (left). Place cards are simply initials done in calligraphy. The narrow dining table, which was made by the host, is conducive to conversation and meals served right from the table.* HIMMEL

*Guests are surrounded by the classic beauty of garden roses, antique objects, and elegant comfort (right). The setting is bathed in candlelight and the melody of easy conversation. All antiques from Didier Aaron in New York.* HIMMEL

## American Homestyle

On this heartland American farm, entertaining revolves around the family and their neighbors. In the winter they eat in the kitchen where it is warm; in the summer they eat on the screened porch while insects buzz outside and breezes rustle the trees. Meals are made from local produce—corn from the field, home-cured hams, fresh eggs from the yard chickens, pears from the orchard, and lots of sweet butter and homemade jams to go on hot-from-the-oven bread. Social events revolve around christenings, weddings and funerals, barn raisings, and church socials. No matter who shows up, there is always room at the table and plenty of food and iced tea.

## Formal with Flair

Dinners at this home on the outskirts of Philadelphia are always formal. Fine antique silver and crystal glisten by candlelight; there are fragrant garden roses arranged by the hostess, and subtle piano music fills the air. The setting always makes guests feel they are glowing with wit and grace. The food, elegant but unpretentious, is prepared to perfection: turtle soup, poached chicken with tarragon, and peach melba. There is just enough of it; no one feels they have overeaten. The servants perform their duties with such proficiency they are never noticed and conversation is not interrupted. The evening is traditional, but in an unstuffy, relaxed, and enjoyable manner.

# Chapter 2

# THE ADEPT
# ENTERTAINER

*W*hether you are having one friend over for an evening of chess and pizza in front of the fire or one hundred of the world's social elite for a weekend gala at a Newport estate, the ultimate effect should be the same— your guests should feel they are special. There are as many ways of accomplishing this as there are successful hosts. One hostess who is a gardener likes to use her prize-winning vegetables as a centerpiece and sends guests  home with individual baskets of her fresh produce and homemade jams. A Louisiana hostess who entertained the governor and his entourage for dinner sent everyone home with a bag full of homemade chocolate chip cookies. It is thoughtful, unexpected treats like these that make guests leave your company with smiling faces. The idea is to care for your friends, not overwhelm them. By definition, inviting people into your home is a personal and flattering gesture. It is a time to show your guests who you are and to share the things you enjoy with them. As the host it is up to you to plan an evening around what you can afford and what you can prepare and serve graciously. Your budget, where you live, whether or not you cook, and how much time you have to prepare for a party should simply be guidelines that determine how you entertain, not deterrents to enjoying the company of others. A one-dish meal of chili, spaghetti, or jambalaya with beer or jug wine served by a relaxed, genial host is far more enjoyable than overdone prime rib and

*A solarium filled with pots of blooming plants and garden furniture provides a relaxed setting for a luncheon for two. A favorite room can be the perfect spot for entertaining because it reflects the interests of its owner.* HIMMEL

warm, flat champagne served by an overeager one.

Analyze your favorite parties and you'll find that many times you can't even remember what you were served. What actually mattered was the host's ability to please people with the setting, the combination of guests, and the quality of the food. Remember, everyone has problems giving parties, even His Highness the Maharaja of Jaipur, at whose parties guests must sometimes cease talking because of the deafening crescendo of monkeys thudding about on the roof overhead. Yet no one would ever refuse a second invitation to dine with him because he is such a congenial host.

In a sense, you are producing theater. You create the setting and provide the cast of characters against a backdrop that is you—your style, your imagination, your concept. If all goes according to plan, the party will be a success and conversation will take over. No one will want to go home, and invitations to your next party will be more sought-after than an evening at a four-star restaurant.

Entertaining should be a pleasure for both you and your guests. Whether you give a luncheon on Super Bowl Sunday or a formal seated dinner for fifty, guests should feel relaxed. The host or hostess who bobs up and down and rushes back and forth to the kitchen will do nothing to add to the conviviality of a party. So what if the hired waiter has drunk himself silly and passed out? Tell your guests what has happened and they'll all have a good laugh. Wouldn't you if you were the guest? Remember, they haven't come just to eat and drink at your expense, they've come to have a good time and enjoy your company.

## Choosing the Guests

If there is one element that will make or break a party, it is the choice of guests. "I feel that an interesting, diverse guest list is the main ingredient in a successful dinner, whether it is an official state function or a small private dinner party," says First Lady Nancy Reagan. "We use our best effort to bring together an assortment of people in whom our honored guest will have an interest. I try to gather people from many different walks of life so that their various experiences and interests lead to good conversation and an enjoyable evening. It's always nice to know that guests leave an event at the White House with special memories.

"I think all details—the guest list, the menu, the flowers, the entertainment—are important in contributing to a successful dinner, and they should blend together to provide a special flow and sparkle," she explains.

A party made up of the people to whom you owe invitations can be dreadful, much like a social rummage sale. One New York designer says that on occasions when he must mix incompatible people, he invites some of his sparkling friends and counts on them to spice up the party. "If they do a good job," he quips, "I return the favor!" Another problem, especially in small towns, is having the same people at party after party. The only hope in both cases is to introduce some fascinating new faces to the group. Peggy Fisher, a scintillating Tulsa hostess, calls these people kickers, "and without them," she says, "the party hasn't a prayer of success."

When internationally known executives

Carolina and Reinaldo Herrera have a dinner party, those guests who cannot come to dinner are invited for after-dinner drinks and coffee. New blood is infused into the party and the conversation takes off as "old" and "new" guests fill one another in on what has transpired during the earlier part of the evening.

"A good mix of people guarantees success," says New York art patron Judith Rothschild. "First I start with an idea. For example, a guest of honor who is from Chicago recently published a book on Indian art and is from a family that collects Abstract Expressionist paintings. That way I can have couples from three different interest groups and the party will come to life."

When planning the guest list, cast the party as you would a play. Let's say that your aunt and uncle are visiting. She tends to be stuffy, though interested in birds; he is very witty on the subject of Proust. You add a couple in which the husband is the national authority on yellow-breasted sapsuckers and the wife is the president of Planned Parenthood. Then, to round out the group, you include the delightful French teacher from the local college and the new, unmarried Episcopal minister. The guest list has some potential, although you would probably never have had the opportunity or desire to put the group together had it not been for the visit of your relatives. If you are fortunate, one or two of your guests will turn out to be great fun and you will want to have them back with your regular group of friends.

Keep notes on your friends' interests and try to invite other guests whom they will enjoy. There are exceptions to this, of course. If you put three couples together simply because the wives are all in the Junior League or because the husbands are all proctologists, the party will be extremely dull for all those who are not members of the group. Even the best-laid plans can backfire. One hostess thought it would be fun to invite all of her friends who didn't know one another. The party was so dreadful that no one would leave for fear that those remaining would talk about them.

You can generate plenty of electricity if you invite attorneys who are on opposing sides of a publicized case, but invite two attorneys from the same firm and the party will be dull, dull, dull. Ever sat by while two women monopolized the entire conversation arguing about the meaning of last Sunday's sermon? The solution to this is to pack the guest list with people who have diverse interests and who aren't shy about expressing their views.

Knowing the right number of people to invite is an art in itself. Noted hostess Pat Buckley likes to invite no more than twenty for lunch and thirty for dinner so that she can have a chance to chat with each of the guests. Many hostesses stress that if there were a magic number it would be eight at each table. Four people can exhaust all avenues of conversation unless they are brilliant talkers. On the other hand, ten people may cause an individual to get "stage fright" having to address nine people, or the table talk may be reduced to lectures given by the overbearing to the unwitting. The secret when giving a party for a group is to have multiple tables that seat six to eight people.

## Getting Organized

The key to successful and worry-free entertaining is organization—that dreary word that conjures up memories of your old home ec teacher. Have you ever been putting the lasagna on the table when you remembered that your husband's boss abhors cheese? Have you ever noticed two of your guests sitting in stony silence and realized that you've seated your guest of honor next to the wife of a man he is suing? Have you ever sat by and watched your daughter's fiancé beset by a violent attack of sneezing because you forgot he is allergic to carnations?

These things have happened to nearly everyone once, but with the help of a good party diary, they may never happen to you again. Keep notes about who does and does not eat what. Remember that Dr. Frankenstein's wife will eat beef only if it is mooing, that the director of your local art museum prefers kosher food, that your wife's partner has a heart condition and can't eat salt. Who is on a diet? Who likes to smoke at the table and who is offended by it?

Write down your menus and critique the meals. Was the meat overdone? Did everyone leave half of their stuffed squash? Was there not enough dessert to go around? Where did you get the coffee that everyone raved about? Be sure to note where the recipes came from. You'd hate to serve a dessert to a guest from whom the caterer stole the recipe.

Who sat next to whom? Which combinations of people worked, and which ones didn't? Write down the names of people you might want to in-

*Louellen Berger keeps her social life perfectly organized by making file cards for each party, complete with guest list, menu, and photographs of flower arrangements and centerpieces. A master list gives her the names of all the resource people she may need for each event, from deejays to skywriters. HIMMEL*

vite in the future because they have something in common with a friend of yours.

Who always comes late? Consider the doctor who might be on call; if his beeper sounds and he has to leave, will the meal be palatable upon his return? Remember this so you can plan a meal that won't be ruined if it must be held for an extra hour. Who tends to go to sleep and fall face down in her cream puff if the meal goes on for too long?

One format that works well is a card file. In one section prepare a card on each of your regular guests, what they like and dislike, what they've been served at your house, whom they sat next to. In another section write up each party. At the top of the card put the date of the party and the occasion, the guest list, menu and recipe notes, table appointments, seating arrangements, favors and general notes, perhaps even noting what you wore. If you are lucky enough to have a home computer, you can enter all of this into its memory and give yours a rest.

You may want to keep a file of ideas, recipes, and menus you want to try. You should also keep an index of your favorite recipes from your cookbooks. On each card write a type of food—cold soup, vegetable, salad—with a reference to the name of the cookbook, the page number, and the name of the recipe. If you cook for large numbers of people, put the quantity of ingredients on the card, as well as your favorite variations.

No matter how hard you plan to have the right food for guests, there will be times when someone just simply cannot or will not eat what you have prepared. Although there are many reli-

Collect paper cocktail and dinner napkins with bold, imaginative designs. They are perfect for informal picnics, dinners, and luncheons.

Have dozens of votive and tall candles on hand. (Store them in a freezer if possible, and they will burn longer.) Votive candles can be used all over the house—along walkways (to create an entrance), on dining tables, and on side tables and coffee tables in groupings (always use an odd number). Masses of votive candles in a nonworking fireplace create a glow better than a real fire.

It's a good idea to have enough tall candles to change your candlesticks twice during a party. If you use a lot of candles, order them by the case and store them in a cool place. You may want to order them through a church, funeral home, or ecclesiastical supply store.

Matches are a must in your party closet: wooden kitchen matches to light candles and Sterno, cedar matches to light cigars, and matchbooks to place on tables for guests to use. You can buy colorful assortments imprinted with your name or collect an interesting variety from restaurants and clubs you patronize. Have enough Sterno or alcohol for several chafing dishes.

People who entertain a lot never have enough trays and ashtrays. Ashtrays that serve more than one purpose are extremely handy: real shells from the beach, ceramic shell dishes, demitasse saucers, small stackable, rectangular plastic hors d'oeuvres plates printed with works of art, and oyster plates. Trays can range from plastic to

*Change the appearance of your dining room to a beach party in the middle of winter by adding objects from your garden, sheets from your bed, and hand-painted place mats for guests to take home after the party.* BOYD

*Once party supplies are corralled into one area, party giving becomes a breeze. You'll know at once what you have and what you need—paints, markers, tape, holiday decorations, candles and candlesticks, napkin rings, place and menu cards, ribbons, balloons, place mats, napkins, tablecloths, and bits of fabric and wallpaper left over from your decorating scheme. Heirloom tablecloths should be rolled on dowels and stored in acid-free paper. Vintage postcards from Archives of Louisiana Trade Labels.* HIMMEL

silver, and warming trays are invaluable when serving large groups.

If you don't have a special place for flower arranging, it might be a good idea to keep your flower-arranging tools in a basket along with your party supplies. Keep just the things you use the most: clippers, scissors, wire, oases, water vials, smooth rocks, frogs, stickum.

Remember all those presents that people have brought you from trips or things you've collected from yours? Go through them all and pick out the items you can use as decorations and fill a basket with paper kites, lanterns and flowers, seashells, pieces of fabric, fans, carved animals, bongo drums, and the rest. This is also the place where you can combine gift-wrapping materials and party supplies: ribbons, markers, balloons and place cards, paper stock, and special pens.

Collect a great assortment of napkin rings or make your own from papier-mâché. Keep your old silver spoons and forks that have gone through the garbage disposal and have a silversmith make the ends into napkin rings.

If you do a lot of outdoor entertaining, keep a fifteen-pound bag of sand (which can be reused), paper lunch bags, and candle stubs to make luminarias. You also need kerosene or alcohol to go in outdoor lanterns. Keep plenty of pink light bulbs on hand to create flattering light for a party. And don't forget an assortment of extension cords for plate warmers, hot trays, and special lights. Keep a list of friends you can borrow things from.

gious taboos, some are easy to remember: Orthodox Jews will not eat pork, shellfish, or scavenger fish; Moslems will not eat pork or shellfish either or have alcohol of any kind, not even wine in a sauce; Hindus will eat no beef, and strict Catholics prefer not to eat meat during Lent. Not only do these various religions prohibit eating certain foods, but their followers should not even be in close proximity to them.

Food allergies are another problem. The most common food allergens are dairy products (including eggs and cheese), wheat, sugar, chocolate, coffee, nuts, and shellfish, and many people do not like to even think about garlic. When in doubt, have the guests for cocktails and serve lots of fresh fruit and vegetables as hors d'oeuvres.

*Bright invitations and favors are irresistible. Who could turn down a silk-screened apron or a vase of flowers cut from plywood; a painted watermelon canvas place mat or a personalized lunch box? The invitation can be placed in a box wrapped in fabulous paper, which can also be incorporated into the table setting. Give each guest a miniature swan with the invitation attached to its neck, then carry out the theme in your centerpiece by "floating" more tiny swans and fresh flowers on a Mylar lake. HIMMEL.*

Organize all of your party supplies. Have a party ready room, closet, hamper, box, chest of drawers. You can use an armoire, trunk, or old wooden icebox. This is the place where you can keep all the supplies you need for each party. You can collect these from an antiques store, the dime store, or a flea market. Use your creativity and have fun putting your collection together. Fort Worth hostess Mary D. Walsh keeps each theme party's supplies in a different basket. When she travels, if she sees a mug, napkin, or invitation she likes, she buys sixty of them for her party baskets.

## Designing the Invitation

How the invitation is presented, whether it is verbal, handwritten, or printed, has a lot to do with how a guest will feel about accepting it. The more excited you seem about having a guest, the more he or she will look forward to coming. A printed invitation must be representative of the event. Make even the envelope appealing by using commemorative stamps and having the address done in calligraphy. You can use a felt-tip calligraphy pen or nonrun watercolor markers, but it is crucial that the envelope be hand addressed, not typed. Colored stickers also add to the look of an informal invitation, both inside and out. They can even be added to a printed invitation. Silver swans or gold unicorns can do wonders, even for an invitation that has been run off on a photocopier.

Remember, a formal lunch or dinner invitation should be written entirely by hand or on partially engraved cards on white or cream-colored heavy card stock, 4 1/2 by 5 1/2 inches, with

matching envelopes. They are always done in black ink.

When ordering any invitation from a printer, especially engraved or thermographed ones, be certain that the printer can guarantee the date of delivery and show you proofs before the final invitation has been run off and that the quoted price includes the plates, scoring, folding, and delivery. For engraving, use the best paper stock, which is by Crane. Engraving is costly because each invitation is hand pressed. The plate may cost only eight to fifteen dollars per line, but the hand labor is expensive. For example, 500 engraved wedding invitations will cost between $600 and $1,000.

Thermographing is a resin and heat process that leaves the ink raised on top of the paper. It is easier, faster, and less expensive than engraving, though not top of the line. Another cost saver is using Linwood paper stock. Some people have a large number of engraved cards made with their monogram and then, when they need an invitation quickly, have them thermographed onto the cards.

The least expensive way to do invitations is by using a photocopier. Take, for example, a "Poverty Party." The IRS tax form can be run off on red paper, the invitation printed on the back and put in a copying machine. A brunch after a big party the night before can be a "Hangover Party" with invitations on a doctor's prescription form done on green paper. You can make a crossword puzzle that guests have to fill in themselves with the date, time, and place. If your regular invitation looks too dull, cut it up like a jigsaw puzzle and let the guest put it together. Museums

and bookstores are good sources of oversized, pretty, or antique postcards. Put the "boring" invitation in a gift-wrapped box and tie a regular balloon to it—now *that* looks like fun!

Unfortunately, people today are getting worse and worse about responding to invitations. In order to get an answer, you must mail the invitation no later than two weeks before the party, although a phoned invitation can happen up to the minute the food is put on the table. If invitations go out three to four weeks in advance, be certain to mail a reminder card. This is also a nice way to reconfirm phoned invitations. *Regrets*, when written on an invitation, tends to signal the guest that the party will have a cast of thousands or will be, as it has been nicknamed, a "garbage party" or a "phone book party." With an RSVP (*répondez s'il vous plaît*, or "please reply"), you can include a stamped, self-addressed card, but some people still won't answer.

Indicating your address for the RSVP, as well as a phone number where someone is available to answer the phone all day, will save you hours of chitchatting with all of the callers. An answering machine can help too. If you haven't heard from some people and you need an answer, you or a secretary should call and ask if they plan to come. Even then, for a party with more than ten guests, about 10 percent of the acceptances will probably not come at party time.

Occasionally an invitation goes astray and a person you hoped to have doesn't get your message. Usually you won't find out until after the party. Send flowers or balloons with a note saying

Write the invitation on a beach ball or balloon and attach a note instructing the recipient to blow it up.

Roll the invitation into a tube resembling a firecracker. Assemble so the "cracker" pops and releases confetti when the string is pulled.

Send a whole watermelon with the invitation affixed on a skewer.

Tie the invitation with a bow to a bunch of daisies or orchids.

Fill a plastic lock-top bag with sand and tiny seashells. Using a gold marker, write a phone number on a large shell. On an answering machine, record the invitation with Hawaiian music in the background: "Come to a swimming party . . ."

Attach the invitation to a kite.

Create a beach scene in a small goldfish bowl using sand and miniature sand toys. Write the invitation on a paper umbrella or a mini beach towel.

Silk-screen the invitation on a hand towel or billed cap.

Send a real flowering plant or a bowl of fish with the invitation attached to a wire.

Make a miniature picnic basket. Line a tiny basket with red and white checkered material with the edges pinked and fill with miniature food replicas or refrigerator magnets. Curl up the invitation and attach with colored yarn.

For a cocktail party, take an empty single-serving bottle of liquor or wine (the kind you get on an airplane) and attach your invitation over the label. Fill the bottle with tiny flowers and deliver it.

Create a potted flower by sandwiching the invitation between two oatmeal-raisin cookies. For the stem, use a thin dowel, sticking one end between the cookies and the other into plastic foam in a flowerpot. Cover the plastic foam with jelly beans and the cookies with plastic wrap tied on with a piece of wire and ribbon.

Fill fortune cookies with small bits of an invitation and enclose them in a black lacquered box. Recipients must open each cookie to get all the party details.

Louellen Berger recycles old 45-rpm records by applying invitations directly over the labels. Other hosts may want to compose musical invitations and have them recorded.

how embarrassed you are, or at least call the person. Never describe how great the party was!

Remember, when you are hosting a party with other people, the person whose house or apartment is used for the party will get all of the credit unless the invitation makes it clear who the hosts are. To ensure against this confusion, put the other people's names first on the invitation and give their names, addresses, and phone numbers for the RSVP. They should stand near the front door to greet guests or bid them good night. When the hosts are unknown to the guests, a receiving line can be a sensible idea. Some people solve the problem by having the hosts wear funny matching neckties or the hostesses add flowers to their hair.

## Letting Guests Know What to Expect

Have you ever arrived at someone's house for "just a barbecue" to find everyone else in suits and ties? Have you ever been to a party in another city where the host said, "It isn't formal," to find that your silk daytime dress was out of place next to the other women in shorts and slacks?

Guests should come to your home knowing exactly what time they are expected and what the majority of the other guests will be wearing. Standards and customs differ from city to city and from one group to another. A well-mannered lady from South Carolina who lives in Aspen was given a vague verbal invitation to dine après ski with a certain male star at a wealthy producer's house. She assumed that après ski meant five and dinner meant eight, so she compromised and showed up at six-thirty. Although she was raised in a culture where a lady would never wear pants in the evening, she reasoned that since it was Aspen she'd wear a pair of designer trousers and a gorgeous beaded sweater. When she arrived, she was handed a towel by the butler and told to take her clothes off. "The other guests have been in the hot tub for an hour waiting for you to come so that they could start dinner, and now my soufflé is ruined!" moaned the simpering servant. Without batting an eye she smiled sweetly and said, "Oh, I'm so sorry. I bathed before I came and never get hungry before nine!" With that she fled, vowing never to go out again without first determining the exact nature of the party.

The considerate host and hostess will tell a first-time guest specifically how they will dress. Don't be vague; instead say, "We always dress for dinner" or "I'll be wearing a silk sari and Bubba will be in his kilt." Or maybe you can say, "Just be comfortable. Everyone in our group wears whatever they like. My wife usually wears jeans and I never wear a tie or a jacket, but some of our guests will come in the same clothes they wear to the office." A written invitation that says casual can mean anything short of white tie and tails. As the hostess you may not care what your guests wear, but they might not want to show up in a new cocktail dress when everyone else is in running clothes.

It is fine for the host and hostess to be a bit more dressed up than the guests. There are certain hazards to avoid, however. If you are going to be moving around, passing food or cooking, wear something that you won't trip over, spill on, or set afire. Spiked heels and bangle bracelets are fabulous as long as you don't have to dash up and down stairs, chase children across the lawn, or whisk egg whites. A flambéed host or one with a broken leg won't do much for the merriment of a party.

The bane of all cooks is the late guest, yet how many times have you been invited for seven o'clock and arrived on time to find your host still in his bathrobe? It is socially acceptable for a guest to be ten minutes late to lunch and twenty minutes late to dinner. Etiquette authorities agree, however, that it is up to the person who is giving the party to tell the first-time guest, "We serve at ten, so many of our friends who don't like a long cocktail period come at nine." Be consistent. Once a guest who arrives at eight-fifteen for a seven-thirty invitation finds that he isn't offered a drink and that all the other guests are at the table, he will get the message. If the guest hasn't turned up after one hour, call and then proceed with the party, since it is rude to hold things up for those who arrived on time.

The worst of all possible information comes from the hostess who says, "Just drop over at sevenish." Most guests would prefer for you to say, "I hope you'll come right on time, because I want to have a chance to visit with you before everyone else arrives." This accomplishes two things—first, it gets the guest to your house on time and, second, it makes him or her feel special.

There are those hostesses—smokers and vicarious smokers—who are more than happy to put ashtrays on the table for guests who smoke.

After all, they reckon, it is the courteous thing to do. Then there are those hostesses—reformed smokers and never-have-been/never-will-be smokers—who find smoking at the table the height of rudeness.

This is not a middle-of-the-road issue. Each host and hostess must take a stand and be consistent. However, if you don't put an ashtray on the table and a guest asks for one, you must furnish it; to do otherwise would be discourteous. Of course, you may say in your sweetest voice, "I hope I have one, no one ever smokes in here." Maybe next time the guest will be too embarrassed to ask.

## Including Yourself in the Fun

No matter how frantically you have had to rush to get the house or food ready, give yourself about fifteen minutes in a hot bathtub to relax before "show time." A nap rarely works because the second you hit the bed you remember that you forgot to preheat the oven or get any cocktail napkins. Once you are in the tub, though, you are trapped. If you are truly compulsive, leave a piece of paper and pencil by the side of the tub to write down any last-minute chores. If you have small children, arrange for an out-of-house babysitter or have your sitter arrive at five o'clock and get the children bathed and fed before the party.

Proper ladies are taught that the perfect hostess never lets on that she has been in any way inconvenienced by the arrival of sixteen extra people for dinner; after all, it is all she has had to look forward to all day. (She would never let on that she was up at dawn icing the cake, polishing the silver, and shopping for the freshest ingredients.) The party should appear effortless. So what if you forget to serve a course or if you let the dessert soufflé burn because you were having fun and lost track of the time? Substitute sherbet and no one will ever know except you. Isn't it, after all, terribly flattering to your guests that you enjoyed them so much you forgot about the food?

## Encouraging Guests to Mingle

No matter how you do it, be certain that you are near the front door to greet guests as they arrive. You should be one of the first people they see. Introduce each guest to a few others before they enter the party, even if it is an informal outdoor party.

The introduction of guests should always be done with the inferior introduced to the superior. Therefore you introduce your guest to the guest of honor by saying, "Archibald [guest of honor], I'd like to present my sister-in-law, Alixe Zander." Then add a bit about her to make conversation easier: "She's appearing in the show *The Vampire Returns Again* off Broadway and wants to be a veterinarian."

At very formal parties, the guest's name is announced by the butler as he or she is brought into the living room. Congresswoman Lindy Boggs says that this is crucially important if there is any chance at all that the host or hostess won't recognize a guest.

Carol Price, the wife of Charles Price, United States ambassador to the Court of St. James's, finds that guests from out of town or those who will not know the other people at the party appreciate receiving a list of the other guests' names with a bit of information about them. One Pasadena host prides himself on giving fascinating information about guests to ensure that people will mingle. A sample might read: "Boo Boo and Nicky Hellman—he's Boo Boo and she's Nicky. They import snakes from the Amazon. Their son, Honoré, is at school with your niece at Yale. Nicky is a tall blonde and Boo Boo used to be a quarterback for the Rams." Your guest will be a great deal more interested in getting to know them and will certainly remember their names.

The good hostess should make it her business to help guests avoid embarrassment. For example, a host and hostess should try to keep a handle on the conversation and warn guests (discreetly) of conversational "land mines." Inform Jimmie Sue Houlihan, the lady wrestler and militant feminist, that the man in the Hawaiian shirt is Father O'Flanagan, a firm believer that a woman's place is in the home, and that it might be a good idea to confine their conversation to famous Irish athletes.

No matter what the host and hostess do, guests at parties sometimes just will not mingle. The problem often occurs when there are several groups of couples at the same party who don't know one another. Everyone talks to their friends and makes no effort to meet anyone new.

You can force people to talk to one another by using place cards to seat them at dinner. Put talkers next to listeners or put all the bores at one

*An unusual assortment of people may have an easier time mingling if the party is out of doors and very informal. Guests can even pick part of the meal straight from the garden.* BRONSON

table, especially those who like to hear themselves talk, and put the interesting people at another. Mixing the two groups is hopeless. Remember, the quickest way to take the life out of a party is to break up an animated table conversation by moving into the living room where guests must regroup. Let the party have a life of its own.

Lee Copley Thaw, an international representative for Sotheby's, believes in the French saying *"Le but de la société c'est l'intimité"* ("The object of company is closeness"). To promote intimacy, Lee sets up small tables at which she mixes new faces with familiar ones. Since she serves only three courses, her seating is an invitation to conversation, not imprisonment.

At cocktail parties or dinners where guests are not seated at tables, you can employ a few tricks to get people to mix. (They work well at singles parties too.) For example, as guests arrive, tell them they all have one thing in common and, in order to get dinner, they must find out what it is. When dinner is announced, each guest must present you with the answer as he or she enters the dining room. The answer might be that they all were born in July, have three children, go to the same dentist, have broken their legs skiing, drink J&B Scotch, ride the bus to work, have fathers who were doctors. It *does* get people talking.

Another trick is to take oversized postcards (or old Christmas cards, invitations, or photographs) and cut them into four pieces. Each arriving guest must draw a piece out of a basket (couples draw from different baskets). In order to

get dinner, the guests must complete their puzzles and eat as a group. Another possibility is to put a message on each guest's back as he or she enters the party (written on Post-it pads). To get dessert, the guest must figure out his or her message by asking others for a hint—only one hint from each person. Messages can be: "My favorite spectator sport is women's track," "In college I was known as Sewer Snood," "Tomorrow is my birthday." Some guests are painfully shy and the worst thing you can do is plop them down in the middle of all the talkers. Ask one of your friends who is thoughtful and vivacious to look after the quiet guest throughout the party and that person will feel secure and special.

One hostess who was having a large number of guests from out of town decided to get her party rolling by creating topic rooms and assigning her local friends to each room. There was a "name-dropping" room, a "sports" room, a "parents of kids who go or want to go to a good school" room, a "politically active" room, and an "I hate large parties" room. The last one filled up first and seemed to attract the liveliest conversationalists.

## Serving Cocktails

The first offering made by the host is usually a drink. If the host says simply, "And what will you have?" the guest is left wondering whether the host is offering a cocktail, wine, or chilled root beer. Of course, in some homes this is never a problem because the host has everything. "Oh, I'll have Mouton Rothschild 1965, please," you can say, and within seconds there it is. By the same token, you can say, "I'll have a beer," and find that everyone at the party is drinking vintage port and that your request is out of the question. To save the guest embarrassment, the host should say, "Will you have a drink? I'm having a mint julep and my wife is having a wine spritzer. We've got everything except gin and Dubonnet." In other words, give the guest some sort of guidelines about what you have to offer.

Don't fall into the trap of believing that no one notices the quality of liquor served at a party. Forget it—they do! If you cannot afford good Scotch, bourbon, or vodka, serve moderately priced wines; even good beer beats bad hard liquor. If your funds are limited, offer the guests a "special" drink—sangria with lots of fresh fruit, pitchers of Bloody Marys or screwdrivers.

If you do luck into an off brand of liquor that tastes like the good stuff, put it in a fabulous decanter and hide the empty bottle in the bottom of the neighbor's trash can. The late designer Angelo Donghia used to display his wine on a round wooden vase stand. "A seven-dollar bottle of wine is instantly transformed into a twenty-seven-dollar bottle," he quipped. Remember that red wine should be uncorked and allowed to "breathe" for about an hour before it is served, but white wine and rosé will lose their crispness if they are exposed to the air before serving.

A good rule of thumb is that there are four servings in each bottle of wine (a fifth), so for four people plan on two to three bottles. There are twenty drinks per quart bottle of liquor. Plan on one ten-ounce bottle of mixer per person, with

*For those informal parties at home, set up an easily accessible bar area with a wide variety of drink choices. Make the area appealing but uncluttered. Carts make wonderful bars because they can be rolled from room to room and stored in a closet when not in use. Courtesy* Food & Wine *magazine. HAGIWARA*

more soda water than tonic, cola, and ginger ale. Flavored seltzers, such as pear, raspberry, and lemon, are a nice alternative to sweetened soft drinks (see Appendix A, "Cocktail Savvy").

Champagne adds pizzazz to any occasion or meal, even leftover turkey, and it is proper to serve it anytime from cocktails through dessert. It is the wine for love, achievement, and celebration. With few exceptions you cannot get away with anything that costs less than six dollars per bottle; ten to fifteen dollars is average, and for more than that you can get something that champagne aficionados will particularly enjoy. There are six glasses per bottle. If you are having lots of people, they probably won't notice how good the champagne is, but they will notice if it is bad. One alternative is to ask a knowledgeable wine merchant to find a sparkling wine labeled *méthode champenoise*, which is dry and palatable and won't be classified by the average guest as cheap. Although white sparkling wine produced in this country is often labeled champagne, French law prohibits any champagne-style wine from being labeled as such unless the grapes are grown and the fermentation takes place in the French province of Champagne. Other European countries, such as Spain, a great producer of white sparkling wines, respect the French position. The only alternative to cheap "champagne" is to forget a sparkling wine and serve a good white wine.

There is a theory that the larger the bottle in which the champagne has matured, the better it will be. The magnum holds the equivalent of two bottles, the Jeroboam or double magnum holds four. The Rehoboam holds six; the Methuselah, eight; the Salmanazar, twelve; the Balthazar, sixteen; and the Nebuchadnezzar, twenty (beware: it weighs about eighty pounds).

Wine experts seem to agree that there are certain rules that those in the know should adhere to when they serve champagne. It must be cold but not frozen or icy. Two and a half hours in the bottom of the refrigerator will do, although sitting in a bucket of ice for twenty minutes is proper for fine champagne. It must be served immediately after it is opened (see page 309 for instructions).

Among those secure souls who drink beer, foreign brands are very popular, and there also are good locally brewed American brands. If you plan to return empty or unopened beer bottles, stick to one or two brands to avoid confusion. For mob-scene parties, keg beer is fine. A keg will serve about thirty to forty serious imbibers. It should be placed in a large tub with ice to keep it cold and catch the overflow. Heineken in the keg or any light beer is a good choice.

Another idea is to put out pitchers of nonalcoholic beverages to which alcohol can be added

*Brian Hagiwara and Peter Flanagan make their drinks irresistible by blending fresh fruit juices, flavored sparkling waters, aperitifs with a low alcohol content, beautiful glasses, and a touch of imagination. Courtesy* Food & Wine *magazine.* HAGIWARA

—Virgin Marys, bloody shames, dry dock Manhattans, whiskeyless sours. There are also some wonderful sparkling ciders, fruit-flavored seltzers, and mineral waters on the market. You can serve the drinks in pretty stemmed glasses, and if the party is a big success, your guests might even forget to add the alcohol.

Always measure drinks with a jigger and serve them in smallish glasses to discourage doubles and triples. Many smart hostesses say that glasses should never be more than half full, as they look more elegant that way. Don't keep refilling guests' glasses before they have finished a drink. They too will lose track of how much alcohol they have consumed.

Consider that one drink counts as 1 1/4 ounces of 80-proof liquor, a 12-ounce can of beer, or a 4-ounce glass of table wine. At a cocktail party, try to pace guests at one drink per hour. A 120-pound woman who has four drinks in an hour and a half will test as being intoxicated, whereas a 200-pound man who consumes six drinks in two hours will test the same way. Admittedly, some people absorb alcohol even quicker than this.

The host can inhibit his guests' consumption by serving plenty of food with cocktails. The best choices are solid cheese, fresh vegetables, high-fiber foods, meats (not processed or salty), or anything greasy because they slow the absorption of alcohol. On the other hand, starches and carbonated mixers (cola, seltzer, ginger ale) escalate the absorption of alcohol and therefore should be avoided. Salty snacks are also bad because they encourage people to drink more and faster.

## A FEW SOBERING THOUGHTS

Many hosts and hostesses become annoyed when the subject of drunken guests comes up. After all, as good hosts we are all taught to show guests a good time and doesn't that mean keeping their glasses filled? While in many states the host can be held legally accountable if a drunken guest kills someone in an automobile accident, it certainly puts a damper on a good party when the host must refuse a guest another drink. Tragically, every twenty-three minutes in the United States, someone dies in an alcohol-related accident, and about half of all automobile accidents involve drunken drivers.

Jimmy Moran, one of the nation's most renowned restaurateurs, has solved the problem for the guests at his parties. He sends chauffeured limousines to pick them up! They feel pampered and, once at one of his parties, they can drink all they wish without having to worry. Other hosts like to ask several nondrinkers to drive the other guests home after a fun evening. Elaine Lehman has only a forty-minute cocktail hour, allowing twenty minutes per drink. Her guests know beforehand that cocktails will begin at 8:30 and dinner will be served promptly at 9:10 p.m.

As the host, you should be familiar with how much is too much and pace the evening accordingly. When you know there will be an extended period before dinner, you might serve cold soup, such as vichyssoise, cucumber, or tomato mandarin, in elegant wide-mouthed wine glasses. Dr. Rise Ochsner likes to serve a cream soup before cocktails to reduce her guests' absorption of alcohol.

Try to stop the flow of alcohol about an hour before a dinner disbands; at a cocktail party, put the liquor away and leave the mixers. Have a long dessert-and-coffee period. Although this will not sober anyone up, it will give guests time to begin to metabolize what they've consumed. Remember that once someone is drunk, there is no way to sober him or her up quickly. Coffee merely creates a wide-awake drunk as opposed to a sleepy drunk. All you can do is provide the guest with plenty of water and a place to sleep off the booze.

Studies show that men and women tend to drink less when there is a one-to-one ratio of males to females at a party. Another conclusion of the studies is that the faster the beat of the music played at a party, the less the guests seem to drink. Hurray for rock 'n' roll!

*Boston artist Barbara Dunn makes special place cards for her friends, painting pictures of things that are close to their hearts. Here Sweet Pea, a Springer spaniel, has been immortalized on a tiny canvas for a doting owner as a take-home place card/favor.*
HIMMEL

## Getting Guests to the Table

The polite hostess will ask her guests if they would like to freshen up before dinner. Often hosts assume that a guest who wants to use the facilities will know where they are by telepathy or that everyone has built-in radar to sense exactly when dinner will be served. It is a good idea for the host or hostess to announce, "We'll be eating in fifteen minutes. Would anyone like to have a fresh drink or go to the powder room?" At that point the guest who must make a phone call can do so without delaying the meal.

At a restaurant the food arrives when it is at its peak because the guests sit and wait for it. At your home the food must wait for the guests, and all too often the longer it waits, the more it will deteriorate. It is up to you to lead the move to the table with the guest of honor in tow. Have the other host or another friend bring up the rear and get the guests moving in the right direction.

When there are many important people attending a seated meal, events planner Nancy Winton of Minneapolis and San Francisco suggests that the host find a subtle way to direct them to their tables. At one luncheon for women in banking, there were six tables, each with a different color tablecloth. She stood at the door and handed a rose to each guest. The flower was color coordinated to the table where the guest was to sit. While this appeared to the guests to be a haphazard approach to seating, she knew exactly who she was placing where.

No matter how informal the party, the guest of honor, if female, sits to the right of the host and, if male, to the right of the hostess. If there is no guest of honor, age and clerical status are given deference.

Place cards are a great help in getting people to sit down. Ruth Jackson of San Francisco likes to purchase raffle tickets in her guests' names to use as place cards. If you don't care where people sit, you might find it fun to put their names in two baskets—one for the men and another for the women. Franny will sit with Zooey, Steve with Edie, Spic with Span, McNeil with Lehrer, Price with Waterhouse—any pairs you can think of. Once drawn, the pairs can proceed to the table together.

You can have laminated place mats made using blowups of pictures of each guest, their dogs, baby pictures, automobiles, or whatever. Small picture frames at each place with individual photographs also work well.

Favors and place cards can be combined. You might silk-screen the guest's name on a hand towel, napkin, or T-shirt to go at his or her place. Or you could paint the name on a clear glass plate or miniature fishbowl complete with fish.

At other times, especially if you have invited the same old group, you can add a little zest to the party by writing witty, descriptive phrases such as "Best Set of Legs," "Highest Score on the SAT," "Fastest Driver," "Best Tennis Player," or "Highest IQ." It can be quite amusing to see who sits where. After the meal you can switch the cards according to who you thought fit each description.

A printed menu card on the table is a nice touch. Guests will know how much food they will be served and can pace themselves accordingly. Some artistic hostesses can even do a poster with illustrations of the food and place it on an easel in the corner.

## Serving the Meal

While the meal is being served, it is the hostess who must give the guests their cues on what to do. There is a story about some good ol' boys who went to visit their friend Andrew Jackson in the White House and were told not to worry, just do what the President does. When coffee was served, they watched him carefully remove his coffee cup from the saucer, which they did. Next he poured milk into the saucer, which they did. Then he set his saucer of milk on the floor, which they did—only to find he was feeding his pet cat under the table!

At the other extreme there is the hostess who saves her guests embarrassment at all costs. Queen Victoria was giving a dinner for a visiting foreign dignitary. When a finger bowl was presented to him, he picked it up and drank the contents. Being a good hostess, the Queen picked up her finger bowl and followed suit—as did all of her guests!

When hosting an informal meal, relax. Serve the first course as an hors d'oeuvre before the meal or have it on the table when the guests are seated. Then clear away the plates and let the guests serve themselves from the buffet or even the stove. A two-shelf rolling cart can be an invaluable aid.

Wine is poured as soon as the food is brought to the table. It is generally the male host who serves the wine and keeps the guests' glasses replenished, and he should never fill wineglasses to the top but only halfway to allow space for the bouquet.

At a formal meal, the host and hostess never, ever serve themselves first. *Service à la Russe*, made popular in the late nineteenth century by a Russian aristocrat, dictates that the food be passed by a servant. Carried to the hilt, as it was in Europe in the late 1800s, there was a servant behind each place to serve the guest. Prior to this, *service à la Français* or *l'Anglais* was popular, with elaborate food being placed directly on the table for both decoration and eating.

There are several schools of thought on when the host and hostess should be served at an informal meal. The meal seems to progress more smoothly (in the case of a buffet, for example) if the hostess serves several of the guests first. This style, *service Américain*, shows the guest the average portion size and takes the responsibility away from the guest for making a gash in the mousse. Then the hostess should serve herself and begin eating so that the guests who have already served themselves may start.

If a blessing is to be said, the hostess should indicate this by not putting her napkin in her lap when she sits down. The well-mannered guest, trained to follow the hostess's lead, will follow suit and wait for grace to be said.

The hostess should be the last to finish eating and should take seconds, however meager the portion, to encourage others to do so. Polite ladies are taught that they are never to allude to the amount

*An elegant luncheon with antique menu card is all perfectly proper, yet Anne Strachan Crounse makes it more interesting by using contemporary cotton napkins from Pierre Deux, and colorful peppers combined with a Spode dessert service, circa 1820. In the background she has created an arrangement of flowers complementing the colors of the napkins and peppers—full-blown red roses and maidenhair fern from her garden, mixed with a few lilies.*

*French champagne flutes, circa 1850; Louis Philippe vermeil flatware; English wine glasses, circa 1880; early seventeenth-century allegorical painting; English Regency tea urn. All from Lucullus. HIMMEL*

a guest has eaten but should merely say, "Do have some," without adding "more." If for some reason you need to excuse yourself, leave your napkin in your chair, not on the table, to indicate you will be returning to the table and allow your guests to remain seated.

Even at the most informal of meals, it is incorrect to stack dishes when clearing a table. Even lazy people realize that when dishes are stacked they must be washed on the bottom as well as the top. It is fine to have one guest help clear the table, taking plates two at a time. But try to discourage more than one person helping, as too many will cause pandemonium. Once the plates are cleared, return to your seat. Never start to clean up the kitchen between courses and never let a guest do it.

Mary D. Walsh has continued one of her family's ranch traditions by having an open house for lunch every day which attracts a dozen or so people. She serves roast beef, chicken, and just about everything else you could think of. So that guests feel at home, she lets them pick a job card. One might pour the tea, another pass the rolls, another pass seconds. Servants stand by to do the real work, but the guests feel they are doing something a little special and it helps bridge the gap between the wide variety of guests, who range from diplomats to foreign college students to good friends.

Johann Bultman, whose dining room accommodates four tables of eight, has figured out how to get thirty-two people to rise at the same time: he asks a friend to be the host at each table. To signal the end of the meal, he raises a toast to his guest of honor and his assembled friends. The hosts at each table rise and do likewise. They then lead the guests out to continue the festive evening.

## Saying Good Night

A yawn from the host or hostess is a good sign that the hour is getting late but will not persuade some guests to go home. Even going in to clean up the kitchen won't help. Handing the guests their coats and standing by the door should do the trick. Keep saying over and over, "This has been such a treat, let's get together again real soon." It is difficult to have a conversation with a standing host, especially one holding the door open.

Occasionally a host will have the opposite problem. A guest will have to leave early. The host must help him or her make an easy exit that does not break up the party. One solution is simply to tell the guest beforehand to slip out without making a big hoorah of thanks.

After the last guest has left, no matter how tired you are, dispose of the dead cigarettes, air out the room, dry off the tabletops, soak the soiled linen, and at least move the mess into one place. Don't wait; it will look worse the next day. The best thing to do with leftover food is to give it to guests to take home, except for dessert—it's great for breakfast the next morning.

## Entertaining a Crowd

Whether the big party is a wedding reception, the office Christmas party, or a cocktail buffet, there are certain constants. Be sure the room is well cooled before the party (even in winter). Move

## FORMAL MEAL SERVICE

### Dinner

The very mention of the word *formal* tends to make all those within earshot sit up a bit straighter in their chairs and adopt a barely discernible grimace. A formal meal does not have to be a painful experience. Sometimes the ritual and structure of a formally served meal can be a refreshing change—for example, on New Year's Eve or at a corporate dinner. The party does not have to be stilted but should be carried out with leisurely ceremony. After all, no one has to have a formal party, but it is a good idea to know how to do it, just in case.

Here's how to pull it off, taking the liberty of assuming the optimal case of having both a man and a woman to serve. Servants should be dressed appropriately, the butler in black trousers, black shoes and socks, white shirt, black bow tie, and a white cotton or linen jacket. The female servant wears a black, white, or gray cotton uniform and a bib apron, white or black shoes, and neutral stockings. Keep a supply of crisp aprons on hand so they can be changed if need be.

In a pinch there should be at least one server for every six guests, although Urania Ristow of San Francisco recommends one server for every three guests so that service is impeccable and warm foods are served promptly. If this servant ratio isn't possible, modify the rules to suit your needs.

The doorbell rings and your butler answers the door. With a slight bow he opens the door, saying "Good evening" to the guests, taking their coats, and directing them into the living room where the host and hostess are waiting to greet their guests. At a formal dinner the hosts never open the door.

Cocktails are offered and are brought to the guest on a silver tray. Hors d'oeuvres are passed during the half-hour to hour cocktail period.

The meal is announced by the butler. Guests enter the dining room two by two, the host leading the lady who will sit to his right, the hostess bringing up the rear with her male dinner partner, the male guest of honor. At a large function there should be a plan of the tables displayed in an adjacent reception room. To help the guests find their places, their place cards should be displayed on a cloth-covered table. They should be in alphabetical order and keyed to the table—Mr. Benjamin Franklin, table 16, with the red flowers and blue china, place 6. (For formal table settings, see pages 125, 126.)

If the first course is soup or oysters, it should be on the table when the guests are seated. First-course food is to be placed on a service plate and on the more elaborate place plate. Soup plates should never be more than three-quarters full. If the first course is fish or salad, the place plates are on the table when guests are seated. The napkins are folded on the plates. After the guest removes the napkin, the butler removes the place plate from the right side.

The butler then offers the first course to each guest. This is presented in a serving dish or on a platter with the serving fork and spoon in place with their handles toward the guest. Food

*At a small dinner party at the Windsor Court Hotel, the gentlemen retire to a private area of the bar for brandy and cigars while the ladies enjoy coffee and liqueurs in another part of the room away from the smoke.*

*Cigars should be of the finest quality, as fresh as possible, and served directly from a humidor. They should be handled as little as possible and kept away from any "offensive" odors such as perfume or flowers. After the guest has selected his cigar from the humidor, he should be offered a cutter. There are those who eschew a cutter and prefer to bite off the cap of the cigar or remove it with a fingernail. The cigar is then lit with a nontoxic flame. A cedar taper or match with the sulfur burned off or a butane lighter is best.* HIMMEL

is always served from the guest's left side. Platters and serving dishes are held on the palm of the hand, never by the rim. The server may steady the dish with his right hand. If the dish is too hot, a folded napkin is placed under it to protect the server's hand. The waitress follows the butler with any accompanying sauce, to be served from the left side. When this service is completed, the butler serves the wine from the guest's right side and the waitress passes the bread. (It is prebuttered because bread and butter plates are not used at a formal meal.)

At the completion of the course, the plates are removed from the right and replaced by the dinner plates (or the fish plates if there is a fish course). If the first course was soup or oysters, the place plates are removed simultaneously. The butler then serves the main course and is followed by the waitress with the vegetables.

The butler serves the wine for the course. Even if a different wine is served, the first course glasses are not removed.

Salads are always served separately. The butler serves the salad from a large bowl or tray. The dinner plate is removed and replaced with the salad. If there is dressing to be served separately, the waitress passes it and then any accompanying bread or toast. If the salad is to be accompanied by cheese, the butler passes the cheese tray and then refills the wineglasses.

For dessert the table is completely cleared of plates, salt and pepper, menu and place cards. The table is crumbed by the waitress using a napkin to brush the crumbs onto a small silver tray. The dessert service is placed in front of each guest. This includes the dessert plate, finger bowl (half filled) on a doily (never paper), and dessert spoon and fork. While a slice of lemon is never used in a finger bowl at a formal dinner, a few rose petals or violets may be floated in it. The finger bowl is presented on a dessert plate and placed in front of each guest with the silverware for dessert on either side of the plate. As the host, you lead the way by removing the silver, placing the fork to the left and the spoon to the right of the plate. Then with your right hand, lift the bowl and, with your left, its doily, and put the bowl to the front left of the place setting. The dessert is served by the butler with the waitress following with sauces, cakes, or cookies. The butler then serves the dessert wine.

## The Formal Lunch

The luncheon is quite similar to the dinner but with a few exceptions. There is usually only one wine served and there is a goblet of water at the place. When wine is not served, there is a coaster and a highball glass for iced tea. Hot breads are also served with the main course—biscuits, croissants, muffins—and placed on a bread and butter plate.

*A marvelous piece of aged blue cheese, Costa Rican coffee with chicory, port, and good conversation by the fire (facing page) offer the perfect end to a meal. Antiques from Didier Aaron.* HIMMEL

*Little touches can add appeal to a coffee tray (below). Present your guests with the options of whipped cream or hot milk; amber sugar crystals, white sugar, or artificial sweetener; dark chocolate shavings or Kahlua; and cinnamon sticks for stirring.* HIMMEL

furniture out of the way and put away fragile objects. At any large party ask friends to play hostess in various rooms or in different areas. Be certain that they get people introduced to one another.

The best way to plan where food, bars, and coat areas should be is to walk through your house as a guest would. Start by pretending that you've had to park three blocks away in the pouring rain. Walk in with a dripping coat and go to the powder room to pull yourself together. When moving from the powder room to the bar and the bar to the food, is there furniture or a crush of people in your way? Can the food be easily eaten without a knife and fork? Where will you put your empty glass and plate?

Provide plenty of coat racks. A six-foot rack will hold about twenty-five winter coats or thirty-five raincoats. Improvise coat checks by cutting playing cards in half or use colored hangers so that a guest will remember that his Burberry trench coat or her full-length sable is on a blue hanger on coat rack A with the blue balloons. You can put the coat racks on a side porch, in a spare bedroom, or in the hall upstairs. If this isn't possible, divide the coats into separate rooms. Guests whose names begin with A-L put their coats in one room, M-Z in another.

One bar is needed for every twenty-five people, but only three bars when you reach one hundred people. To be on the safe side, allow a twelve-by-twelve foot cleared space in front and on the sides of a bar that will serve twenty-five to forty people. Even if you have a built-in bar, remove the stools for easy access. Keep the bar away from entrances, the coat area, food areas, or any part of your house that could become congested. Try to put each bar in a space that has both a way in and a separate way out—not, for example, at the end of a narrow hall. Another good idea is to have a separate self-serve wine and soft-drink bar.

Cover each bar with a floor-length cloth. Store all the liquor mixes on ice in a large picnic-sized ice chest under the bar. Ice tubs or old metal washbasins can be wrapped in sheets or fabric for a spiffy look and added insulation. Block ice chipped into chunks lasts longer than crushed ice

or cubes. If there is snow on the ground, utilize it. For drinks you will need about one pound of ice per guest.

Consider that it is necessary to have one food "station" to feed twenty guests buffet-style. For one hundred guests, set up at least two buffet tables (each in a different room) with two food stations per table. Set up one opulent food display. Don't put out all the food at once, but when it has run out, remove the platters immediately. Avoid highly perishable foods such as sushi or gelatin-based mousses unless you can control the room temperature.

No matter how elegant, the food set out for a big party will get messed up before it is completely eaten. A gorgeous salmon mousse begins to look like the victim of a grisly accident after a few nibblers have hacked into it; there are broken-off bits of crackers, and garnishes strewn on the table and pink stuff all over the knife handle. Therefore it is a good idea to have a food maintenance person who does nothing but keep the food looking its best: the ham sliced, the mustard replenished, and the table dusted off. (Unless you want to cut food consumption—people eat less when they have to slice meat or fill patty shells themselves.)

Having bite-sized food passed on trays is a nice way to feed people, especially those who are involved in conversation a long way from the food table. As the host, however, do not be the one to pass the food because your presence will disrupt the conversation among your guests and make them feel compelled to help. Hired waiters aren't necessary; get some teenagers to help. The party theme can even be played out by having the servers dress in costume—anything from cowboys to tap-dancing dice. Having the food passed will keep guests moving and will not leave the hungry grazing in the dining room.

Have you ever had a tray of succulent golden fried shrimp passed to you at a party? You get a toothpick with which to dip the shrimp into the sauce, and if you're lucky you get a napkin. Just as you get your teeth around the morsel, it begins to char the roof of your mouth. As tears run down your cheeks, the server says with a smile, "It's hot." At that point you realize that she is warning you about the sauce, which hits the open wound in the roof of your mouth and gives new meaning to the word *sizzle*. What is so irksome is that in five minutes the same hors d'oeuvre would have been stone cold. Now you are left with a sauce-stained paper napkin clutched around a toothpick and a drink with a soggy paper napkin around it. Forget finding an ashtray or getting the server passing the tray of caviar-filled cherry tomatoes to take your trash.

One hostess has solved the problem. First, nothing gets passed that is hot enough to pass the medieval torture test. Second, she has her servers wear little gingham aprons with pockets (like a carpenter's apron for nails). As they pass through the crowd, they can collect used toothpicks and napkins, which disappear into the pockets.

## The Do-It-Yourself Affair

Mounting an extravagant affair is different from simply having a big party because the preparations

*No matter how small your entertaining space, food should be served in an intriguing manner. Anne Strachan Crounse has arranged iced tea and dessert on an eighteenth-century Irish Georgian pine dresser and cupboard. Guests can actually serve themselves on whichever majolica piece strikes their fancy. Flowers and food complete the visual picture of a glorious still life— iris, heather, alstroemeria, and a luscious almond cake with marzipan icing shaped like a cabbage from La Marquise. Antiques and majolica from Lucullus.* HIMMEL

are far more elaborate and demand precision planning. Whether it is a debutante ball or a corporate bash, it requires months of advance preparation. Of course, the easy answer is to hire a party planner, caterer, or hotel or restaurant manager to handle everything. There are times, however, when you will want to—or need to—do the planning yourself. The following will give you some idea of how to schedule the major tasks.

*To do several months in advance:*

1. Determine your budget. Figure out what must be paid for in advance and be sure your checking account has the money to cover these costs.

2. Figure out the type of party, the theme, where and when it will be held, and make the arrangements. Get all commitments in writing.

3. Decide on the guest list. Put it on a computer or on file cards so you can easily keep track of rejections and acceptances.

4. Have the invitations printed, but not until you are certain of the location, time, and date of the party.

5. Order all equipment that will be needed and specify when it should be delivered and returned: tables, chairs, tablecloths, napkins, heating and cooling systems, dance floors, security and cleanup equipment. Be certain you have arranged for a place to store everything before it arrives.

6. Plan the decorations and order the flowers (don't let them be delivered too soon), candles, special lighting, and favors.

7. Book the entertainment. Besides music, decide what else you may want—photographers, caricature artists, face painters, jugglers, magicians, mimes, carolers, fortune tellers, fireworks, or other entertainment.

8. If you want the event publicized, you must arrange this with each publication. Find out who to call and follow up with a letter detailing the time, place, location, and so on. Be certain each press person you contact gets a personal invitation in addition to their press information.

*To do six weeks to one month in advance:*

1. Mail the invitations. They can go out under a bulk mail permit if they exceed two hundred and are delivered to a bulk mailing service, which will charge a flat rate for Zip coding, processing, and the use of its bulk mail permit. If you are a nonprofit organization, you can apply for your own permit, but it takes a few weeks. The post office will supply bundling labels.

2. Have a system set up for recording acceptances. Keep a count for the food preparers and those who will be arranging the seating.

3. Walk through the event in your mind. Do you have a contingency plan if it should rain? Do you have adequate parking? If children will be at the event, will they be safely entertained?

4. Figure out a game plan for the event. Hire all the help you need, arrange for their uniforms, trays, and other details. Prepare a printed sheet of instructions for the servers: when to pass things, when to stop serving (especially if there is to be entertainment), what times the band will take intermissions, and so on.

*To do the week before the event:*

1. Don't take anything for granted.

2. Plan to spend twenty-four hours a day on the event.

3. Call everyone to double-check that things will be delivered at the specified times.

4. Check each order as it arrives.

5. Delegate responsibility so that you can act as host. Have only one person in charge to answer questions.

## Selecting the Right Kind of Assistance

There are many different people who can help you have a successful party. It is up to you to find exactly the right person to make your life easy. For decades estimable social secretaries have handled the social affairs of old-line families across America. Today many social secretaries are young, personable, and have computers. Morrell Taggart, a vivacious southerner, explains that in her role as a social secretary she does the invitations and handles the RSVPs, but when she puts on her party planner hat, she does everything from concept to cleanup. Pat Ryan of Party Planners West has even choreographed a party in which one of her clients arrived via hang glider and swooped down into his party. The best way to find the right planner is to ask friends who have had parties you enjoyed.

Caterers can provide a variety of services, from doing literally everything (except providing the guest list) to simply preparing a few dishes. One of New York's most successful caterers is Sean Driscoll of Glorious Food. He says that the client-caterer relationship must be based on trust. A party, especially an important one, can make any host nervous. The caterer should meet with you and listen carefully to all of your needs and wants, look over the party location, and figure out all the logistics, menu, and budget. He should also suggest the price range for the type of party you are having. It is up to you to make it clear to the caterer what the budget is so there is no worry about overspending. At big-city prices, dinner can cost between $75 and $150 per person.

The services of a security guard or police officer may be necessary in some communities to ensure the safety of the guests. The police department can advise you about what you will need and may even offer the service free of charge if you will have a certain number of guests. Valet parking is necessary if there will be many cars in a tight space, but check your liability insurance before hiring anyone.

### Rent-a-Staff

A good staff is essential if you want to enjoy a party at all. Of course, many parties can be pulled off with no help whatsoever, but more formal seated dinners and large cocktail parties move easily when you are not working your way through the whole event. The ideal is a staff that displays the efficiency of a good maitre d' at a fine restaurant, giving the impression that they could do anything from piloting the *QE II* through rough seas to efficiently disposing of the body after a murder.

If you can't find an agency that provides temporary help, ask your friends for referrals; try local

*Capitalize on your assets. Set out food and drink in a visually pleasing space because that is where guests will congregate. Catering by Bespoke Foods.*
JEFFERY

56

clubs, restaurants, or hotels; put notices on the bulletin boards of colleges or high schools (or call up the guidance counselor or employment office); or contact a nearby military base to find someone.

The best way to choose the staff is by interviewing. Ask them their thoughts on parties and find out what kinds of parties they are accustomed to serving. If the bartender has only worked the "prune juice circuit," then beware. If the waitress has never served a party before and tells you at length that she disapproves of imbibing—watch out. Other sure-fire losers are those whose first question is how often they can take breaks or how much of the leftover liquor they can take home.

Establish the fee and hours. It will take a good bartender about an hour to set up before a big party; a waitress will want about half an hour to become accustomed to the layout of the kitchen. A good rule of thumb is that you will need one waiter or waitress for every six guests; for twelve you will need a waiter or waitress and a bartender. Decide on what uniforms you want them to wear. Do you want the male help in tuxedos, tails, or white jackets; the women in black dresses with white aprons or white uniforms?

The type of bartender needed for a small, intimate dinner is entirely different from the type needed for a "blowout" cocktail party. You wouldn't ask the venerable family butler, a Mr. Hudson lookalike, to tend bar at a fraternity toga party. The bartender hired for an elegant party at home should be courteous, remember guests' names or at least what they are drinking, and act as though he has been on staff forever. He should not be chatty. He should be efficient, polite, and knowledgeable. The bartender for a long loud party is yet another breed. He must be aloof yet polite, methodical, efficient, and able to concentrate, no matter how many glasses are being held in his face for refills. He must be highly professional and able to deal with long hours of standing. The bartender should be dressed appropriately—in summer, white jacket, white starched shirt, and black bow tie, trousers, and socks; in winter, black jacket, although the white jacket may be used year round.

Explain the type of people the bartender will be serving. For example: "Most of our friends will want two drinks before dinner. The Gilbeys drink gin martinis up with a twist; the Rothschilds will drink only champagne. It is in the bottom of the fridge. The Muscadines like only sparkling, non-alcoholic grape juice, which I keep next to the champagne." Explain your overall game plan. "People are invited for seven-thirty, but all except the Gilbeys will arrive at eight. There will be sixteen people and we'll have drinks on the terrace until nine."

In your mind, walk through your house as if you were the first-time waitress, butler, or bartender. Remember to tell them things like when to light the candles, how to handle overindulgent guests, when and where to empty ashtrays, whether to straighten the living room while you are at dinner, as well as how to serve the meal.

Write down all the crucial details: when to turn on the broiler, when to pour the wine, where the fire extinguisher is, how to find extra liquor

# SECURITY

Hosts and hostesses who entertain the rich, the famous, and the powerful must consider security. Most upper-echelon politicians have their own security team that accompanies them, whereas most movie stars, and other guests who may arrive at your home dripping in diamonds, do not.

If you are responsible for security, find a firm that is both licensed and bonded, preferably one recommended by a friend. The firm will generally send out a person to survey the party location. On the night of the function, there are usually two security men at the front (dressed in the same attire as the guests); one checks the guest list and the other keeps a vigilant eye. There are additional people who unobtrusively patrol the property. The liaison person stays in the kitchen in radio contact with the other guards.

Sid Moreland, executive assistant to the governor of Louisiana, explains what happens when you have an important political guest. First, you will be carefully checked out. You must provide a guest list and a list of the party helpers, who also will be scrutinized. A short physical description of the people and a brief biography stating especially "what they do" will be helpful. It is greatly appreciated if the host and hostess find out what food the politician likes and how long he or she will be able to stay. An added courtesy is to send a menu to the guest of honor.

On the day of the party, a team of security men will come to the party site to do a comprehensive check. They must locate all entrances and exits, bathrooms, phones, parking, and plan escape routes in case of an emergency.

A staff of security personnel will be on duty from before the event until the politician departs. It is courteous to provide food and soft drinks for them, so be sure to find out how many of these "guests" will be at the function.

and mixers. Be certain to explain how you want things cleaned up: what does and doesn't go in the dishwasher, where to put the washed and dried dishes, what to do with badly soiled linen.

About ten minutes before the guests arrive, have a nice chat with the help. Tell them your contingency plans: "If the flan burns, there's a frozen lemon icebox pie." "If we run out of ice, the neighbors said we could borrow some if their lights are still on." Ask if they have any questions and go over all of the service equipment (which, of course, you have already laid out). Use your own judgment about whether they should come to you with questions once the guests have arrived. Some people will needle you to death asking whether or not to put the frilly toothpicks on the tray with the cocktail weenies. On the other hand, if candles are dripping on your priceless oriental rug, you want to be told.

In some cases you may want to let the staff enjoy a drink and a cigarette before the party, but make it clear that once the guests have arrived, this is not to be done. If they are to take breaks, tell them where to spend them—in other words, not mingling with the guests.

Some hosts and hostesses make it a policy to have bartenders spread out their empties to count and waitresses to do the same with the silver. This shows a lack of trust and is demeaning. If you cannot trust the help, then they should not be in your house at all. If you ever find something missing, you should take it up with the server or the agency the next morning. Remember that most waiters, bartenders, and waitresses do this work

for a living and therefore rely on a good reputation. After all, maybe it was your son's college roommate who actually took the 1898 bottle of Mouton Cadet Rothschild.

If the help wants to be paid in cash, be sure to have it on hand. If the service has been good, a 15 to 20 percent tip is recommended if you ever want them to work for you again. Even more important, however, is to express your appreciation for what they have done and adequately thank them. If it seems appropriate, you may want to offer them a bottle of wine, champagne, or liquor, some of the party flowers, or leftover food.

After you have seen how difficult it is to prepare the help, you might see why many people prefer to host parties they can manage themselves. After dealing with employees all day, some hosts would rather come home and cook and clean themselves. The world won't stop if guests have to serve themselves, and dishes can always be done the next day. It really depends on the mood and feeling you want.

## Omigod

Everyone has given a few parties they would rather forget. One of the most renowned artists of this century invited a group of his friends over for *brandade* (a special salt cod and cream dish). After hours of waiting for the meal to be served, they were ravenous. As they took the first bite, they all frantically reached for their wineglasses. Their host had forgotten to soak the cod before he prepared the dish, and it was so salty that it was inedible. The guests all thought it was hysterically funny. Someone ordered in Chinese food and they had a great evening—one that, five years later, they still laugh about.

Analyze any crisis as if it were happening to someone else. Never panic. Consider what you would advise a friend to do in a similar situation.

### General Disasters
*Your child comes down with the chicken pox or you or your husband gets the flu just minutes before the guests arrive.*

If the illness is serious, ask one of the guests to take the others to dinner at your expense.

*A guest at a large party has charged several hundred dollars in phone calls to your phone.*

Don't embarrass yourself by playing detective and accusing guests. Call the business office of your phone company and explain that the calls were made without your knowledge or consent. The phone company will find out who received the calls and, from there, who made the calls.

*You run into one of your least favorite people at the florist while you are planning a party. She says, "So you're having a party. I can't wait—when is it?"*

The best way to handle tactless invitation-fishers is to ignore them. "Isn't having parties work?" you might reply. "I never know what to expect when Goober brings his frat brothers home." Then walk away before the "fisher" has another opportunity to snare an invitation.

*Every time you have a backyard party, the neighbors wander over.*

Since they are neighbors, you can't really throw them out. You can, however, say loudly, "I'd like for all of my guests to meet our darling neighbors, the Bizzibotties. Weren't they sweet to come?" Then put your hand firmly on their backs and walk them back to their yard, all the while telling them how nice it was for them to drop by.

*Your husband, wife, or best friend gets in a foul temper whenever you give a party together.*

Giving parties with people, especially those with "great personal style," can be problematic, especially when your styles clash. Also, parties can bring out people's insecurities. Many couples say that their worst fights occur as the result of parties.

There is nothing worse than a public row. Confide in a guest who is a friend and hope that he or she can "jolly" the grumpy host into retracting his fangs. If this doesn't work, keep clear of any problem, especially the other host.

*Two of your female guests show up in the same wildly expensive dress.*

Make the best of it. Tell them how marvelous they look and what a treat it is to see them dressed alike. You might also relate the story about Prime Minister Margaret Thatcher arriving for her weekly conference with Queen Elizabeth to find they were both wearing the same dress. The next morning the Prime Minister's secretary called the Queen's secretary with the purpose of initiating the custom of a weekly call to discover what the Queen would be wearing so the problem wouldn't arise again. The Queen's secretary replied that Her Majesty never notices what her guests wear.

*A guest puts out a cigarette on your floor.*

Make a deliberate effort to clean up the mess in front of the guest wearing the most disquieted look on your face that you can muster. Hope that you will never again have to have that rude and thoughtless person in your home.

*Two of your friends become so angry that they start throwing punches at each other.*

When Norman Mailer punched Gore Vidal at a Manhattan dinner party, it became even more widely publicized than one of Ali's fights. Get both guests calmed down and out of the party as soon as possible. Turn up the music and create a diversion. Don't make a big fuss over the incident—tomorrow your party might be headline news!

*One of your guests is being insulting and rude to your other guests.*

As the host, you have a duty to break up the problem. In a polite manner explain quietly to the rude guest that you have no other recourse but to ask him to leave since he is obviously not enjoying the company of your other guests. Once the unpleasant guest has departed, change the subject and direct positive attention toward the affronted guests.

*At a large party you notice half a dozen people packed into your tiny powder room. On closer inspection you smell marijuana or find traces of cocaine being cut on your great-grandmother's silver hand mirror.*

Drugs are definitely a party hazard when you or your guests don't approve of them. You have the right to take a hardline: "Please don't do this in my house, it is against the law." Or you may prefer the mischievous approach: Saunter over to a drug user and whisper, "My cousin Louie is a DEA agent and I wondered why he was asking us if you'd be at this party." The offender not only will be scared to death but will be unlikely to bring drugs into your home again.

### Mealtime Disasters

*While guests wait for dinner, the family Doberman eats all of the steaks right off the grill.*

Laughingly tell the guests what has happened. Substitute something else (such as take-out fried chicken) but serve it on your best silver platter. Presumably the rest of the food for the meal is still intact, so the guests will be fine as long as they are fed quickly.

*You are giving the perfect cocktail buffet in your newly landscaped country garden. You notice that the food line has been stalled for fifteen minutes. A visit to the kitchen confirms your worst fear—the hired waitress has neglected to take all of the casseroles for the main course out of the freezer.*

Having no restaurants, fast-food franchises, or a microwave oven in the country, you are faced with fifty unfed guests and thirty who have eaten and are ready for dessert. You and the waitress boil up all the pasta in the house and toss in chopped ham, tomatoes, olive oil, some herbs, and lots of cheese. Within fifteen minutes the remaining guests have "pasta frantico"—an instant hit. In a pinch, eggs can be scrambled and English muffins made into pizzas.

## THE PARTY NEVERS

Never try to impress people by spending more than you can afford. An authority on snobs once said that an exaggerated predilection for caviar and lobster is a sure sign of recently acquired wealth. After all, people who have grown up with money are unimpressed by these delicacies.

Never rely on the consumption of alcohol to create a party atmosphere.

Never invite guests you don't like. This will interfere with your enjoyment of the party and will put a damper on everyone's good time.

Never keep guests standing while you decide where people should sit. Make a plan ahead of time, do place cards, or let people sit wherever they want.

Never apologize for the food. If you know the food is bad and serve it anyway, you are telling guests they are not important to you. If you discover the food is not to your taste after the first bite, do not call anyone's attention to it. Be so witty and charming that no one remembers what they ate. If the food is genuinely inedible, make a joke about it, remove it quickly, and serve something else.

Never treat guests as if they are secondary to the food. Don't jerk away half-finished first-course plates just because the main course is ready. Maybe your guest is enjoying the conversation and isn't ready for the main course. Next time plan the cooking time better or warn guests of your miscalculation before the meal.

Never expect guests to stay outside if it is too hot or too cold. Even though a band and the food are outside, guests will pack into the house rather than brave the elements.

*You've waited until the last possible minute to make the lemon mousse for dessert. It's all ready before you realize there is no room left in the fridge.*

First, take out everything that doesn't have to be refrigerated. Second, determine if any of the other food can go into the freezer. Can you "borrow" space in a neighbor's refrigerator? Fill an ice chest with ice and unload some of the permanent inhabitants, like mayonnaise, butter, and salad dressing. Now all should be well.

*An unavoidably detained guest arrives just as you are getting guests to the table. He arrives with six enormous bunches of flowers in need of immediate attention.*

As the gracious hostess, you offer sincere thanks, disappear into the kitchen with your flowers, and plunge them in water to soak. After the meal, ask the guest to help you arrange them. They'll add a wonderful splash of color to the room where you'll have coffee and after-dinner drinks.

*You are having cocktails with your guests while the prime rib is roasting. Suddenly, the electricity shuts off.*

Light the candles and see if a neighbor has a gas oven in which you can finish cooking the meal. If not, this is when you make the best of it and switch the menu to fondue by chopping all of the barely cooked meat into chunks.

*The hired waitress and waiter are becoming progressively more tipsy and begin to splatter your guests with food as they pass it.*

Slip into the kitchen, pay the help off, and get rid of them. Face a crisis with poise and good humor. Explain *all* to the guests, have a hearty laugh, and let those who volunteer help out.

*The cook breaks her leg on the morning of an important formal dinner party.*

Call a restaurant, club, caterer, or several friends and have the food brought in from elsewhere (after first calling an ambulance, of course).

*A guest begins to choke.*

Don't take choking lightly. If a guest begins to choke don't let him leave the table and politely slip away from the party. Ask if he needs help and if he nods, you or someone who feels competent must administer the Heimlich maneuver.

*You have invited a friend to meet a friend of the opposite sex for dinner. The lady has had her hair done, bought a new dress, and taken a day off work to prepare for the evening. After an hour the gentleman still hasn't shown up.*

Begin dinner, put a stuffed animal in the guest's place, and turn an awkward situation into a joke on the guest who did not show up.

# Chapter 3
# THE CONSUMMATE DESIGNER

The impression made by your entertaining space has more to do with the mood you create than with the cost and quality of the furnishings. The space you choose—large or small, a favorite room or outdoors—depends greatly on the kind of party you are giving, but the mood depends on what you do with it. You can design any mood you like by choosing special lighting, special music, special scents, and special effects. 🫖 Set designer

Candy Davey suggests that the mood you want to create can begin at the front door, which should be decorated to create excitement and interest. After all, it gives the first impression of what is going on inside. Give the decoration an *S* or *C* shape for visual motion and keep it in proportion to the house or the apartment hallway. Remember that the door will be used, so don't use things that stick out too far. For special parties, add battery-powered lights and fresh flowers. 🌷 Landscape architect Charles Caplinger advises that party schemes should carry some surprise. When he cooks, he lets guests walk into a house that isn't dressed up for the party. After cocktails, they walk into the kitchen and—wow!—there is a spectacular display of food. A roast beef hangs on a hook from the ceiling, and a mammoth platter is piled with vegetables and roast turkeys. Three-foot-tall arrangements of evergreens and exotic flowers are accentuated by special spotlights. 🫖 In her exquisite English manor house in Middletown, Rhode Island, Fran Vanliew

Virginia Weinmann has created an arrangement that greets her guests outside the front door. She has combined elephant ears and their white flower, ginger, split-leaf philodendron, and pumpkins to say "welcome." HIMMEL

likes to bring the colors and fragrance of her cutting garden inside. Throughout the house, furnishings echo the spirit of the flowers from her garden. At seated parties, each table is alive with different styles of baskets filled with yellow pansies, Queen Anne's lace, black-eyed Susans, or whatever is in bloom.

## Setting Up for Entertaining

In the eighteenth century, dining didn't require a separate room. Then came the nineteenth century when the ideal was a palatial room that could accommodate forty. Today most people would rather entertain in more intimate surroundings. More and more dinner parties are being held in the library, on the front gallery, by the poolside, or in a cozy kitchen. If your favorite room is the bedroom, you can serve a dinner oriental style on the bed or a low table. A bed with a headboard and lots of pillows is a comfortable place to sit.

The best way to evaluate your entertaining spaces is to watch a party in action. Where do people congregate? Do they cluster in the kitchen? End up sitting on the bed? After the party, examine the way your rooms look. If the chairs have been moved, your conversational groupings are wrong.

Sit down in different chairs in your house. Do they hug you and make you relax or are they stiff, rickety, and uncomfortable? Can guests become trapped in the middle of the banquette? Are there throw rugs that guests can slip on or sharp-edged coffee tables that will bruise shins? Does the phone ring loudly in the room where you will entertain? If it can't be unplugged, at least tape the bell to muffle the sound.

Look at your rooms as a first-time guest would. Is your living room dark and dingy? If you don't like to go into it, your guests probably won't either. A hole in the ceiling, a crack in the plaster, or a stain on the carpet will probably not be noticed, but if the problem bothers you, camouflage it with decorations.

String up a banner, drape the room with sheets held with pushpins, attach a clump of balloons with dangling streamers. Serve your hors d'oeuvres on a table covered with fabric and place it strategically to mask any imperfection on the floor. Big plants on casters are invaluable for instant camouflage. Attach little twinkle lights to a big plant and turn off the other lights in the room —the atmosphere will be magical.

Some busy souls have given up entertaining at home altogether. Instead, they have glorious parties in the private rooms of clubs and restaurants or even take over the whole place for their guests. The surroundings become their own, however, when they add their own table linens, decorations, and special favors. They literally become guests at their own parties and no one feels as if they are having just another restaurant meal.

### Tables

The table you eat from certainly doesn't have to be in a dining room, although it should work well enough so that it can transform a chosen room into a gracious dining room. There should be enough elbow room for the people gathered

*At large parties let each table be its own island. At left, Mary Lou Ochsner has repeated only two elements on each table—the flowers and the antique napkins—to create visual continuity. Each table has its own serving bowls, and one guest acts as hostess to serve the other guests.* HIMMEL

*Joanne Creveling has created a dining room that functions as an empty stage, where mood and color are supplied by food, friends, and flowers. She bought the house furnished and then added her own touch by lacquering the dining room table and assembling an assortment of chairs from all over the house.* HIMMEL

*Memphis-style tables and chairs create a style and mood that cry out for classic American food served with informal grace. Chef Seppi Renggli of the Four Seasons in New York has provided this host with a tureen of hearty American barley soup.* HAGIWARA

around it to sit comfortably. Look for a table having a nice surface, even if it will be covered with a mat or a cloth.

Tables for eating should be located 45 to 50 inches from the wall or other furniture to allow for the maximum comfort of the guests. The ideal size for each place at the table is 24 inches wide and 29 inches deep. This gives each person about two feet of table. (Never place people more than 30 inches apart if you want them to talk without shouting.) Whether you eat at a coffee table seated on the floor or at a formal dining table, you need to allow 10 to 12 inches of knee room between the table and the seat of the chair.

Before you decide on a table, think about the number of people who will usually be using it at mealtimes. Will it be used primarily for meals or will it be used as a worktable for dressmaking? Do you need to have a table that will extend? If it does extend, will the extra legs be in the wrong place to fit chairs under it?

Remember, tables always look smaller in stores than they do in your dining room. After you find a table you like, get the measurements, then go home and make a pattern out of newspaper to the exact dimensions. Put chairs around it and see how it looks. If the table is too big but you must have it, knowing you'll move eventually, push it up against a wall. Mirror the wall and the room will look endless.

A round table is fine for a square room; oval tables are attractive in boxy rooms—they add pleasantly curved lines. A rectangular table needs a rather long, wide room so that it doesn't make the room look like a train car. A refectory table is handy because it has a minimum of legs. When not in use, it can be placed behind a sofa or pushed against a wall for use as a lamp table.

Even though a series of round tables seating eight people is ideal for conversation, some hostesses are reverting back to the custom of using one long table. Reinaldo and Carolina Herrera recently hosted a seated luncheon for fifty at one long table. They felt it was one of their most successful parties because the closeness of the people promoted conversation. No one can complain about being at the wrong table or with a dull group.

The ideal solution for a small space is a box-shaped coffee table that, when turned on its side, becomes a dining table. A 48-inch round or a 30-by-72-inch folding top can be placed on it for larger parties. (When not in use, the top can be stored under a bed.) There are also chests that transform into rectangular dining surfaces and tables with screw-in legs.

Writer B. H. Friedman and his wife, Abby, commissioned sculptor Ed Higgins to make a series of geometric stainless steel components that can be used as separate tables for six or combined to make one table seating twenty-four.

Jewelry designer Mignon Faget had a boring late-nineteenth-century dining room table. She took it to an auto body shop and had it painted with a high-gloss automobile lacquer, "Fire Mist Plum," which she accessorizes with pale blue Porthault linens and massive arrangements of deep green palm fronds. Other hostesses have painted their tables in *trompe l'oeil* patterns or transformed them into *faux marbre* surfaces.

In a pinch, tables can be made out of unpainted flush doors placed on sawhorses and covered with fabulous cloths. Do-it-yourself tops can be made for your card tables. Have the lumber yard cut 3/4-inch chipboard or particle board into the necessary shapes. Clip the tops to the tables with wooden swivel clips.

A rolling cart is the ideal accessory. It can serve as a bar or provide a place to put dirty plates and glasses at a large buffet or cocktail party. A folding stand with a butler's tray is also invaluable. It is ideal as a do-it-yourself bar for a large party or can be set with dessert plates and dessert in a small dining room.

### Chairs

For the conventional dining room you need to determine how many chairs can be placed around the table when it is fully extended with all its leaves. If you haven't enough chairs, there are many perfectly acceptable, inexpensive alternatives. Buy several dozen canvas director's chairs with natural frames. Use dark-colored covers for everyday use and change to white or natural canvas for parties. Anything can be silk-screened on the backs, from your family crest or monogram to whimsical designs or flowers.

White enameled or acrylic stackable or folding chairs work especially well if you add a cushion covered in your own fabric. One hostess has several tie-on covers that match her napkins. Philanthropist Sunny Norman has slipcovered extra

*Designer Eric Bernard has solved Claire Fishbein's problem of how to use a museum-quality Josef Hoffman tea table in her New Jersey penthouse without damaging it. To transform the small table into a dining table for eight, Bernard has encased the wooden frame in Plexiglas. A rotating glass buffet has been sandwiched between a new glass top and the original marble of the tea table.* VITALE

There's something very appealing about having one long table where all friends and family can sit together (facing page). Producer Michael Ulick and his wife, Denise Flamino, painted chairs in different colors to designate various family members. HIMMEL

Replace your usual seating with Chinese garden benches (left) and cover your floor or carpet with straw matting for a change of scene. If you've given up the idea of a dining table altogether, place oversized pillows on the floor around a card table. BEADLE

Designer John Saladino and his wife, Virginia, have set up their kitchen (right) for reading the paper over leisurely breakfasts. Saladino has combined contemporary lacquer chairs, which he designed for Baker, with antique Directoire metal chairs and a banquette covered in pale celadon leather. HIMMEL

David Sanders loves the lightweight, stackable quality of these French garden chairs (left) made of black steel frames and plastic cording. Chairs available through D.F. Sanders & Company in New York. Wall relief by Rosemarie Costoro. HIMMEL

A small oriental dining table (right) can seat two people as comfortably as eight. Flowers are always kept to a minimum. Bulbs have been taken out of their pots and placed in antique porcelain bowls for the evening. HIMMEL

## THE IDEAL POWDER ROOM

The powder room is likely to be the room least used by the family and most used by guests. In a sense it is a public place and should be decorated with that thought in mind. Don't make the mistake of the couple who had a fabulous powder room, complete with brass fixtures, marvelous antiques, and eighteenth-century erotic English etchings that could be reversed to floral prints. One day their young son's teacher dropped by unexpectedly and had to use the powder room, saw the naughty etchings, and was so shocked that she left before she had a chance to ask little Petie's mother to bake ten dozen cookies for the school bazaar. Petie's mother didn't miss making the cookies, but she was embarrassed by the etchings.

*At a beach house in Amagansett, Long Island, designer Richard Lowell Neas has transformed a dark second-floor closet into a bathroom overlooking the sand dunes and ocean. An octagonal window frames the beautiful environs; a skirted marble-topped vanity provides storage space; and a faux bamboo chair is used instead of a towel rack to hold stacks of thick terry cloth towels.* HIMMEL

Instead, take the advice of the late designer Angelo Donghia, who suggested that small bathrooms are more appealing when they are reminiscent of the sea. Paint the walls and ceiling pale blue and spray-paint white clouds on the walls. Use a shell motif on bath towels and accessories. Lots of mirrors on all the surfaces will also help enlarge the space.

Too often the powder room isn't furnished with the things guests may need. Provide a full-length mirror, as well as a small magnifying mirror. Many people don't wear their glasses when they go out, and a good hand mirror is essential for makeup repairs. Make certain there is good lighting, perhaps on a rheostat. There should be facial tissues in plain sight, as well as a supply of helpful products under the sink—safety pins, dental floss, mouthwash, aspirin, antacid, drinking glasses, and the like. Then there is the ultimate luxury—a tray full of bottles of perfume and men's cologne. Scented toilet paper and air freshener are no-nos. They will never smell as luxurious as good perfume and too many smells can clash. You can use potpourri or a scented candle (placed on a high shelf) if the fragrance is subtle.

Guests seem reluctant to defile freshly pressed linen hand towels. They'd rather wipe their hands on a wildly expensive cocktail dress or the toilet paper. The solution is to give them a choice—have the nice linen towels on the towel rack and set out a basket of good, rolled terry-cloth towels. (Remember at a large party to keep the towels replenished.)

Designers Ann Holden and Ann Dupuy in New Orleans have created a satirical powder room based on an ancient Roman bath (below). Draped walls and slipcovered fixtures have been coated with gesso to ensure their permanent texture. Cornice and frieze by Sculptor's Inc.; wall treatment and slipcover drapings by Alain Simard; sisal rug painted by Marcia Schenthal; bronze faucets by Mario Villa. FREEMAN

Mark Hampton has designed an elegant guest boudoir and powder room. If guests will be using your dressing table, clear away some of the clutter but leave all of the special treats ladies love to try—an array of perfumes, powders, rouges, and eye pencils. HIMMEL

What may be slightly impractical for everyday use can be a great pleasure for guests. Since the guest bathroom is small, designer Stephen Chappell created an elegant dressing table in an adjoining room. WHICKER

folding chairs with silk-screened material designed by artist Philip Mayberry.

Inexpensive Basque chairs with rush seats can be dressed up with paint to coordinate with your color scheme. Add a festive touch by tying balloons to their ladder backs.

There may be occasions when you need dozens of extra chairs, which even the most accomplished hostess would not have on hand. Find a regular source from which they can be rented or borrowed. Churches, funeral homes, and schools often have a better quality chair than do rental places. Otherwise, keep an eye out for sets of inexpensive dining chairs and have an auto body shop paint them in outlandish colors like Cadillac fuchsia or Liz Taylor violet. These can be strewn about in the kitchen, utility room, and children's rooms until they are needed.

Pamela Pipes and Priscilla Claverie, two busy New Orleans career women, bought a large set of chairs at an auction of restaurant furniture. Each stores a group in her garage. At party time, there they are—sixty matching chairs.

## Creating an Illusion

A simple meal can be transformed into a feast with the addition of a little imagination. You can change your dining room into a romantic setting with the help of special lighting, music, and scents. Architect Arthur Davis has created such an intricate computer system in a home that when dinner is served a button can be pushed and the lights dim, specially selected music comes on, and a wall opens up to reveal an elegant dining room.

You don't have to spend a fortune, however, to create an illusion when you entertain. After the Great Depression, some of the grandes dames of the South found that all they had left was a decaying family home, a little silver, and lots of good china. Nevertheless, they continued to entertain and no one suspected that the roaring fire was taking the place of electricity and heat. Neither did their guests realize they were being served course after course of corn, beans, and greens, because they were presented so ceremoniously.

### Lighting

Next to comfortable seating, lighting is the single most important factor in comfortable entertaining. Observe how other people look in your rooms. If they don't look good, neither do you.

The first thing to do is put all of your lamps and overhead lights on rheostats. The lights can be gradually dimmed as the evening progresses. Reinaldo Herrera suggests removing the bulbs from chandeliers and adding candles to soften the light. (Be sure to protect the sockets with plastic wrap so the bulbs can easily be reinserted.) A bright overhead light makes everyone look deadly, wrinkled, and pale. Pink bulbs are a must for anyone over thirty-five; they give a soft, flattering light. Amber bulbs used in corners, away from people, create sultry warmth.

The choice of lampshade can also make a difference. Designer Angelo Donghia liked to drape a scarf or a square of sheer fabric over the shade to change the lighting to a muted and more romantic mood.

*Noguchi lamps provide the mood for this oriental buffet. Crudités are arranged like a garden under three tall candlesticks, and the low bowl of pomegranates echoes the shape of the lamps. Bento box on floor from Naga Antiques. Courtesy* New York *magazine.* HEYERT

One instant way to create drama is to up-light a plant in the corner with a clip-on work light and a low-wattage spotlight bulb. The shadows of the foliage will create a dramatic effect on the entrance hall, dining room, or living room walls. Actress Joan Crawford had an up-lighted garden of bamboo plants in the corner of her living room.

Install picture lights over your good paintings (or those you wish to pass off as good). They will change the room's appearance considerably. Show off a display of plates, photographs, or pictures using dimmed track lighting, but be certain these lights are never directed at the eyes of anyone who is sitting or standing.

Marvelous effects can be created with exterior and interior lighting. At one party in a re-adapted, small nineteenth-century fire station, the only light came from the flickering flames of the gas lights in the garden and hundreds of tiny votive candles placed inside on the floor and low tables. They were banked around flats of single-colored pansies. The same romantic effect can be created with fires in the fireplace. Buy copper sulfate at the drugstore and sprinkle a bit on the fire to make colorful flames.

Straight white candles, 7 7/8 by 7/8 inches, are classic for the dining room table. You must be certain the candles will not cast ghoulish shadows on your guests. There should be no direct candlelight from the hairline to the chin. Candle-holding chandeliers and wall sconces give off soft, flattering light. Don't forget to allow enough time to light all of the candles before the party or meal.

If you use a lot of candles, it is better to order them by the case. Remember that cheap candles contain a lot of air and burn very quickly. The more expensive ones from ecclesiastical supply houses last much longer. Putting the candles in the freezer will slow their burning. You should also be careful not to place them in a draft from an open window or an air-conditioner.

Many times the base of a candle will not fit into the holder. If the candle is too large, trim it with a knife run under hot water or simply hold the end of the candle under hot water to soften it. If a candle is too small, use a bit of stickum (florist's clay) or melted candlewax to hold the candle securely in place. Another idea that works well is to wrap a small strip of tin foil or masking tape around the base.

Spike holders for large candles pose a problem. Many times the candle will split when impaled on the spike. To prevent this from happening, make a hole in the bottom of the candle with a hot, pointed awl, ice pick, or nail, or heat the spike before placing the candle on it.

Votive candles are a must for any party at night. They can be banked on a glass or chrome étagère, a mirrored place mat, or any reflective surface to create magic. Writer B. H. Friedman and his wife, Abby, have an enormous heart-shaped, graduated, wrought-iron stand filled with red votive candles in front of their dining room window overlooking the harbor in Provincetown. When the candles are lit, the heart seems to pulsate. Other people make serpentine patterns on tabletops with their votive candles. Instead of the usual glass containers, votive candles can be put in cut artichokes. (Cut off the stem of the artichoke so it sits flat; open the leaves and insert the candle.) A 1 1/2-by-1 3/4-inch votive candle should burn about twelve hours, and a 2 1/2-by-4-inch votive for forty-eight hours. When purchasing votive candles, choose the unscented ones. In a pinch, the vanilla-scented ones are all right, but the others tend to smell like room deodorizer.

Liquid candles, which consist of clear plastic disks and wicks, have many uses. You can fill any object with water topped by 1/2 inch of vegetable oil, float the disks, and voilà, instant candles. They can be floated in a Steuben bowl with gardenias or camellias or put into crystal cocktail glasses or clear or cranberry glass compotes. They will burn for up to three hours.

Outdoors you can use luminarias, a Mexican tradition, to make your house look inviting. Fill small colored or brown paper bags about one-third full of sand and nestle a candle in each. The glow of lighted luminarias is gorgeous around a pond, lining a path, or around the back of a garden. Be certain not to place them too close to grass, flowers, or shrubbery, especially if it is dry or brittle, and do not use in windy weather.

Up-lights can be placed on trees so that they shine through the foliage to create a sense of drama. Tiny twinkle lights placed on bushes and in hanging baskets will make the garden come alive. Light a party outside with paper lanterns, kerosene lanterns, or candles with hurricane shades. Be certain no outside light shines directly on anyone's face.

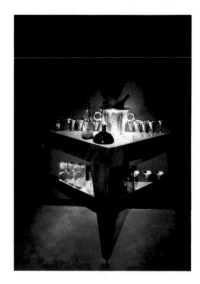

## Music

Music sets the mood for a party and shouldn't be considered at the last minute. Many hosts and hostesses make long tapes of their favorite music. Each tape has a different mood, from quiet and romantic to upbeat and jazzy. Some people go a step further and make tapes of forties, fifties, sixties, and seventies music. They like to play music from an era that will make a first-time guest feel at home.

Vocal music, especially opera, with dinner is overbearing. In general, music during a meal distracts from good conversation and must therefore recede to the background. If you have a marvelous sound system and a penchant for Wagner, invite your carefully chosen friends with a similar interest for an evening of their favorite composer. After dinner, dim the lights and let people relax over cognac in the living room while listening to an hour of music.

Live music immediately makes a party into an event and gives it a focus. Even the crush of a giant cocktail party is lessened by the tones of live music. It may be a kazoo band at the front door, but it livens up the party.

Piano music is terrific if you have the space. Have the pianist start out playing quiet classical music and end up with contemporary jazz after dinner to quicken the pace of the party. The synthesizer is the accordion of the 1980s and can do anything at the hands of a skilled musician. A harp provides elegant, ethereal background music; a saxophone or clarinet can be moody and sexy; the flute, perky and happy.

Talented musicians in any community welcome the opportunity to earn some money playing at a party. Then there are people who simply like to play music. One Minneapolis psychiatrist offers to play for his friends' parties just because he finds it relaxing—and he is very talented to boot. New Orleans coroner Frank Minyard blows the horn at his parties. If you don't have a booking agent in your area, ask local music teachers or church choirmasters to suggest good musicians.

A good booking agent can be the key to getting the right music. Jean Nathan, a top booking agent in New Orleans, explains: "It is very important to find out what an agency's focus is. Do they do only large parties and events or do they also specialize in small, intimate affairs? Call as many agents as you can find because their advice is free." She further advises that you explain the theme of your party, the type of guests you will invite, and the mood you want to create. Most importantly, tell the agent what your budget is for the music. The agent also needs to know what limitations your location may have, such as lack of electrical outlets outside, no space to dance, neighbors who will complain about loud music.

Another consideration is accommodating the musicians themselves. One member of a baroque music quartet, Catherine Bull, tells of times they literally could not hear what they were playing because of the noise level of a party. If music is to be background, place the musicians on a raised platform, in a gallery, or in an area where they won't be stepped on and can perform. A makeshift screen of potted palms can help.

*Live piano music is a marvelous way to end an evening. Designer Nancy Wong has created an eminently comfortable room around a grand piano, where guests can gather for after-dinner coffee and liqueurs.* HIMMEL

Special live music at a party can work well unless the music turns into a concert. Concerts only work if the guests have been forewarned. Imagine studying music and practicing for a lifetime, only to find yourself performing a complex aria in competition with a matron regaling several other guests with stories about her face-lift. Find out if the musician will be bothered by guests smoking or talking during the performance. If the answer is yes, either invite only guests who know how to behave or skip the concert.

Dancing at parties can be terrific fun. Sometimes it is spontaneous—someone turns up the music and people begin dancing—and other times you can put on a lively record or tape and encourage guests to dance. You can also hire a deejay to keep the music going and gear it to the pace of the party. For live dance music, you can hire anything from a synthesizer or three-piece combo to a full-scale orchestra. A word of warning —be sure to ask whether or not you have to furnish the sound system, what kind of electric requirements the musicians have, what special lighting they need, and how loud they will be.

Never hire musicians sight unseen (or rather, sound unheard). Go see them perform first, and if that is not possible, ask to hear a tape and speak to someone for whom they have played. Imagine the horror of the quiet, elderly hostess who hired the Larry Welk combo for her husband's eightieth birthday party. Larry was a punk rocker with a pierced nose, and the combo consisted of four sparsely clad women who played the drums. Larry needed the money badly and tried very hard to please by playing what he considered "easy listening" music over and over—a medley of Barry Manilow classics. Luckily, the guests thought it was a joke.

### Scents

Scents, when they are pleasant and not overbearing, can set a party mood. Baking bread, roasting meat, and freshly ground coffee are luscious aromas that make guests eagerly anticipate a meal. One Fort Worth hostess places freshly roasted and ground coffee beans in the potted plants before a breakfast or brunch to fill the house with a rich coffee smell. Designer Darrell Schmitt studs oranges with cloves and sets them to boil in red wine before he hosts a dinner in the winter. Simmering a pot of spices—cinnamon, allspice, nutmeg, cloves, lemon and orange rinds —not only will fill your house with a glorious aroma but also will mask kitchen odors.

Fragrant flowers are delightful but should never be placed where food will be consumed. The worst offenders are gardenias, magnolias, narcissus, and jasmine. Potpourri, incense, scented candles, room sprays, or perfumed lightbulb rings are fine when discreetly used. They should be so subtle that a guest wonders if the fragrance isn't your perfume.

For an outside party, the hostess can give each female guest a sprig of freesia or a gardenia to wear in her hair. They will fill the party with the smell of flowers. Other hostesses use scented oil in oil-burning lamps or plant jasmine or sweet olive to welcome their guests.

At Mary Lou Ochsner's, dining need not take place in the dining room to be elegant. After a concert guests sit down to a supper of she-crab soup followed by a hearts of palm and tangerine salad —all prepared in advance and served immediately upon returning home. Fragrant narcissus are kept on the sideboard away from the table, where they would compete with the aroma of the soup. In place of an elaborate centerpiece, orchids, iris, and calla lilies are first placed in water vials, then wired into curly willow and placed in an up-lit vase on a pedestal. HIMMEL

## Entertaining in a Small Space

Some people live in fear that someone will actually see where they live. Perhaps they think that their homes are too small, poorly furnished, or uncomfortable. If you feel this way and are faced with the prospect of entertaining at home, don't panic. Create such a unique atmosphere that no one will notice any shortcomings.

One celebrated novelist tells of a time, many years ago, when his sweetheart brought her parents from Savannah to his dingy, one-room apartment in New York. The struggling writer had returned home one day to find a note tacked to the door: "Darling, Mama and Daddy have just come to town and are dying to see you, so I asked them to have dinner with us here at 6:30. I'm certain they will love you just as much as I do." The poor young man got the note at 5:00 p.m. Having only $8.49 to spend, he didn't hold much hope of making a good impression.

Six-thirty arrived and his sweetheart and her parents were shown into a marvelously exotic scene out of the Arabian Nights. With the help of his French landlady, the writer had cut huge branches from the flowering fruit trees in his neighborhood and put them into a trash can and bucket. He had draped his coffee table with an Indian bedspread and borrowed pillows to use as seating on the floor around the table. The room was illuminated with dozens of yellow and red votive candles that he bought from a neighborhood church. For dinner, he spent his remaining six dollars on Middle Eastern and Indian take-out food, which he laid out on a borrowed black lacquer tray, and invited his guests to eat with their hands. (His landlady had provided him with finger bowls.) "I'm so sorry that we have to eat in my kitchen," he told his soon-to-be mother-in-law, "but I've stayed up all night editing my novel and the pages are all over the living room and bedroom." Luckily for him, none of his guests had to use the bathroom, which was down the hall.

Any space, no matter how small, should have two areas, one for easing into the party, greeting and talking, and the other for eating. You can change the mood by laying straw matting on the floor or throwing a quilt over the back of a sofa. Joshua Greene, noted design photographer, puts white muslin and white pillows all over the floor of his one-room loft apartment. Everyone feels instantly comfortable and relaxed.

Your apartment or vacation condo, which is cozy for one and crowded for two, can become the setting for a mob scene. It may be an impromptu party or a cocktail buffet in a rented condominium in Vail. Before you know it, there are twenty people coming and they tell you they have asked others to drop by.

First of all, get rid of as much furniture as you can. Don't strip the place, however, because removing everything will remove the character of the room. Three people can stand wherever there is a chair, so get rid of all the little chairs, armchairs, and small tables. Clear off a few shelves in your bookcase to hold food, napkins, and ashtrays. Transform any bed that can't be removed into a couch by adding lots of pillows and pushing it against the wall.

*When space is small, a cart can work as the perfect place from which to serve a buffet.* LIZA-NINA

*Create two spaces in the room where the meal will be served—one for eating and another for before-dinner cocktails and after-dinner coffee. Be certain guests are seated so they are not looking at the dirty dishes.* LIZA-NINA

*When space is a problem, set the food out on the staircase (right) and hope that guests have enough sense not to go upstairs. Popular New York eatery Arizona 206 has provided a southwestern buffet that is easily accessible.* HEYERT

Forget about decorations unless you can hang streamers, balloons, mobiles, or banners from the ceiling. Fill the space with cool air before party time. Keep the lights dim—maybe no one will notice how small the space is. Serve only finger food. There is no way to manage plates, knives, and forks with a crowd on hand. Have a big trash can and plenty of heavy trash bags. Make a sweep of plastic glasses (there's no way you can even consider using anything else) every half-hour to clear spaces for newly abandoned drinks.

The logical place to put the food is on the dining room table. Try to place the table in the center of the room so that the guests can easily "graze" around it. If the space is too crowded, push the table close to a wall, leaving a small space for the food maintenance person to stand. Remember that all the food does not have to be in one place and you can make several smaller food areas. You can also set up a bar on the balcony or even in the powder room if you have a second bathroom.

No doubt the quaint cottage you have rented on the same weekend you have six houseguests will not have a dishwasher. If you just can't cope, be inventive! But whatever you do, don't complain to your guests. You can scrape the plates and make them disappear until later, when you are more kindly disposed toward washing them. One man in Martha's Vineyard keeps large buckets by his back door. Before a party he fills them half full with water and dishwashing detergent. As guests finish each course, he scrapes the plates, slips out the back door, and plops them into the sudsy

water to soak. His kitchen, where the guests eat, stays clean, and he can do the dishes the next day. An Alaskan hostess puts her scraped plates into the bathtub, which she has filled with soapy water, and closes the shower curtain.

## Entertaining in a Large Space

The new rule of thumb is that a party's success varies inversely to the size of the room. The more crowded and cozy the room, the more at ease the guests will feel and the better the conversation will flow. Therefore, if you want to entertain in a room that seats forty, have forty-five guests! Don't, however, pack guests in like matches in a box.

If the room for a party is too big, divide up the space to make it more intimate. Folding hinged screens work well. A less expensive solution is to run a ribbon across part of the space and tie helium-filled balloons at different heights or to bank lots of tall plants together to make a forest.

One terrific big-space divider is the "diversion centerpiece." In Wichita Falls, Texas, the large dance floor of the country club was transformed by the use of a red lacquered Japanese bridge flanked by a sea of red flowering plants. Guests could walk over or around the bridge to get to the dance floor.

When you are stuck having to decorate a gymnasium, the first thing you need to do is visually lower the ceiling. This can be accomplished by hanging large air- or fiber-filled shapes with clear fishing line suspended from the metal stripping around the acoustical tile ceiling.

John Funt, the head of display at Tiffany's,

who does lots of decorating in big spaces, has these tips: "Don't try to camouflage an entire room," he says. "Instead, do one or two massive decorations that are eye-catching. Each tabletop should be aglow with light, thus creating islands of interest. By leaving the undecorated areas of the big space in the dark, they will disappear. Create pathways with inexpensive indoor/outdoor carpeting that will make a wide space look narrow."

## Entertaining Outdoors

A party in your rose garden or on the top of a hill when the wildflowers are in bloom is sure to be a success because it is also a visual feast. A front yard can be transformed into the English country-side by adding a few grazing sheep. Some hostesses have rented peacocks to add atmosphere to their outdoor receptions. Beverly Hills designer David Jones had flocks of swans at his all-white garden party benefit at Robinson Gardens.

Even the roof of your apartment building can be an exciting place to have a party. So what if the roof itself is a bit ugly? The idea is to enjoy the fresh air and scenery. Have a sunset champagne party and let the view be the entertainment. If the roof looks better in the dark, have a late-night "West Side Story" picnic and ask guests to come as gang members or their honeys. Rig up clotheslines as dividers to camouflage unsightly rooftop equipment or structures. Spread out red-checkered tablecloths and put candles in Chianti bottles. Record lots of romantic music for slow dancing, and serve pizzas with beer and Italian ice for dessert.

The late Hale Boggs, who was majority leader of the House, and his wife, Lindy (now a congresswoman), used to host garden parties for 2,000! They didn't want to host a party in a hotel because that was too impersonal, but their house couldn't hold such a large crowd, so they decided to entertain outdoors. Lindy did all of the cooking and her friends cleared out their freezers to store food for her before the party. The congressman was in charge of the guest list and the weather. The parties were a huge success because they were outside. "We had the congressional community, old Washington society, visiting dignitaries with their children," says Lindy. "The children would all hide in the bushes and peek out. That would break the ice."

The whole party doesn't have to be outside. The biggest pitfall of an outside party is that the hostess must continually run back and forth from the house. If this is a problem, serve cocktails outside while the food is cooking and go inside to eat. Alternatively, have cocktails inside, and let the guests fill their own plates and go outside to eat.

Picnics and barbecues are the most popular form of outdoor entertaining. If you've become bored with conventional outdoor parties, try a theme party, such as a nineteenth-century ice cream social, a luau, a clambake, a Texas chuckwagon barbecue, or a New York pushcart dinner with vendors "selling" hot pretzels, hot dogs, falafel, knishes, sodas, and ice cream.

At a picnic at a ranch near Goliad, Texas, friends mowed a lawn-sized patch of the tall grass and wildflowers in a pasture. The guests sat on

small rugs and quilts and were served food from large hampers set on picnic benches. After the party, the benches, rugs, and hampers went back into a station wagon and the landscape went back to nature.

Edith and Merton Carlson of Eolia, Missouri, like to take guests over their pastures in a Jeep. They hike through the bed of a stream and end up at a cave and "picnic rock," a picturesque spot miles from their house. They take their willow baskets and spread crisp Greek homespun cloths across the earth's fresh surface. When they are very fortunate, they are serenaded by birds singing from a tree overhead.

Fran, Willis, Stew, Robin, and Phil Baker like to saddle up their horses and have an early morning ride, stopping at a favorite wildflower-filled Kansas meadow for a barbecue breakfast. Diana and George Wilson and their children, Amelie, Nancy, George, and Tristan, also like early morning picnics at their Mississippi plantation. They each pull a child's red wagon down to the pond, where they roast sausages over an open fire and pick gallons of dewberries to eat with cream. After years of picnics, all of these families stress that the choice of picnic spot is crucial. Stay away from swamps and thickets because that is where bugs and "varmints" live. Also beware of ant piles. The ideal way to picnic is to stretch out the eating so that the experience of eating alfresco can be savored as long as possible.

Many people with swimming pools take them for granted, but not Broadway financier Mickey Easterling. Her favorite place to entertain is by her

*Friends can be invited over for lunch midweek as a break from lunch in the office or a restaurant. An hour in the sun can do wonders for the psyche.*
SCHLNZ

pool. In the winter she even has the area tented. Lighting is provided by hundreds of tiny lights in the trees and silver candelabra on each table. Exotic flowers are flown in from all over the world, and rechargeable lighting tubes are wrapped around branches, umbrellas, and poles to create a sculptured effect.

Decorating outside is easy. At night, outdoor umbrellas can be taken down and the hole in the middle of the patio tables filled with enormous dried branches, spray-painted silver and decorated with tiny twinkle lights and masses of flowers wired to them. Large baskets of potted plants in bright colors are splendid. The bigger the space, the bigger the arrangements you will need.

A pool can become the centerpiece of the party. Karl and Bette Ewald like to fill their pool with floating gardenias or camellias and miniature floating candles. They surround the pool area with primitive kerosene lanterns on spikes, which they brought from Haiti. Another hostess filled her swimming pool with a carpet of red balloons for her "Red Ball" several years ago.

Of course, outside entertaining isn't without its problems. The most obvious is bugs. You can have your garden professionally sprayed—at least six hours before the party so the smell will dissipate. There are also do-it-yourself sprays that you should concentrate on dense foliage and low-lying green areas near where people will be standing. You can line the area of the party with citronella candles or small commercial bug torches. (Keep both away from food areas because the smell is not appealing.) Electronic devices are fine if you

don't mind the sizzling sound of frying bugs as an accompaniment to your meal. The most pleasant solution is to use aromatic plants and herbs around the food area. Put together bunches of lavender and marigold flowers or burn oil of lavender in a lantern.

For the mental well-being of guests who fear being gobbled up by bugs, buy about six different types of insect repellent and put them in an accessible place. If a guest should be stung by a wasp or a bee, apply a cold compress or wet tobacco immediately and then apply calamine lotion. Remove the stinger from the wound with tweezers. A severe allergic reaction can involve the respiratory system. Get the afflicted person to an emergency room immediately.

If it is very windy, be certain to anchor the tablecloth to the table with clips. Another solution is to thread the corners of the tablecloth through heavy napkin rings and tie them into knots to hold them down. Napkins can be held by placing them under heavy seashells.

When it is very sunny, an outside meal can be hard on the eyes. If shade is impossible, remember to use dark-colored cloths, napkins, and plates, which won't reflect the light so brightly. If it is very hot, be certain to keep food either cooler than 42 degrees or hotter than 140 degrees. Meat, anything containing eggs (like mayonnaise), and cheese will spoil very rapidly in hot weather.

What do you do on the day of your daughter's garden wedding when it is 93 degrees in the shade —even under the tents you rented at great expense? If there is any chance it will be a hot day, arrange for a company to pump air-conditioning into the tented area. If this service is unavailable in your area, revert to the tricks people used before the advent of air-conditioning. Set giant blocks of ice in front of electric fans. Some hostesses in the South used to seat guests in uncushioned caned chairs with an ice bucket under each chair. Give each guest a fan tied with a pretty ribbon. Have lots of umbrellas and parasols for shade and move very slowly. No matter how hot it is, you must ignore the heat and hope that no one will be concerned if you are cool and collected. (Every so often, sneak into a corner and hold ice on your wrists to cool yourself off.)

The opposite can also happen. You are having a formal after-theater dinner for sixty people around your pool and the temperature drops to 35 degrees. If you can, tent the space and pump in heat. If this isn't possible, have old oil drums cut in half and build bonfires in them with charcoal. Change the theme of the party to "Winter Wonderland." Put out lots of candles and kerosene lanterns, arrange twinkle lights in the trees, and serve hot food. Don't act as if you're cold. Put on layers of long underwear and act as if you're warm in your coatless formal attire.

# *Chapter 4*
# THE STYLISH ARRANGER

*N*o matter how busy they are, today's successful hosts and hostesses are finding creative ways to interject style and taste into table decorations. They might use a small piece of sculpture or a decorative bird cage, a model boat, an antique teddy bear, several pieces of jade or Steuben glass, a collection of Venetian paper boxes, a pincushion filled with antique stick pins, or an American Indian water vessel. Combine these treasures with

one single flower in a bud vase and—voilà—a personal table decoration. Hedi Kravis and Ellie Cullman, designers and antiques consultants in New York City, may be partners, but each has a special style when it comes to table settings. Hedi uses her collection of antique tortoiseshell, while Ellie and her husband use their excellent collection of eighteenth- and nineteenth-century decanters. "I like to use something *for* the garden with something *from* the garden," says gardening expert Marybeth Weston. "I'll unpot a new blue sage, bleeding heart, chrysanthemum, or aster for temporary use in a porcelain bowl on the dining table." She then uses a pencil to stick in leaves, being careful not to injure the plant's roots, and creates a garden-like arrangement. After the party the plant can go back to its original pot in the garden for a long, happy life. In the fall and spring, Mary Williams, an accomplished fund-raiser, weaves the stems of branches together in an oriental vase with a narrow neck. She advises that symmetry isn't

*A platter of sliced kiwi, pineapple, and oranges is dressed up with three antique bottles and a few blossoms (top). A Guatemalan handwoven tablecloth is a nice accompaniment to an unmatched collection of white and blue antique ironstone and contemporary wall graphics by artist Merri Pruitt. HIMMEL*

*Even leftovers can be dressed up when the spirit is fun (left). If no fresh flowers are available, you can cut shapes out of plywood and paint them (in whatever colors and patterns strike your fancy). In the corner of the table is a whimsical "Fingerbowl" by artist George Febres from the collection of Marjorie and Walter Davis. HIMMEL*

visually pleasing. After the branches have been anchored to one another, she adds bright flowers. Then she places a few clear votives underneath to give the arrangement a glow.

Table accessories are like fashion accessories. Mix the expensive with the cheap, the antique with the modern. Kay Church, a retired doctor's wife from Fort Worth, likes to use an antique wooden Pinocchio doll, which stands eighteen inches tall, surrounded by a garden of clay flowerpots filled with bright red geraniums, impatiens, pansies, ranunculus, and sweet peas. At each guest's place, she puts a miniature tin watering can that has the guest's name painted on it; in it are three bread sticks tied with a red and white striped ribbon.

Look around your house, your attic, or even an antiques or junk shop to find objects that will lend new character to the mood and style you want to project. Those Victorian jardinieres, statues, and epergnes festooned with roses might be just the thing for a tea party.

There are times and places when it is a good idea to have an old standby that can be reused. One Aspen hostess uses a clear acrylic flowerpot in which she places an acrylic tube or a cardboard mailing tube spray-painted silver. She anchors it in the flowerpot with red or green grapes, red cherries, cranberries, or marbles (or layers of several). Into the top of the tube she places feathers or flowering branches.

Peggy Kennedy, the executive editor of *House Beautiful*, keeps a ceramic rabbit tureen on hand at her country cottage. When flowers are unavail-

*Make each object used in a table setting provide impact, not visual noise. Designer Larry Laslo began this table setting (top, left) on an empty white Formica table. Bare windows and classic Josef Hoffman dining chairs give him clean, simple lines to work with. As Laslo says, "Decorating is like theater. The table is its own stage." Here he has set a dramatically spare table with tableware of his own design and strikingly simple objects. A bunch of curly willow adds dimension to a few rubrum lilies on the mantel. The containers on the table hold anthurium and birds of paradise. HIMMEL*

*After ice skating, guests are treated to a winter luncheon in the kitchen surrounded by some of J. Allen Murphy's favorite objects. The centerpiece is a replica of Marshall Field's private railroad car. Ivy print napkins and place mats made from a Brunschweig fabric accent the Wedgwood china. VITALE*

able she fills it with a large bunch of fresh parsley, carrots or radishes, ties a bow around the bunny's neck and one around each napkin, and has an instantly festive table. Nancy and John Poynor use their collection of Boehm porcelains on their table. The porcelains are surrounded by crystal candlesticks and camellias.

Edith Mary Carlson and her husband moved from an ultra-modern estate in St. Louis to an unpretentious farm outside Eolia, Missouri. For her table she relies on seven cranberry glass fingerbowls which she fills with garden flowers or fruit. She lines them down the middle of her table, clusters them on smaller tables, or uses one on each of several card tables.

You can have special items made in chocolate —a Mercedes Benz, a tennis racquet, or a guest's initials. After the meal, the centerpiece becomes dessert. For informal dinners, create an enormous hero sandwich. Take three two-foot loaves of Italian or French bread and slice them lengthwise. Cut the ends off all the loaves except for the pieces that will be at either end. Spread with mayonnaise and mustard and fill with sliced meats, cheese, lettuce, and tomato. Put each sandwich end to end and construct one very long sandwich. If you don't want a real sandwich, you can slice the bread horizontally and fill with greenery and flowers for an unusual centerpiece.

Helium balloons can be tied to anything to add height and interest. Tie bunches of asparagus or leeks with plaid ribbon. Pile the bundles at odd angles in a flat basket with a handle. Using streamers of the same ribbon, attach helium balloons to

Containers almost have more impact on a floral decoration than the actual flowers. Imagine a spring bouquet of wildflowers, white roses, daisies, anemones, and daffodils. Picture it in a light blue spatterware pitcher. It makes a pretty country statement. Picture the same spring bouquet arranged in a low silver bowl, and it makes an elegant statement.

Having the right containers on hand can be a tremendous asset. When your best friend surprises you with a dozen roses for your birthday, you'll have all sorts of options. You can display them in a clear fishbowl, divide and place them into two clear cylinder vases, or place them in individual small bottles, bud vases, and aperitif glasses to create twelve little arrangements.

A variety of painted baskets festooned with ribbons can be an elegant alternative to silver bowls (and they don't have to be polished). Clear bowls in various sizes and shapes are extremely versatile, since they will fit into almost any decor and can be formal or informal. Lush, opulent arrangements can be created inexpensively by placing branches or weeds—pussy willow, pine and holly boughs, chinaberry branches, cattails, eucalyptus, autumn branches from maple or oak—in an oversized container such as a porcelain umbrella stand or an old coal bucket. The secret is to put together a collection of containers that works for you and your lifestyle, then choose your flowers accordingly.

*Don't be afraid to use your best vases for flowers. They make a personal statement and certainly show off your special objects. Flowers can be displayed in any objects that can hold water to give color and life to an otherwise dark corner. Art vases from the collection of Rosie and Pierre Levai; containers and flowers from Twigs.* HIMMEL

*The combination of roses and silver is magical, opulent, and elegant. A tea or coffee service makes an enchanting series of vases for your favorite flowers.* FREEMAN

the handle. An elegant effect can be created using clear balloons tied to an arrangement of dime-store pearls, twinkle lights, and white roses in a silver bowl.

Even small tables can be decorated. A card table can have a decorative fan opened on a stand. On either side there can be a votive candle and a vase with one small flower. Another solution is bunches of wheat tied with raffia or baskets covered with an opened napkin and topped with a variety of edible decorative breads.

No matter what you do, never duplicate it exactly. Bill Blass stresses that if the same flowers are used in the same vase in the same location, they virtually become invisible. Guests become so accustomed to seeing them that they no longer pay attention to them.

## The Ideal Assortment of Vases

Almost anything that holds water can be used as a vase. If you want to use an unusual item that doesn't hold water, such as a pair of boots, hat box, brown paper bag, picnic basket, or especially fine pieces of porcelain, you can insert simple plastic or glass containers to serve as liners. Don't overlook fruits and vegetables—pears, pumpkins, eggplants, melons, artichokes—which can be scooped out and cored to hold flowers.

For period arrangements or theme parties, dig out all those old epergnes, jardinieres, wine coolers, cut-glass and silverplate vases. These objects look romantic and elegant with arrangements done in the French or English style.

When there is absolutely no room on the table for anything, buy a pair of candelabra; one of the sockets can be modified to hold water and flowers by making a collar out of aluminum foil and sticking in a piece of oasis.

A good supply of small vases that hold one or two blossoms is invaluable because they are low. Being no more than 6 inches tall, they become virtually invisible, making them compatible with any decorating scheme. The most versatile are bubble-bottomed clear vases, beakers with or without raffia, 4-inch fishbowls, little copper or pewter vials, and cordial glasses. The ones with a lip can be hung from a chandelier or from heavy branches with raffia or ribbon.

Vases 7 to 11 inches tall work well for bouquets of flowers. For example, a 9-inch fishbowl is ideal for a dozen medium-stemmed roses, irises, or daffodils. Other vases in this category that are particularly versatile include cylinders and ginger jars that have mouths no wider than 4 to 6 inches. They work nicely with simple arrangements not requiring a lot of flowers (such as aspidistra mixed with three anthuriums).

Straight-sided low bowls (3 inches high, 6 to 14 inches in diameter) can be used in several different ways. You can float one or two large blossoms (magnolias, camellias, peonies) in them or put a small bud vase with a dendrobium orchid in the center and surround it with river rocks, marbles, or smooth black stones.

The most versatile of all the larger vases is the fishbowl (12 to 20 inches high), which works well for two dozen long-stemmed roses, assorted greens, branches, and flowers. The stems of iris,

*Dress up flower arrangements with objects that make a visual statement. Wallpaper by Carefree Wallcoverings.* SIMMS

*Fresh fruits and vegetables make interesting containers for flowers (left). Hollow out the center and either use a nonperishable flower, such as a daisy or an orchid, or place your favorite flower in a water vial and insert it. Fruit and vegetable containers can also be used for sauces and dips to add pizzazz to a buffet.* HAGIWARA

*Denise Flamino and Michael Ulick use antique glass bottles (right) found in Venice to set off the simple flowers bought at a corner market.* HIMMEL

*Collect all the things you have that will hold flowers (right) and experiment with shapes and colors to create different moods. Accessorize your party as you would your wardrobe, with looks for morning, noon, and evening.* HIMMEL

*Use vegetables and fruits as you would flowers and plants (page 108). North Carolina designer Gail L. McAllister of Panache has used wallpaper from Sterling Prints, Dufour Ltd.* WHICKER

gladiola, and ginger can be woven to create an interesting pattern. The shape also works well for a dozen or so of the more exotic plants, such as anthurium and bird of paradise.

Very large containers (20 to 24 inches high) with small mouths 6 to 8 inches can hold large branches without artificial anchoring. They work well for peach, pear, and apple blossoms, lilac, dogwood, and magnolia leaves. (Be extremely careful because these arrangements can weigh up to 60 pounds when filled with water.)

Opulent dried arrangements can be created in sculptured vases by simply stacking giant branches of bleached or natural curly willow.

## Baskets

A versatile part of your supply of containers, baskets can hold plants, bread and rolls, or silverware and napkins. They can be painted with a guest's name and used at each place to hold a favor. They can hold flower arrangements, hors d'oeuvres, potpourri, hand towels, or anything else you like. A rustic country basket, a colorful African or Indian basket, or a romantic painted basket tied with ribbons, lace, and dried flowers can be a marvelous way to add some texture and character to your decor. Ribbons, helium balloons, and napkins can always be used to give an old basket a fresh look.

Inexpensive baskets or woven paper plate holders from the dime store can be completely transformed with a bit of paint. First use gesso or spray paint to cover any stains or imperfections. Then paint or spray on colors and patterns— splattered pastels, bold colored stripes, muted

## PRACTICAL SHAPES AND USES FOR BASKETS

Groupings of four 8-inch baskets can be used to hold cocktail napkins in various parts of a room or can be grouped together in the center of a table to hold plants and flowers as centerpieces.

A series of round baskets with liners can be used for crackers and hors d'oeuvres or tiny pots of flowers. Since they are inexpensive, you'll find it handy to have two sets, one of natural straw and another that has been painted. The most versatile sizes are 2 1/2 to 3 inches high by 8 1/2 to 11 inches in diameter.

Market baskets with handles are useful for breads, potted plants, vegetables, or fruits. The most flexible sizes are 6 to 7 inches high, 15 to 18 inches long, and 11 to 15 inches wide. Deep baskets are handy for such things as popcorn or potato chips. Oblong or square baskets are particularly good for displaying flats of tulips or other flowering bulbs or holding mounds of fresh strawberries, apples, or tomatoes. Grapevine baskets in heart shapes make an unusual centerpiece when festooned with ribbons and filled with white eggs or camellias.

Wall baskets with flat backs can be filled with dried arrangements and placed on the wall or filled with blooming plants and put on the front door.

Everyone needs a picnic basket. Decorate the top with silk flowers or gingham bows and sprigs of fragrant fresh rosemary.

Animal baskets can add a whimsical touch to your table decorations. You might choose a large lacquered rooster, bamboo ducks, large and small painted swans, or baskets in the shapes of

baby chicks, pigeons, rabbits, pigs, frogs, and turtles.

Painted baskets can hold clay pots of geraniums, mums, or other flowering plants. You should have lots of shapes and sizes and make sure the construction is sturdy.

Giant woven clothes hampers can be lined with a plastic tub to make an ideal cooler for ice and wine or beer.

*As in ancient times, baskets remain one of the most decorative and useful items in the house. They come in handy for everything from gathering flowers to collecting all those children's toys that come in hundreds of pieces. Anita Walker has filled her corner cupboard with a collection of primitive and Louisiana Indian baskets. HIMMEL.*

109

Designer *Myra Densmore sprays baskets with color and combines colorful fruits and vegetables (right) to create an inexpensive centerpiece that can be used for a visual lift every day.*
PROCTOR

*Natural baskets overflowing with mounds of apples, cranberries, pinecones, and nuts make an appealing, easy, and aromatic holiday display (bottom, left). For special celebrations add a profusion of bayberry- or cinnamon-scented votive candles.*
HIMMEL

*Anita Walker sets a table with three rag rugs (far right). At each place she uses a different set of china, yet the table is visually tied together by antique bottles of daisies and a mass of pink and blue candles. Balls of rag yarn in baskets are used as the focal point of the table.* HIMMEL

*Place baskets on shelves to decorate a dining room during the winter (facing page), and in the summer pull them down and fill them with potted plants to use throughout the house. Decorate the shelves with your favorite bowls and plates when baskets are needed elsewhere.* BEADLE

grays and beiges applied with a sponge. Finish with a coat of polyurethane. Some baskets can be painted over and over again to fit different party color schemes.

When buying a basket, be certain that the bottom is sturdy. Always line the bottom of a basket if it will hold flowers, plants, or food. Plastic containers, tin foil, or sheets of plastic wrap can be used to keep dirt and crumbs from falling through.

*To create an illusion straight out of an eighteenth-century still life painting (left), Marlo Phillips has draped a piece of silk fabric underneath an antique vase filled with full-blown roses in pale hues.* FREEMAN

*These flowers (right) have been meticulously arranged to look as if they have jumped straight from the garden into the vase.* FREEMAN

*For this party under a tent in Beverly Hills (pages 114–115), spring flowers have been arranged in baskets on each table. More flowers and loaves of bread seem ready to spill out of the jumble of baskets suspended from the ceiling.* FROGER

## Flowers with Flourish and Fantasy

Remember when the only flowers that the florist offered were carnations, mums, daisies, gladiola, and roses, and the only greenery that came with an arrangement was leatherleaf fern? Today, not only are there more flowers available than ever before but the variety is endless. Three agapanthus can be the dramatic focal point of three arrangements with the addition of ligustrum, laurel, Japanese yew, podocarpus, and variegated croton leaves. Our environment is filled with all manner of weeds and wildflowers that can lend a unique quality to any arrangement—milkweed, bitter sweet, pokeweed, black-eyed Susan, Queen Anne's lace, dogwood, pussy willow, lilac, and quince, among others. (Note: Bitter sweet and pokeweed are poisonous, so do not use them near food.)

Reinaldo and Carolina Herrera arrange all their own flowers. "Nature never makes a mistake," says Reinaldo. "All sorts of flowers grow together in a garden—that is what should be created in an arrangement." They mix all types of flowers together into great bouquets.

The ideal thing to do is to keep something blooming in your apartment or garden all year round—bulbs, violets, cyclamen, red verbena, begonias, or geraniums. At party time, just transfer them to clay pots, if necessary, or decorative baskets and set them directly on the table.

For simplicity, there is nothing easier than grouping potted plants in a basket or on a platter or tray. Fill a large painted basket with a few potted plants and surround them with artichokes and Queen Anne's lace. Use three white amaryllis in 6-inch pots and five 4-inch pots of impatiens or begonias. Alternate in a serpentine pattern down the center of the table. To make the arrangement more formal, you can paint the pots or tie them with pretty ribbons.

Fran Baker of Pleasanton, Kansas, likes to use three ornamental peppers and three cherry tomato plants. Around each one she scatters a few cacti and single blossoms in old bottles. The peppers and cherry tomato pots can be wrapped in burlap, painted, or tied up in fabric.

In her home at the beach in Perdido Key, Jane Ingram likes to bank the center of the table with a collection of low green plants (fern, ivy, verbena) or pots of herbs (parsley, dill, rosemary, chervil). She either adds blossoms floating in liqueur glasses, which can be elevated to various heights, or puts blossoms in single vials, which

## HOW TO TALK TO YOUR FLORIST

There are many talented floral designers in this country. To find the one who will be right for you, ask your friends, funeral homes, churches, and clubs for recommendations. If you have a limited budget, you may want to find a legitimate way to buy from a flower wholesaler, or find a florist who will understand your limitations and will give you ideas about how to arrange the flowers you have ordered. The new cash-and-carry flower markets are terrific. Whenever possible, buy flowers by the bunch because they are much cheaper. Be realistic about your budget. If you have an unlimited budget, however, and want to make a big statement, be certain the florist understands exactly what you expect.

Explain the types and varieties of colors of the flowers you like as well as those you loathe. Take in samples of the fabrics in your rooms. Show the florist photographs of your rooms and your table setting, or ask him or her to come to your house and make suggestions. Explain the type of party and the mood you want to create. Show the florist photographs out of magazines depicting arrangements you like, styles you'd like to try, or even containers you'd like to duplicate. Then be flexible and listen to the florist's ideas.

If you like an arrangement, find out the name of the person who did it. Call and express your appreciation. Remember the person's name and ask for him or her next time. If you have a problem with what the florist sends you, call immediately and explain what is wrong. Don't wait until the following week.

E*dible flowers can be interspersed on serving platters and used as garnishes to make colorful complements to any food. These include day lilies, roses, borage flowers (floating in the glass of mineral water), zucchini blossoms, and calendulas.* SCHINZ

B*askets of fresh fruit and potted plants can bring any space to life (far right). Even in the dead of winter, the sun streaming in on great green plants gives the illusion of summer in some tropical paradise.* J. B. O'ROURKE

can be placed directly into the plants. Then she intersperses her favorite pieces of coral or shells.

Even if you can't grow things at home, keep in mind that friends or neighbors might have a glorious array of blooming things that you could borrow, buy, or barter for. Keep an eye out for what grows locally in your community. Often there are wholesale nurseries that can supply all of your needs.

Use what you've got. Tim Trapolin, a New Orleans artist, makes big arrangements of a variety of green things that he's brought in from the garden or gone into the woods and picked. If all you can find are a dozen little impatiens blossoms, float them in the saucer of a tureen filled with greens.

If all that is available are mums and carnations, you can make a huge pom-pom with eight to ten carnations or three to five mums. Wrap the stems with ribbon all the way down to the base and place in a clear plastic pot filled with wet sand. (Be sure to plug the hole with stickum.) Place the arrangement in a soup plate filled with low green leaves floating in water.

If you must use artificial flowers, put them where no one can smell them and intersperse just a few of them in bouquets of fresh greens. One silk magnolia blossom nestled in a large fishbowl will work well if the arrangement can be set atop a platter of real magnolia leaves. A few pink full-blown silk roses mixed into a pitcher of daisies and baby's breath are also lovely. Well-made artificial calla lilies will fool almost anyone if they are put in water with a few aspidistra or palm fronds.

## China and Crystal

Porcelain and bone china are the only kinds of china considered appropriate for formal dining. Porcelain is made from kaolin. The term *bone* means that oxidized bone ash is added to the kaolin. Bone china is valued for its translucence and resistance to chipping. It should not go in the dishwasher, especially if it is edged in gold.

Ovenware is fired by a relatively new method that makes the dinnerware resistant to heat and cold. Made of clay, it is highly practical, but not nearly as fine as real china. Ironstone is heavy and durable and generally white, although there are several popular patterns. Stoneware is thick, opaque, and similar to ironstone. Pottery is porous and thick and tends to chip rather easily.

Platters are important. Choose several platters to complement the sizes, shapes, and colors of your food. Large ones that can hold a large roast or turkey are also useful for serving small canapés, making constant replenishment unnecessary.

When buying or renting china, get more dinner and salad plates because you will use them most often. Service or buffet plates (which are slightly larger) can be in the same pattern or in a complementary one. Many times it is attractive to mix new with antique, unusual with conservative.

Clear glass first-course plates are more attractive than almost any service plate. They can be used as salad or dessert plates as well. If you plan to entertain large groups, purchase three or four dozen. Clear glass bowls are also useful. Antique finger bowls are perfect for soup, salad, or dessert.

Soup bowls and flat soup plates are essential.

Collect small covered tureens in complementary colors. You can also use abalone shells as soup bowls. For a different look, hollow out a cabbage to hold a glass bowl of clear soup.

Brighten up the mood of your table by topping a white plate with a slice of watermelon, 1 1/4 inches thick and 6 to 8 inches in diameter. On one side of the slice insert three short stems of lilac, freesia, pink statice, and a white orchid. Plan each course so that it can be served on a small plate or shell. For example, start the meal with spinach and mandarin orange salad served on a clear plate. For the main dish, serve a chicken and grape curry baked in a shell or an individual casserole. Dessert can be any pretty pink sorbet or ice cream mounded into a hollowed-out navel orange shell and garnished with a sprig of mint.

## Flatware

Good silver flatware is a must for formal dining, but for less formal entertaining there are many choices. Don't be reluctant to use plastic-handled or stainless steel flatware. They can add the perfect textural effect to a table setting. A heavy, sculptural set of stainless can look marvelous next to your old ironstone; blue plastic-handled flatware can add zest to blue and white oriental porcelain or spatterware. A collection of commemorative spoons is great fun to use for serving *pot-de-crème* or demitasse.

Sharp knives are essential for cutting meat. They might have china or silver handles for use at formal meals, or bone, plastic, wood, or stainless steel for less formal occasions.

*Place settings should reflect the style, taste, and interests of the host. At right, a clear plate is used atop a whale bone picked up along the beach on Cape Cod. At each place is a small platter of wishbones from geese, fish mouths, or other unusual bones. Salt is served in the vertebra of a whale. Wine is served in a Baccarat highball glass in the Rotary pattern. HIMMEL*

*The contrast of a sleek black table topped with an antique lace cloth provides a striking change of pace in this stark, modern room (right). Food is served directly from antique silver serving pieces onto contemporary black plates that match the surface of the table. Individual orchids are used in the Two's Company napkin rings to soften the effect. HIMMEL*

Having all the right silver serving pieces (right) certainly adds a touch of elegance to everything you serve. James Robinson in New York has provided an asparagus server, fish knife and fork servers, Stilton cheese server, egg topper, and tea skimmer. Plate from Wolfman Gold & Good; butter server from Kentshire Galleries; fabric in Medici pattern from Yves Gonnet.
*HIMMEL*

The typical crystal "trousseau" (right) contains a water goblet, red wine glass, white wine glass, champagne coup, and sherry/sauterne glass (from left to right on bottom shelf). Champagne aficionados know that champagne must be served in a tulip-shaped glass to preserve the bouquet, so relegate that coup glass to the cupboard for use as a serving dish for sorbet.

Fabric by Gretchen Bellinger; stemware by Baccarat; crystal and silver decanter by Kentshire Galleries; silver champagne bucket by James Robinson.
*HIMMEL*

*Architect Warren Platner designed a glass buffet cabinet that contains Plexiglas trays of glistening silverware (left). Framing projection lights were designed by Platner to shine through the case and cast the shadows of silver objects on the wall and floor beneath.*
STOLLER

*Great cook and accomplished hostess Marina Schinz treats her guests to osso bucco and provides just the right utensil for eating the delectable marrow.*
SCHINZ

Remember, however, that caviar should never be served with a silver utensil, which will react with the acid in the caviar. Also beware of putting silver and bone- or porcelain-handled cutlery in the dishwasher.

## Linens and Table Covers

It is fairly easy to determine the proper size for a tablecloth. For a square or rectangular dining table, add 30 inches to the dimensions of the table. This allows a gracious overhang of 15 inches on each side. If you have a standard card table (36 by 36 inches), for example, you'll need a cloth measuring 66 by 66 inches.

Whether your table is very fine wood, glass, or extremely homely, pads are necessary. You can make a simple pad out of white, ecru, or flesh-colored felt. (Be sure to sew a few rows of stitches around the edges with loose tension to prevent the cloth from stretching when washed or dry-cleaned.) Most department stores and specialty shops selling linens will make pads. If you have a pretty lace cloth, you may want a colored under-cloth that will be decorative as well as protective. One hostess has a red plaid taffeta undercloth for Christmas and a pale silver-gray polished cotton one for her elegant dinner parties.

There is a rubber material called Bulgomme that has the appearance of linen but is heat resistant. Green baize is another good choice of material because it can be used uncovered or as a pad. Some people use a tablecloth with cork mats where the hot plates will go. For a sparkling effect, have mirrors cut to the exact dimensions of your table and use them in place of a tablecloth or place mats. They must be backed in soft fabric to keep them from scratching the table.

The easiest fabrics to care for are blends of natural and synthetic fibers, such as linen and terylene or polyester and cotton. Other people favor new textures—quilts, hooked rugs, chenille with hanging balls, seersucker, painted canvas, painted floorcloths, artists' drop cloths (artistically splattered with paint), even fabric right off the bolt. Shapes can be cut out of sponges and block-painted onto sheets. Sponge on navy blue stars and spatter with silver paint.

Keep a variety of sheets on hand to put on your tables as underlays. A crisp lace or organdy cloth over deep red or maroon creates a period feeling. The same lacy overlay over a pastel pink or peach cloth can be soft and romantic. Shiny black leather or silver vinyl makes a sleek and sophisticated overlay. You may also want to collect square or round overlays in assorted fabrics—geometrics, solids, or floral designs.

Create special effects in your room. Drape fabric from the ceiling, down a wall, and over a table to add drama. If you have a particularly fine piece of silk, lace, or even a scarf, place it on the table and cover with a piece of glass. Lace between two pieces of glass appears to be floating on the base of the table.

Place mats come in almost every material, from lace to plastic. Even napkins folded into large triangles can be used. One hostess uses nineteenth-century lace runners along either side of her rosewood dining table. Another host has sev-

# TABLECLOTH SIZES

| Shape | Table Size | Cloth to Floor | Tablecloth | Persons Seated Dinner | Buffet |
|-------|-----------|----------------|------------|------------------------|--------|
| Round | 24"-30" | 90" | 60" | 2 | 4 |
|  | 36" | 96" | 66" | 2 | 4 |
|  | 48" | 108" | 78" | 4 | 6 |
|  | 54" | 114" | 84" | 8 | 10 |
|  | 60" | 120" | 90" | 8 | 12 |
|  | 72" | 132" | 102" | 10 | 14 |
| Card Table | 34" x 34" | 94" x 94" | 64" x 64" | 4 | 4 |
|  | 36" x 36" | 96" x 96" | 66" x 66" | 4 | 4 |
| Oblong or Oval | 48" x 36" | 108" x 96" | 78" x 66" | 6 | 6–8 |
|  | 60" x 36" | 120" x 96" | 90" x 66" | 6 | 8 |
|  | 72" x 36" | 132" x 96" | 102" x 66" | 6 | 10 |
|  | 96" x 36" | 156" x 96" | 126" x 66" | 8 | 12 |

Buffet and bar cloths should hang to the floor. Since standard table height is about 30 inches, add 60 inches to both the length and width of the table to reach the floor. In a pinch, a king-sized sheet can be used under a cloth that is not long enough. Having the cloth meet the floor is crucial so that the under-table region can be used to store liquor bottles, kitchen utensils, and even soiled linens.

When linens are rented, be certain to check each cloth and napkin for stains before it is put on the table. Use overcloths or fabric squares to hide spots and holes.

Generally, rented linens come in standard sizes and these can be used in multiples or with the addition of skirting.

A glass-topped table under the trees, while a pleasant place to eat, may present a constant cleaning problem. Almost any green leaves can be spread over the surface to provide a stunning accompaniment to alfresco dining. BEADLE

Bring your favorite things from the inside out, as the Victorians did in the days before air conditioning. Set the table with a skirted cloth to match upholstery fabric. Fabric is from Imperial Wallcoverings' Clarence House. HANDY

eral sets of mirrored place mats in different shapes. For his round table he uses the square mats, turning every other one to make a diamond shape. For his rectangular table he uses round mats on either side and two oblong mats at each end. At more elegant dinners he uses mirrored mats over a silver-gray moiré cloth. You can purchase 12-inch mirror tiles with beveled edges at any large do-it-yourself store. Prices start in the area of six tiles for fifteen dollars. Smaller tiles can be used as coasters. Flatware might have to be positioned off the sides of the mat because of lack of space on the mat itself, but who cares?

Decorative shapes such as swans, watermelons, flowers, and Christmas wreaths can be cut from 3/8-inch plywood. Sand well and apply a white base coat to each. Apply designs with colorful acrylic paints. Add several coats of polyurethane to protect the tops and glue velvet or felt to the undersides to protect the table. If you use a seasonal theme, guests can take their place mats home to use as a door decoration.

Another easy way to make place mats starts with canvas. The concept is the same as painting a canvas rug. Any design can be traced onto gesso-backed canvas and cut with very sharp scissors. Paint with acrylic paints and seal with polyurethane when dry. You can easily make matching coasters in the same way.

The next idea comes from conceptual artist Denise Chenel Vallon. Take a photograph of a dinner plate or a place mat with the silverware on either side. Put something unusual on the plate—Scrabble letters spelling out a seasonal greeting, a

*Nothing is more appealing or versatile than beautifully pressed and softly folded napkins (top, right). Napkins from Anichini; silver tray and napkin ring from James Robinson; fabric from Gretchen Bellinger. HIMMEL*

*A few orchid sprays and ivory armlets from Cameroon used as napkin rings bring this table (bottom, right) to life. HIMMEL*

*Buy single rolls of wallpaper to use under glass to set the stage for special theme dinner parties (below). Wallpaper by Carefree Wallcoverings. HANDY*

heart shape made of red candies, a miniature portrait and a piece of parsley. Have the photograph blown up and laminated and then use it as a place mat. The guest sits down to a picture of an unusual place setting.

Scarves, bandannas, and kitchen or terry cloth hand towels can serve as napkins and be take-home presents for the guests. Silk-screen them with designs or use colorfast, waterproof markers. Write the guest's name or create a design depicting the party theme. You have napkin, place card, and favor all in one.

Napkin rings or distinctive folds can make a splash. Mary McFadden likes to tie her napkins in knots. Interior designer Jule Lang ties her napkins with antique-looking, lacy-edged ribbon. A simple napkin ring can be tied with a helium balloon bearing a guest's name. Ulrania Ristow, a Brazilian aristocrat, often slips napkins through sunglasses as a favor for her guests.

Doilies are indispensable for use on trays and plates. Although they should be cloth, in a pinch you can use paper, but never plastic.

For more formal entertaining, it is generally a good idea to have about one dozen or more white 20- to 24-inch square napkins than the number of guests you plan to entertain. Lovely sets often can be found in antiques shops at bargain prices. So what if they are monogrammed with someone else's initials? Tell inquiring guests that they were given to you by a favorite great-aunt. Wonderful linens can also be bought or ordered from Hong Kong or duty-free shops at airports such as Dublin's Shannon airport.

## FORMAL LUNCHEON SETTING

At a formal breakfast or lunch, the table should be set with linen place mats, although lace mats are acceptable. A luncheon napkin is smaller than a dinner napkin, about 15 inches square, and should be folded like a handkerchief in a square of four thicknesses. Cute napkin folds are never used, even if they are intricate and impressive. Damask cloths are not used at a formal luncheon.

A cloth, if used, should overhang the table by only 7 inches.

The centerpiece at a formal luncheon should be simple and elegant. An antique porcelain bowl filled with fruit and vegetables, flowers, or a few special objects is perfect. There are never candles on the table, even if they are not lit.

For a formal dinner, the table may be left bare or it may be covered with a plain white damask or linen cloth—never lace. (Of course, lace is elegant. It is up to the hostess to decide if she wants to have a correctly formal tabletop or one that is merely beautiful.) The cloth may not overhang the table by more than 12 inches. Embroidery is fine if it is in the same color as the cloth and of fine quality. A bare table demands extra-fine napkins, but nothing fussy or cute, and never in a fancy napkin fold. Dinner napkins should be 20-inch squares, folded simply. Remember that monogrammed linens should be ironed on the wrong side to bring up the design.

The centerpiece at a formal dinner can be elaborate, but not so tall as to obscure the view of the guests. White candles in silver holders may be used on the tables, and they should be lit before the guests are seated. For advice on serving a formal meal, see pages 48–49.

*The place plate with a simply folded napkin is on the table when guests are seated. If the first course is soup or oysters, its plate is on the place plate, and the napkin is to the left of the silverware.*

*At a formal dinner, the table is set with the outside utensils being used first and the glass for the first course being positioned on the outside. For the second course, often fish, the next set of utensils and the appropriate wine glass are used. The utensils for the main course are positioned on either side of the plate with the appropriate wine glass above the dinner knife.*

*While it is not strictly correct to have a water goblet at the place setting when guests are seated, guests should be offered water, which is poured at the table from a silver pitcher. The water goblet is placed to the upper right of the main-course wine glass.*

*At the top of the place setting, if there is to be no finger bowl, are the dessert spoon and fork. To the left of the main-course wine glass is the dessert wine or champagne glass.*

*The table setting for a formal dinner (facing page) should evoke elegance and grandeur with just a hint of understatement to relay the fact that the host has not "just arrived." Interior designer Rubén de Saavedra has created a dining room that simply screams Old World charm. EIFORT*

# Chapter 5

# ALL MANNER OF PARTIES

$\mathcal{L}$ife should be fun and full of variety, and this should be reflected in the way you entertain. There is no good reason to fall into a party-giving rut. Entertaining does not always have to be for a meal in the evening. Just because you cannot entertain in the evening does not mean you should give up having friends over. If you aren't keen on cooking, plan a social occasion around a time that demands little or no cooking. Have friends over for

volleyball or boating and lemonade at three on a Sunday afternoon or have an after-work tea party. ☕ One accomplished married hostess has many women friends she sees infrequently because they are not part of a couple. Twice a year she invites about fourteen of them to an hors d'oeuvres, covered dish, and dessert party. Some show up in new cocktail dresses, others come straight from work, and still others wear jeans and T-shirts. Of all of her parties, this is her favorite. It takes no preparation, and if there isn't enough food (which there always is), "We order a pizza!" Besides food, each friend is asked to bring her favorite record. It is a lively evening, filled with great conversation. 🍾 Another host and hostess in Tampa, Florida, became bored with having their group of friends for the same seven to eleven o'clock cocktail and dinner party. It's not that they were tired of their friends—they merely wanted to add some zest to the festivities. One weekend they sent their children off to stay with their grandparents and invited

Oysters, champagne, and a view of the city at night provide a splendid end to an evening. Anne Rosenzweig of Arcadia has prepared an array of sauces so there are enough options to satisfy every guest. Of course, the guest list must be carefully screened to include only oyster fanciers. HAGIWARA

*Unique presentations of place cards add finesse to any table setting. At this 5 A.M. hunt breakfast (left), the guests are greeted by one of their own calling cards affixed to a twig easel or tucked into a twig basket. These, plus a jar of homemade preserves, are to be taken home as favors after the hunt. Flowers by Paul Bott of Twigs; mug, horn cup, toast rack, flask, and riding crop from James II Galleries.* HIMMEL

*Conceptual artist Denise Vallon re-creates what she calls the "Leave It to Beaver, All-American Suburban Breakfast" (top, right) with her collection of Fiesta Ware, the appropriate American breakfast food, and a replica of the Pillsbury Dough Boy. As she says, "When presentation is the key, even fried eggs become fun to eat."* HIMMEL

*This family (bottom, right) does their entertaining early in the day by inviting friends for a breakfast trail ride near their Snowmass, Colorado, ranch. The secret of success is lots of black coffee—the scenery and sunrise provide all the entertainment needed by the guests. As an added treat, guests catch trout in a mountain stream and cook them over an open grill for breakfast. By nine o'clock, they are back down the mountain and ready for their day's activities.* SNOWMASS

their friends over for a safari-style sleeping bag slumber party. They rented tents and a screen and projector and showed *The African Queen* outside under the stars.

## Breakfast

This could be a hunt breakfast, a pre- or post-christening breakfast, a power breakfast to decide the fate of a corporation, or strictly a social occasion. Breakfast can be made into a special occasion by combining several elements.

First, have the breakfast before another event. Bee Longley of Sun Valley, Idaho, a single mother of four grown children, likes to entertain on her deck in the summer. "My friends and I are very sports minded, so by eleven, everyone has gone off to play golf or tennis." She tells of neighbors who have a breakfast once a year for friends to climb Dollar Mountain. Guests arrive at eight in the morning and begin hiking up the mountain. The host is at the halfway point with a tray of screwdrivers and Bloody Marys. At the top, each guest gets a laminated dollar bill on a rope to wear as a medal, and there is a photo session. Afterward, guests go to their host's home for a champagne breakfast (nonclimbers simply arrive at ten for breakfast).

Second, have food that will make people want to wake up and eat. One Saratoga Springs hostess who has breakfasts before the races says that the portions should be on the small side; vats of scrambled eggs or trays of greasy bacon are off-putting. She advises elegance: blini topped with crème fraîche and fresh cherries or sour cream

and caviar; individual cheese and prosciutto souf-flés; frozen yogurt served in a wide-mouthed wine-glass topped with a favorite breakfast cereal and fresh fruit. These treats can be served with a variety of fresh juices, including the nectar of white or red grapes and imported white peach nectar, with or without champagne.

The southern hunt breakfast favors down-home treats served on antique silver and the finest china. In Camden, South Carolina, one young couple lines the drive of their home with eight-foot papier-mâché horses to welcome their two hundred guests after a morning hunt. Inside, the house is decorated with horse blankets, plaids, fresh greens, pewter, and silver. There are cheese grits, tiny buttered biscuits and popovers, a variety of homemade jams, individual omelettes made to order, medallions of beef served with made-to-order scrambled eggs, banana and apple fritters, thinly sliced Virginia ham, and miniature pecan waffles.

Third, there must be a good reason to be up and dressed early. The meal before something, such as a christening or a meeting, is fine. The individual attention of an important person is fine. Morning is an uncomplicated time of day, especially for people in business.

Bette Ewald, who has homes in Natchez, Mississippi; Snowmass, Colorado; and Perdido Key, Florida, seems always to have houseguests who may or may not want to have breakfast on days when the weather isn't nice. Just to be on the safe side, she makes two or three different coffee cakes, keeps hot and mild beef and pork patties

and link sausage in the freezer, gets three small boxes of breakfast cereal, has a box of oranges on hand for fresh juice, and buys lots of fresh fruit. If she has to do a large breakfast or brunch and isn't certain when the guests will awaken, she makes Hollandaise sauce for eggs Benedict first thing in the morning and keeps it warm in a ther-mos bottle. "My family never eats breakfast," says Bette, "but I've had to prepare breakfast for twelve on occasion when we've got guests at the beach on a rainy day. I've learned!"

## Coffees or Elevenses

Coffees (or elevenses) tend to be "ladies only" events. They are especially good for mothers who have school-aged children. They can replace lun-cheons (where more food is required) for meet-ings of bridge, investment, or sewing clubs; for showers and housewarmings; or to introduce a new person, a product, or a political candidate.

A coffee lasts for one to two hours in the late morning and is relatively simple to prepare if you can round up the needed number of cups and saucers. The food can be simply an assortment of homemade breads (get friends to contribute or buy from a bakery): hot gingerbread with lemon sauce; cranberry, banana-nut, carrot, cheese, pumpkin-spice, and raisin breads; or rum-doused fruitcake, chocolate truffles, and apple strudel. Sweet rolls and fresh fruit tarts alone are also fine.

For a formal coffee, keep the coffee hot in a large urn or pot, preferably one with a flame under it. Do not let the coffee boil or it will become bitter. Put out a pitcher of cream and a bowl filled

*Good conversation, an assortment of imported coffees, and a liberal dash of opulence can go a long way to enliven an otherwise dull day. Use the best china you have and give guests the feel-ing that this is an occasion. HIMMEL*

with lump sugar. (Whipped cream or hot milk is a special touch.) To satisfy today's needs, it is a good idea to have a pot of hot water, instant decaffeinated coffee, nondairy creamer, and packets of artificial sweetener. In a formal setting they can be served from the kitchen and brought to the guests who request them.

At a not-so-formal event you could also serve spiced herbal tea, cocoa, or Moroccan-style mint tea. In the summer, serve iced coffee with whipped cream, with or without a dash of white crème de menthe or Kahlua, or iced mint- or orange-flavored tea.

## Brunch

Brunch parties are the perfect way to while away a day eating and drinking. Leah Chase, famed arts patron and Creole chef, says that brunch is the best time to entertain because guests then have their afternoons and evenings free. The food is usually served buffet-style and therefore can be made ahead of time. Brunches are an ideal way to entertain people the day after a big occasion such as a ball, a wedding, or a sports event. Conversation generally isn't too sparkling, but the party can be. While the guests describe their hangovers, you can revive them with bull shots, spicy Bloody Marys, screwdrivers, and mimosas.

Food can be rich and hearty. In the South the Sunday brunch is an institution. While the dress can be anything from very casual to formal, the food is always lavish. There might be milk punch served from a silver punch bowl, wild quail or doves with cornbread dressing, spicy Creole

*grillades* and grits, fried chicken, eggs Benedict or Sardou, leek tarts, do-it-yourself crepes, pineapple upside-down cake, individual Key lime or pecan tarts, bread pudding with hot whiskey sauce, peach cobbler, and café brûlot. After the feast guests either rush off to nap or will happily dance, usually to a jazz combo. In Texas many hostesses favor *huevos rancheros* with corn tortillas, hash browns with small steaks, corned beef hash with poached eggs topped with Hollandaise sauce, chicken hash, champagne with fresh strawberries, and lemon meringue pie. Californian and Hawaiian hostesses seem to favor healthier fare: poached fish or sushi, platters of fresh fruits and marinated salads, accompanied by Margaritas or planter's punch.

## Lunch

There is lunch, there are luncheons, and there are midday dinners. In much of small-town America, men and women still come home from work in the middle of the day for a hot meal. In other households there is a midday Sunday dinner. Fare may include roast meat, gravy, rice or mashed potatoes, good cornbread or biscuits, and lots of seasonal vegetables. The drink of choice is iced tea, and the desserts are flavored with chocolate, lemon, or custard, rich and satisfying. To be invited to one of these family meals is a treat, a glimpse into the family's tradition.

The formal luncheon is characterized by light elegant foods and good breads, such as croissants, muffins, or rolls. No one wants to continue the day's activities feeling stuffed. The meal may

## THE TENNIS LUNCH

*Invitations:* Guests receive a can of tennis balls with an invitation wrapped around it: "Come at 12:30 for lunch, tennis, and swimming." An alternate rain date is given for the following weekend.

*Decorations:* The tennis court is decorated with red and white helium balloons with long white crepe-paper streamers. Tables for four are set up under umbrellas, and each course is served under a tented table.

The pool, if there is one, has several dozen white and red air-filled balloons floating on it, as well as rafts and inner tubes. There should be an ample supply of towels, deck chairs, sun lotion, and magazines.

*Activities:* Tennis games begin immediately. A tournament can be set up or the guests can organize their own games.

*Refreshments:* There are daiquiris, Margaritas, fresh lemonade, spiced iced tea, wine, and beer to drink. On one table is a selection of three cold soups, and on another is an assortment of vegetables, cheeses, meats, seafood, and greens for make-it-yourself salads. For dessert, there are three kinds of frozen yogurt with a choice of toppings. A jazz pianist plays during lunch. The meal is served at three o'clock, although there is plenty of food to nibble on beforehand—raw vegetables with a variety of dips, stuffed grape leaves, snow peas filled with salmon mousse.

*Favors:* At five, humorous trophies are presented to the guest who slept the longest, the best ball-chaser, and the player who changed clothes most often.

*Retreat to a quiet terrace (right) for lunch between tennis or badminton games. The calming strains of Vivaldi will do wonders to ease sore muscles. HARDIN*

*Coordinate your favorite foods with your favorite flowers for a visual feast. Borscht and roses make ideal companions. SCHINZ*

*The magnificent sea view in Newport is all that is needed to make a luncheon memorable. The dining room of Rock Cliff, designed by architect George Chaplin Mason and designer William Hodgins, will seat up to sixteen comfortably at the dining table or fifty when additional round tables are brought in. Dessert and champagne are served outside on the terrace so that guests can take in the full impact of the view. From* Summer Cottages and Castles *by Patricia Corbin and Ted Hardin (NY: E. P. Dutton, 1983). HARDIN*

well consist of three or four courses, with the main course generally a fish or an egg dish: perhaps a spinach and cheese soufflé, leek or mushroom tart, poached chicken with green mayonnaise, or trout Véronique. There are occasions when the formality of a luncheon helps to cover a lack of conversation, for example, when a mother and daughter must entertain a new husband's great-aunt whom they have never met. An evening dinner tends to need male participation, and lunch at a restaurant might appear inhospitable.

Informal luncheon parties on a Saturday in the country are enjoyable. A few couples or friends can get together for a light meal, after which they can go antiques shopping, go to a matinee or sports event, or go home to nap and read.

On Cape Cod, photographer Renate Ponsold is able to pull off a luncheon party at a moment's notice. She keeps her refrigerator stocked with gourmet delights: prosciutto, caviar, crawfish, various cheeses, and a local Portuguese specialty, *linguisa* (a paprika-flavored sausage). When guests drop in, she fills platters with boiled eggs topped with caviar, prosciutto and melon slices, and cheeses, sausage, and breads. She brings them out on the deck to the lounging guests. Her secret is that she is always prepared for a crowd, she presents the food with visual flair, and there is always plenty of chilled champagne.

## The Club Luncheon

The club luncheon today is alive and well. Added to the traditional bridge and garden clubs are aerobics and exercise clubs, investment clubs, sew-

*Rubén de Saavedra designed a dining patio with a Japanese/tropical feeling for clients with a small wooded property in the Hamptons (left). EIFERT*

*Plan to have your next club luncheon outside (right). Make individual hibachis by filling clay flowerpots with lighted charcoal so that guests can roast their own shish kebabs right at the table. Paper napkins need not look commonplace. Roll two napkins of different colors together and slip them into a Sitting Pretty vase/napkin holder from Two's Company. Instead of place cards, names can be printed right on a leaf with silver marker. HIMMEL*

ing circles, and gourmet clubs. Usually members take turns hosting the luncheons, preparing sinful delicacies. Everyone goes all out because, if the club meets monthly, a member may have to entertain the group only once a year.

For club luncheons, there is an age-old formula. The card tables are covered with pretty "bridge" cloths. The first course is on the table. The main course is served buffet-style. If there is a maid, she clears the table and brings in the preserved desserts, two at a time. Coffee is served in another room while the maid gets the card tables ready for bridge or other activities. Pitchers of tea and coffee (iced or hot) are in the room while the game is going on.

The routine, of course, varies from group to group. Some people like to play first and then have

a cocktail-and-nibble period followed by a meal. Other clubs confess that game playing and meeting take a back seat to socializing. One group of mothers of young children has a nap-time poker game. While their little tykes are napping, they play poker, and the loser has the group the following month. Other groups take salad and sandwich makings to a member's house and watch a rented movie on a video recorder while they mend socks and sew patches on their children's clothes.

## The Afternoon Social

Guests can be invited any time from two to five o'clock and don't really have to be served anything. You can invite friends for a trip to a frozen pond or rink for skating and take along thermoses full of hot buttered rum, cocoa, or mulled wine and a few kinds of cookies tucked in the bottom of a picnic hamper. Closer to home, guests can come for a swim or a game of softball or touch football (a great family or singles activity).

In Santa Fe microbiologist Kitty Brothers and her husband have a volleyball, croquet, basketball, and horseshoe party for eighty of their friends. They provide the barbecued meat and a keg of beer, and friends bring salads and desserts. Everyone gets into the spirit and plays at least two of the games before dinner.

Bill and Sally Walker had a whimsical afternoon social at their palatial New Orleans home. Friends were told to come and bring their own lawn furniture. Much to their guests' surprise, the Walkers decorated their porch with a clothesline filled with clothes, a hand-cranked washing ma-

143

chine, a flashing neon beer sign, some old tires, and a dozen live chickens. Sally even went to a used furniture store and bought a sofa with a hole in it for those guests who forgot to bring their own chairs. After the elegantly attired guests had assembled, Sally and Bill appeared dressed like Ma and Pa Kettle, complete with blacked-out teeth and corncob pipes. Music was provided by a jazz band, and the food was country ham, fried chicken, and potato salad.

## The Tea

Traditionally, tea is served at four o'clock, although high tea is a meal served a bit later and is very like an early supper. Formal teas are still given for brides, graduates, debutantes, and visiting dignitaries, to celebrate christenings or anniversaries, or as an organization's social event.

The invitation is sent on the face of folded notepaper or inside the paper if there is a monogram on the front.

In honor of
_____
(name)
_____
(date)

Tea at 4 o'clock
1988 Converse Lane

If there is a guest of honor at a formal tea, the hostess and guest should stand near the front door (not in a receiving line) and talk to each guest as he or she arrives. Guests who don't know one another should be introduced to a few people before they join the party.

The tea table can be laid in any room. The conventional cloth is lace or linen with a design. The cloth should overhang the table by 18 to 20 inches. At a formal party the napkins must match the cloth. Dessert forks are a must if there will be any cake with gooey icing. English dessert forks have a broad tine on one side so that more firm desserts, like fruitcake, can be easily cut.

The tea trolley holds a pot of very hot water, a full pot of freshly made tea, a cream pitcher

_Friends in Jackson, New Hampshire, meet on the mountain after a day of skiing for a light tea (left) catered by Christina's Farm Inn._ JEFFERY

_Tea for two (right) after a civilized game of croquet on the lawn is a courtship ritual that should be revived by all serious lovers. From_ Summer Cottages and Castles _by Patricia Corbin and Ted Hardin (NY: E. P. Dutton, 1983)._ HARDIN

(milk is often preferred in Great Britain), a sugar bowl, a small plate of thin slices of lemon, and a tea strainer.

Many excellent teas are produced by such English firms as Twining's, Fortnum & Mason, and Harrods, and the favorite is Earl Grey. The vast majority of experts (especially the British), however, prefer stronger brands, such as Ty-Phoo and PG Tips, sometimes available at gourmet shops and those catering to Anglophiles. Store any unused portion of tea in an airtight container.

Making a proper pot of tea is an art. A china pot is preferable to silver, except when the formality of the occasion takes precedence. First, you must warm the pot by pouring in some boiling water and swirling it around. When the pot is well warmed, pour out the water. Put one-half teaspoon of tea (a full teaspoon is preferred in Britain) in the teapot for each cup of boiling water. Take the teapot to the kettle, in which the water has just started to boil, and immediately pour in the desired quantity of water. (Best not to use great-grandmama's delicate Royal Doulton teapot; the heat of the water may cause it to crack or break.) Allow the pot of tea to stand for three to four minutes, never longer. The tea may be gently stirred before pouring into individual cups through a tea strainer. For those who prefer weaker tea, pour two-thirds tea and fill up with very hot water.

The proper foods to serve are little tea sandwiches of thinly sliced, peeled cucumber, watercress, or fish or meat pastes on thin bread with the crusts removed and simply spread with butter. Anchovy paste mixed with hard-boiled egg yolk and a little mayonnaise is a popular filling, as are wafer-thin slices of roast beef with a little horseradish sauce. Bite-sized pastry savories, such as tiny English sausage rolls (morsels of tasty sausage rolled in light, flaky pastry), scones, sweet cakes, cream-filled pastries, fruit tarts, and cookies are all suitable for a tea table.

At the Windsor Court Hotel in New Orleans, Kurt Stielhack says, "Tea is an *event*," frequented by little girls and ladies dressed fit to kill. Besides the twelve varieties of tea served from silver pots, the hotel offers champagne, Harvey's Bristol Cream sherry, and port. Cucumber and apple, cream cheese and watercress sandwiches; hot scones with real Devon cream, lemon curd, raspberry jam, and sweet butter; strawberries dipped in chocolate; truffles and miniature sweets—all conspire to conjure up visions of the Ritz in London on a fine June afternoon.

Rosemary Bryant, an internal medicine specialist from Northern Ireland who runs a catering business in Provincetown, Massachusetts, prefers to do all her entertaining at teas held each Sunday afternoon. She and her husband, architect George Bryant, invite friends with children the age of their son, Eric, to go sailing on their boat. Afterward, it is home for an elegant tea party on the deck of their eighteenth-century bayside cottage. Rosemary serves her walnut shortbread, her burned-butter tart with bing cherry glaze, egg and watercress sandwiches, and orange pekoe tea. Guests leave around six-thirty, after a glorious day and enough to eat to tide them over until morning.

*Tea at the Windsor Court Hotel is a civilized way to spend the afternoon, listening to a string quartet and enjoying glorious food. The china is Villeroy and Boch in the Indian Summer pattern.* HIMMEL

*Make decorations at a tea dance as pretty as possible. It is the perfect opportunity to parade your lovely old linens and pretty tea sets, even if they are only used as decorations.* LIZA-NINA

The Tea Dance

The Friday afternoon tea dance is an elegant way to end the work week and begin the weekend. It is regaining popularity among the singles set, especially those who don't want to go home after work, only to fight the traffic to come back downtown later. A tea dance can also be given to honor a debutante, graduate, or engaged couple, or to precede a fund-raiser or dinner party. Usually it is given in a club, a garden or park tent, a cocktail lounge, hotel, or restaurant, or in the atrium of a public building on a Sunday. An office building can be taken over for a tea dance in lieu of the usual Christmas party.

The space, no matter where it is, needs to be intimate. People are reluctant to dance in the daytime and like to feel a bit crowded. The best arrangement is to have a small dance floor surrounded by tables for two or four, covered with crisp white cloths. Small bouquets of pink and white roses can be arranged in silver sugar bowls on each table. Potted palms can be banked to enclose the party.

The invitation to a formal tea dance is written on an engraved fill-in invitation, whereas an informal invitation can be made on a folded notecard. Traditionally, guests are invited for five o'clock on a Friday afternoon.

Tea and champagne are passed on trolleys. Dancing is to an orchestra playing fox-trots or Viennese waltz music. An opulent display of tea cakes and hors d'oeuvres is served on a banquet table. The band stops playing at seven, and guests waltz on, refreshed, to their next activity.

*147*

## The Cocktail Party

Cocktail parties come in many varieties. The term has come to mean that guests will not be seated at a table to eat a meal; it's fend-for-yourself food. There are the straight cocktail parties that generally begin between five and seven o'clock. They don't demand very much food. This is the kind of party you have when you want to have a dinner party but don't have enough space or when you aren't sure how many people you will be entertaining. Guests may drift in and out. Some will have eaten beforehand and others will eat afterward. Passed food can be combined with food that must be eaten on a plate.

Another cocktail party is the mini-buffet, designed to give guests the stand-up qualities of a cocktail party mixed with the sustenance of a dinner. They are held from six to nine in the evening, generally before the theater, a meeting, a parade, or other event. The food should be passed in courses, beginning with hors d'oeuvres—perhaps bite-sized puff pastries filled with *duxelles*, spinach, or cheese; tiny vegetable and seafood tarts; and individual *daube glacé* on toast points. Next you could serve open-faced deli sandwiches piled high with brie, salmon, chicken, or other meats and cheeses. Desserts should be finger foods, such as individual lemon cheese squares or hot chocolate fondue with fruit.

There are several guidelines for giving a successful cocktail party. The first is to plan the party around the space. In Western society, people tend to avoid being physically close to other people. If your party space is too large, tiny groups of people

will hug the walls in clusters and refuse to penetrate another group's cluster. Too small an area and your guests won't be able to move, will become claustrophobic, and leave early. The ideal is cozy crowding, where people can move but are still close enough to produce close contact, nervous energy, talking, laughing, and eating.

If the party will be small, arrange the furniture to make conversational groupings accommodating eight to ten people each. If you want to have dancing, clear a room of furniture and have

## THE "BLOWOUT" PARTY

Any run-of-the-mill cocktail party can be transformed into a real blowout if you adhere to a few guidelines. Understanding group dynamics is essential. Remember that a mob of people acts far differently than a group of people, and the behavior of both bears little resemblance to the behavior of four or five individuals.

Figure out how many people your house or apartment will hold and invite twice that number. You can ensure a memorable party by inviting a liberal smattering of mischief-makers who could easily show up with an entire football team, complete with cheerleaders; some outspoken, pompous types who are sure to offend a few people; a variety of folks who like to dress outlandishly and will give the party pizzazz, as well as a lot of people in all age groups and from diverse backgrounds. If all goes well, someone will put on a Little Richard album and begin to dance.

There is a strange reality about a large party. Three hours into the festivities it will either have taken on a life of its own or be over. Intelligent conversation will no longer be possible because of the noise level. The nonparty crowd will have left and the "party animal" group, who always shows up late, will have taken over.

As the number of guests increases, the cost per guest decreases. The longer the party goes on, the cheaper the booze you can serve, because after three hours of drinking, no one notices. Bring out the jug wine and generic vodka and have plenty of beer, which is what the hard core always seem to want.

After three hours in a noisy, crowded, smoke-filled room, party goers will be in a raw state, saying whatever comes into their minds. At this point, everything seems hysterically funny and the party becomes a legendary success—in early sixties jargon, a blast. By three or four in the morning, the remaining guests may decide to go out to a diner for burgers or breakfast.

Now is the time for ingenuity. Get rid of cigarette butts quickly—outside. Check for any combustible materials or permeating stains. Have the foresight to engage a cleanup crew to come in at eight the next morning and transform the chaos back into your home. Then grab a prepacked suitcase and head for a hotel or a friend's house where you can sleep away the next day.

*Just because a party will be a blowout does not mean that the setting should look like a barroom under siege. Rubén de Saavedra has aided his client by supplying a piece of glass to protect a Louis XV desk when it is used as a bar in the living room. EIFERT*

*Serving food buffet-style need not mean sacrificing your personal style (right). A mass of white tulips, a paisley shawl, and black plaid napkins combine to create a mood for this informal supper party (top) in the fall. Paisley shawl from Kentshire Galleries; stemware by Vietri; napkins from Anichini; white footed bowl, cheese and fruit tray, and bread basket from Wolfman Gold & Good; wooden plates and unglazed terra-cotta candlesticks from Platypus.*

*A late-night buffet in winter (bottom) has a different style and mood, with a crisp white cloth and a profusion of silver. Tablecloth from Anichini; silver champagne bucket and candelabra from James Robinson; crystal and silver decanter, salt servers, silver and jade candlesticks from Kentshire Galleries. HIMMEL*

the space ready; you can even have a moving van load everything up and keep it overnight. If your guest list gets too long, have two parties, with one group on one night and another group on another night. You can also stagger the times on the invitations; invite some people from six to nine and others from seven to ten.

Many people, being who they are, like to make an entrance, especially at a cocktail party where, presumably, guests can mingle to their hearts' content. Single people like to see who is available, so plant a few good-looking men and women within sight of the front door to interest newcomers in mingling. Guests will then tend to float around until they find just the right spot to "colonize" and have a real conversation.

Don't serve overly ambitious drinks. At one party the host made gorgeous old-fashioneds for everyone. Unfortunately, he was mixing second drinks for the first arrivals at the same time he was making first drinks for the late arrivals. He never left the bar. Frozen strawberry daiquiris are fine if they can be made in advance and if guests are offered alternatives. Be careful when you anticipate what your guests will drink. One Atlanta lawyer, fresh out of school, wanted to make a big splash at her first "adult" cocktail party. Instead of having an open bar, she offered three drinks—Seven and Seven (Seagram's Seven and Seven-Up), frozen Kahlua and cream, and made-from-scratch piña coladas. Everyone wanted piña coladas, which ran out quickly. Since no one wanted to switch to the other two choices, the party broke up very quickly.

*151*

## The Dinner Party

The dinner party seems to be the most popular way to entertain today. Couples and single people who want to take a break from entertaining in their own homes are forming dinner clubs. The host for the evening picks the restaurant and orders the food, the chef does a cooking demonstration, and the members eat. The check is split equally.

Several Boston couples have an "international" dinner club. Once a month each couple prepares authentic dishes from a chosen country, complete with an imported beverage.

Mathilde and Prieur Leary like to invite three couples over for a casual evening of Italian cooking. Each couple is responsible for one course. The hosts provide all of the ingredients and set up pasta, gelato, and capuccino machines in the kitchen. Upon arrival, guests are greeted by an accordionist who serenades them throughout the evening—then are given Bellinis, Negronis, or wine *and* their cooking assignments. The hosts make *bagna cauda* (a hot anchovy dip for vegetables) and veal marsala for the main course. Dessert is fresh strawberry gelato and capuccino. It's just as well the cooks are also guests because their kitchen duties are repeatedly interrupted by spontaneous dancing and singing.

Artist Margot Datz, her husband, fisherman Charlie Blair, and daughter, Scarlet, are noted for their dinner parties in Edgartown, Massachusetts. One year they transformed their small cottage into a medieval feasting hall. Margot researched the recipes right down to aphrodisiacs and illusionary foods and asked each guest to prepare one for the party. She herself prepared a roast suckling pig stuffed with pheasant that was stuffed with quail. To be really authentic, Margot and Charlie didn't provide forks for the guests, who came dressed as everything from peasants to crusaders.

The theme of their next dinner was "Dining Atop Mount Olympus." Low tables were wrapped in white sheets and surrounded by fluffy pillows for sitting. The rafters were hung with fifty pounds of polyester fiberfill to look like clouds and strings of twinkle lights to look like stars. The tables were strewn with large pink sequins and icy pink tulips. The menu was raw oysters, sensuous finger foods, and champagne.

Another way to spice up an evening, especially in smaller communities, is to provide some sort of entertainment. Cocktails and hors d'oeuvres can be served for an hour, then the entertainment presented, followed by dinner or vice versa. When there is dancing or a film, dinner is served before the entertainment. Dessert, liqueurs, and coffee can come later in the evening. In some places the host can rent a movie theater, night club, or small auditorium so that the guests can enjoy the show or movie with just their friends.

The whole evening can carry over with the theme of the entertainment. For example, if you are screening a Ginger Rogers and Fred Astaire movie, ask guests to dress in elegant 1930s attire. If you are hosting an evening of Italian Renaissance music, provide an Italian feast in the spirit of the Medicis. For a disco night, tell guests to dress in neon colors, provide washable colored

Guests are sent a red bandanna with a note attached: "Wear this to supper Sunday at 6:30. No shoes required, just a good appetite . . ."

Bottles of beer and soft drinks can be served from old tin washtubs filled with ice. Hors d'oeuvres are bite-sized chunks of a variety of country sausages, individual ribs, and roasted pecans. Background music is provided by B. B. King and Aretha Franklin records, or for a really funky mood, some hard-core blues by Etta James and Leadbelly.

Dinner can be served on anything, from tin pie plates to unmatched dinnerware from the thrift store. The food is served buffet-style from the kitchen. Pots of greens, lima beans with ham, and dirty rice can be left right on the stove. In another area can be baskets of fried chicken and fried fish, a platter of jalapeño cornbread or hush puppies, and cauldrons of tiny ears of sweet corn on the cob.

Guests can eat on the porch, in the yard on quilts, or in the kitchen among the platters of food.

After the debris is cleared away, the guests can serve themselves from another buffet table laden with pecan, sweet potato, apple, and blueberry pies and an enormous bowl of whipped cream.

*North Carolina designer Dennis Anderson has used a drying rack as part of a buffet service so that guests can easily help themselves to plates and silverware before digging into the food. Wallpaper by Imperial Wallcoverings.* PROCTOR

*When Neetsy and Johhny Walker entertain at their country home, they boil shrimp outside and have guests serve the other food right from the stove (right). Once served, everyone goes outside to eat on quilts under the trees while they are serenaded by a blues band.* HIMMEL

hair sprays, and hire a punk makeup artist for the brave. Dr. Tom Reese, art historian at the Getty Art Center, and his wife, Carol, like to have "art dinners" at which each guest must prepare a dish taken from a famous painting. After dinner they have a competition of tableaux vivants in which teams act out famous paintings for the others to guess.

Keep in mind that long evenings and heavy meals don't mix too well. The more courses you serve, the lighter each should be.

## The Supper Party

Supper differs from dinner by being a lighter but not necessarily more informal meal, although it certainly can be. Supper parties are ideal after a heavy brunch or noon meal or after a long day of activities and food. They begin any time from six to eleven in the evening. Hot or cold soup may be the main component of the meal—perhaps bouillabaisse, gumbo, she-crab soup, minestrone, or gazpacho.

During the holidays, attorney and law professor Duncan Low and his wife, Patsy, of Atherton, California, like to have a supper party for law students who aren't able to go home to be with their families. They design meals around what the students like—barbecue or tamale pie, with ice cream sundaes for dessert.

The midnight supper (or breakfast) takes over where the supper party leaves off. Almost always held after another event, it may begin any time after 11 P.M. A midnight supper at home should be for a small number of people and should be served quickly so that guests don't fall asleep waiting for their food. The food should also be light—no heavy sauces or liquor-laced dishes. Scrambled eggs with truffles, fettucine Alfredo with prosciutto, or a simple cheese soufflé would be perfect.

## The Dinner Dance

A dinner dance does not have to be a ball, and it certainly does not have to be a fund-raiser. Consider having a theme dance for a special occasion or an honored guest. Invite friends to an outdoor Caribbean ball with a steel band and fireworks, or close off your block for a Parisian street dance. One Florida couple rents a barge on the Intercoastal Waterway and has a disco party MC'd by a deejay. An Idaho couple has a country-and-western dance and barbecue on their island in a river near Ketchum. Whatever theme you choose, prepare food that goes with it. Movable carts loaded with various bite-sized foods make serving easy.

After returning from one of her world cruises, arts patron Dot Shushan has a splendid international dinner dance to treat her friends to the culture, food, and music she has experienced. Each room in her beautifully appointed apartment is filled with the ambiance of a different country. Guests leave feeling as if they've been on a world tour.

## The Dessert Party

Dessert parties are another easy way to make a big splash. People will generally go out to dinner beforehand, and anticipation will be high. The more

A *quiet supper by the fire can be a relaxing change of pace for informal entertaining. Caroline Wogan Sontheimer is serving mussels and her own Creole version of bouillabaisse with lots of hot French bread.* HIMMEL

Serve dessert in another room after dinner to free guests for conversations with others (left). Desserts can be laid out in advance on a gallery or porch so that guests get to enjoy many different views and moods. JEFFERY

Milton Williams has created more than a hundred different chocolate confections, including tree branches and wine coolers dipped in dark chocolate (top, right). Chocolate-colored chairs, a matching tablecloth with Swiss eyelet overlay, and a profusion of orchids set the scene for the most decadent of dessert parties. KAUFMAN

At an Easter garden party, Milton Williams created a traditional Russian dessert in the center pot (bottom, right). The surrounding flowerpots are filled with baked chocolate and walnut pudding. To re-create these desserts, buy regular clay pots and boil them for twenty minutes, fill with ice cream, crumble chocolate cookies on top to look like dirt, and freeze for an hour. Insert a drinking straw and add the stem of a flower before serving. From The Party Book by Milton Williams (NY: Doubleday, 1981). KAUFMAN

glittering the invitation, the more dressed up guests will be, and the prettier they feel, the more fun they will have. To a thermographed silver card, add a chocolate lollipop shaped like the Eiffel Tower, or send miniature boxes of Krön chocolates with a black and gold invitation attached. Tables can be laden with a dazzling display of your favorite desserts, accompanied by magnums of champagne. At Tommy and Dathel Coleman's parties, the food is sinful, the flowers spectacular, the lighting dim, and the dance music impossible to resist.

One Seattle hostess has annual dessert parties for different holidays. For a chocolate spectacular on New Year's Eve (before people go on their "resolution diets" the next day), her theme is the Hershey's Kiss. She dresses in silver, and the invitation is a silver balloon attached to a kiss. At her Easter custard party she serves a gigantic trifle, Charlotte Russe, crème brûlot, and crème caramel. Since her theme for this party is eggs, each guest receives an Easter egg with the invitation written on it. For Bastille Day, all the desserts are blue, white, or red and contain lots of fresh blueberries, raspberries, and strawberries. Halloween brings an orange and yellow party with lemon- and orange-flavored confections.

## The Cotillion and the Ball

The word *cotillion* conjures up images of dance cards, debutantes, and fresh-faced young men in dress uniforms. Elaborate structured balls by definition, they rarely have theme decorations or trendy music.

*Cap off dinner in a restaurant by asking a few friends home for a spectacular dessert. It might also have come from a restaurant, but no one needs to know. Dim the lights, put on your favorite music, and have a special dessert wine for all to sample.* HARDIN

*Ball* is a term that implies no expense has been spared. There must be continuous music, elaborate decorations, and the finest of everything. Salvador Dali gave a ball at which guests were told to come as their favorite dream. William Randolph Hearst presented a one-pound tin of Beluga caviar and a Methuselah of champagne to each guest at a Christmas Eve ball at San Simeon. Aristotle Onassis once had the ballroom of the Dorchester Hotel in London covered with flowers from floor to ceiling for a ball for Maria Callas.

For the ultimate in opulence, you could have a "Black and Silver" ball. Send each guest an eye mask—black for men and silver for women. Attach an invitation to a dinner dance that tells the men to wear black and the women to wear silver. Decorations, table settings, and party favors should all carry out the black and silver theme. Each course of dinner is served, using masses of silver serving pieces, in a different room. Dessert consists of black chocolate mousse topped with paper-thin strips of edible silver gilding.

## Parties to Breathe Life into the Old Crowd

Joel Cavaness likes to give "Coming Up for Air" or "Out from Under a Rock" parties for friends who are busy professionals. Being one herself, she realizes that when someone is hard at work on a project, he or she rarely gets to see friends and, after finishing the project, is probably too tired to organize any activity. She plans the party a few days after the deadline, be it a major trial or a tax audit. Her favorite invitation shows the honoree literally slithering out from beneath a boulder.

The idea is to treat your guests to something new and different, to lift their spirits. Create a mood and let guests step out of themselves a bit. Plan activities that will entertain but not become tedious. A creative party given in Shreveport had a "Madam Butterfly" theme. The hostess rented a costume for each guest and had a makeup artist to do all of the makeup. Guests could either learn a part or lip-sync to a record.

### Arabian Nights

*Invitations*: Send each guest a dime-store bubble bath or perfume vial resembling Aladdin's lamp. Attach a note that reads: "Sultan Ali Baba of Persia and his Harem demand your presence for dinner to celebrate the Feast of the Arabian Nights. Harem attire is required . . ."

*Decorations*: Remove most of the furniture from the living room and dining room. Cover the floors with borrowed Persian carpets and masses of fluffy pillows surrounding a low table (place pieces of plywood on cinder blocks and cover with Indian bedspreads). Complete the setting with palm trees under which are spread sand-colored sheets covered with gold coins and glitter.

*Features*: Dinner, served from brass trays, is kibbeh, stuffed grape leaves with lamb, couscous, and pita bread stuffed with salad. Everyone eats with their fingers. Dessert is a flaming date pudding presented by two belly dancers, who entertain and give lessons long into the night to those brave enough to learn.

*Favors*: Photographs of each guest learning to belly dance.

## Follow-the-Clues Mystery Party

*Clue No. 1:* Each guest receives an envelope containing a small plastic magnifying glass and pieces of a puzzle with tiny writing on each. The guest must put the puzzle together and read the first clue with the magnifying glass: "Make no plans for 8:00 P.M. on Saturday, April 9. For more information, look for a message to Sherlock in the 'Personals' section of the classifieds on April 3."

*Clue No. 2:* Run a classified ad that reads: "Sherlock, look for my message in your car on April 5. Signed, Watson."

*Clue No. 3:* In the early morning or the night before, place a typed message in the car or under the windshield wiper:

**W**e'll call tonight between 7:00 and 8:00 P.M. to see if you're coming.

**A**nything you wear is fine, as long as it is informal.

**T**rying to guess won't help!

**S**ee you on the 9th at 8:00 P.M.

**O**n time is the way to be.

**N**o excuses!

*Clue No. 4:* Have someone call everyone on the guest list at the appointed time. If the guest can come, give another clue by directing him or her to a particular corner to look for the next clue, which you can place on a telephone pole or tree.

*Clue No. 5:* The guest finds a note to Sherlock that reads: "Your mission, should you choose to accept it, is to go to the corner of _____ and _____ [guests must all start at the same location], then go north on _____ Street for _____ blocks until you get to a house whose number ends in _____ and where there is a blue balloon tied on the back door." When the guests arrive, there is a banner across the back door that says "CONGRATULATIONS, SHERLOCK!"

Guests are given champagne and hors d'oeuvres. Then they must put their powers of deduction to good use. Couples are separated into two teams for Name That Tune and Charades. The winning team gets to eat in the dining room, the losers in the living room.

After dinner the losing team must act out for the winners the location of the dessert. Maybe it's at a nearby saloon for dancing or at a theater for a mystery movie. The losing team arrives first and just hopes that the winners can follow their clues to find the fun.

*Favors:* Mystery novels bought in used book shops, a plastic bubble-blowing pipe, and a stick-on mustache.

## Beer-Tasting Party

*Invitations:* The ideal number of guests is twelve or fewer. Invitations are printed on labels affixed to long-necked beer bottles. If the invitations are to be mailed, make beer cans from cardboard and write the pertinent information on the labels.

*Features:* Select one or two brands of domestic and imported beers from each of the following categories: light beer, malt liquor, lager, ale, and stout. Allow three servings per bottle, with about four bottles (or cans) of each brand for twelve

*Beer need not be pedestrian. After a beer-tasting cocktail party, guests retire to the dining room for hot chicken curry and fresh fruit chutneys. There are no flowers available on this cold Sunday night, so the hostess has improvised with arrangements of dead branches gathered from the side of the road and spray-painted white. The centerpiece is an early nineteenth-century porcelain bowl from which the food will be served. The cartoon in the background was done for a party forty years ago by artist David Smith. The table is an eighteenth-century French butcher's table with a painted faux malachite top. The nineteenth-century chairs of gilded carved pine were made to commemorate Lord Nelson's sea victories. They came from the home of Lord Sitwell in Venice.* HIMMEL

Hoppy—sharpness, bitterness, and aroma
Flavor—short-lived or lingering
Taste and aroma—richness and freshness

Guests drink the beer from spotless tulip-shaped wineglasses to enjoy the optimal aroma and taste. Then they score each one on a scale of 1 to 5.

Do not serve strongly flavored foods during the tasting. Choose something like whole-wheat toast and mild cheeses. After the tasting, prepare Welsh rarebit using the group's favorite beer or serve a German beef carbonnade made with a hearty beer and onion sauce.

*Favors*: Give your guests their favorite beer to take home.

### Bowling Alley Party

This party could be hosted by several people to defray the cost of renting the bowling alley.

*Invitations*: Send a plastic bowling pin or a custom-made bowling shirt with the invitation attached and the guest's team assignment.

*Features*: Music should be vintage 1950s and early 1960s, and the food should be real bowling alley food—hot dogs, pizza, and lots of beer. Divide the group of guests into two leagues, and the leagues into several teams of four that will compete against one another.

*Favors*: The league with the highest score wins their own custom-made extra-large T-shirts emblazoned with their league name and the date of victory.

guests. Chill the beer to no colder than 40 degrees by placing in a bucket of ice for half an hour.

Prepare a score card for each guest, with the names of the beers listed and columns headed:

Malty—sweetness, mellowness, and harshness

# Chapter 6
# HOLIDAY ENTERTAINING

*H*olidays are glorious times to share with friends and family. Never fear, holiday parties need not be mob scenes. Graciousness and imagination need not be replaced by theme paper hats and confetti. Celebrations should remain personal. Many times the greatest gift that you can give to guests is to include them among a wonderful assortment of your dearest friends. What could be a nicer treat than to see your best friend

 from grammar school engrossed in conversation with your next-door neighbor? The happiest memories that many of us have are those relating to the special customs surrounding the holidays. Traditions and rituals can add a spirit of celebration, transforming the holiday from an event into an occasion. There are many things you, your family, and your friends can look forward to year after year. Concoct a special drink or food that you prepare only at that time of year. Do research into your family history and come up with a treat from "the old country." If cooking is not your bent, create a unique decoration to herald the occasion. It could even be as simple as planting a tree each year or repainting a different room in your house to commemorate your favorite holiday. In New Orleans, Al Copeland, founder of Popeyes Famous Fried Chicken, especially likes to share Christmas with the needy of the community. He and his staff get the names of needy families and have a Santa Claus to present each child with three personalized gifts.

*In place of heavy holiday meals, have friends and family come for a long bike ride and picnic. Courtesy* Weight-watcher's *magazine.* SKOTT

*To add splash to your next New Year's Eve party (left), invite guests to come as their favorite characters from the 1930s and show a vintage movie after dinner as the guests sip champagne.* HEYERT

*If the space is small but the guest list is large, suspend decorations from the ceiling (top, right). Balloons with ribbon streamers provide a festive atmosphere. When rooms fill with people, small arrangements tend to disappear from sight, and all that remains is the illusion of clutter and the absence of a place to abandon an empty drink glass.* DOMENECH

*After a night of party hopping, this couple has invited another couple back home for a midnight breakfast (bottom, right). Leaves from the garden are sprayed silver and combined with a few orchid sprays. When the hosts and their guests return, all they must do is scramble some eggs and add pre-chopped sweet peppers and prosciutto.* HIMMEL

## New Year's Eve

New Year's Eve should be an occasion for merriment, yet many people dread the idea of going to a New Year's Eve party as much as they dread the thought of staying home. The problem is the expectation that this must, at all costs, be the most fun-filled night of the year. Those brave souls who entertain on New Year's Eve must be the most self-assured of any party givers, for their parties will be judged along these guidelines.

There is only one way around this—treat New Year's Eve just like any other night, and the pressure will be instantly released. Have a dessert party beginning at ten o'clock. Have an early open house or cocktail party before everyone goes off in quest of the time of their lives. Host a midnight supper after someone else's party, or have a sedate formal dinner with such scintillating guests that no one remembers what night it is. At midnight, serve a flaming dessert and café brûlot.

Do the unexpected. Host a beach party in the winter. Ask the guests to wear shorts, sunglasses, and a favorite sweater. Decorate your house with patio furniture, beach umbrellas, beach towels, pool toys, beach balls, and flowering plants. Serve Margaritas and spicy Mexican food. Play vintage Beach Boys and Jan and Dean music, and no one will notice it's really New Year's Eve.

If, however, you are undeterred from having a New Year's Eve party, make the most of it. Have a masked ball or host a costume party with a special food theme in a restaurant—"Ben Franklin in Paris," "Marco Polo in the Court of Genghis Khan," "Columbus in the New World." No mat-

ter what you choose to do, make the event festive. Guests must be kept occupied every minute with eating and conversing or dancing so they don't have time to stand around waiting to have fun. Put lighted sparklers in the food. Use real top hats, canes and white gloves, plastic pearls, clear balloons, and lots of shiny confetti to set the scene. If possible, have the party in a location where the guests can watch some fireworks. A midnight fireworks display is a terrific means of getting people to go home. Once they go outside to watch, they are already halfway to their cars.

For those with older kids, it could be fun to hire a bus and driver to take them all out for a night of activities. Begin at a bowling alley or skating rink, then have dinner at a Chinese or Italian restaurant, and go to someone's home afterward for dessert, dancing, and fireworks.

One Cincinnati divorcee has a group of her friends and their children over for an annual potluck supper and game-playing marathon. A couple of confirmed New Year's Eve haters in Philadelphia host a slumber party for all of their friends' kids so the adults can go out. They turn the house into a children's paradise, with each age group getting a part of the house all to themselves. They have loads of confetti, paper hats and noisemakers for everyone, and nonalcoholic champagne. They change all the clocks in the house so that midnight is celebrated at ten.

If you want to celebrate early, invite some foreign friends to be the honored guests and hold the party at the time it would be midnight in their country. Find out what foods are traditional for New Year's in their homeland; for instance, twelve bite-sized mincemeat pies must be eaten by each British person to assure good luck in the coming twelve months. It's an especially warm gesture for those of your foreign friends who are unable to get home at this time of the year.

## New Year's Day

New Year's Day brings with it hangovers, football games, and black-eyed peas. Some people have parties to watch the games, but for those who aren't interested, these events can be dreadful.

There is a way to lessen the pain. Set up video recorders and rent some movies for those who hate football. Divide the food and televisions so that in each room the groups are self-contained. Hard-core fans may want to set up three televisions in one room, each tuned to a different game. To add spice to the activities, let the guests bet on the games. Losers must take the winners out to dinner the following weekend.

You may prefer to host a brunch and have all of the televisions hidden away. Ask guests to write their resolutions on slips of paper and let everyone try to guess whose resolution is whose. Six months later have a Fourth of July party and read the resolutions to see who's been naughty and who's been nice.

## Valentine's Day

This is the ideal time to have a party for a couple who is getting married or having an anniversary, or just for your favorite single friends. The invitation can be enclosed in a small, heart-shaped box

*While avid fans are glued to the football games on television, Judi Burrus entertains other friends by showing vintage musicals and classic horror films. The video equipment is hidden in a coffee table designed by Tim Landry. The black china is by Fitz and Floyd. HIMMEL*

## THE ROMANTIC DINNER FOR TWO

One man treated his wife to an intimate dinner at the city's botanical garden, which he had rented for the night. He hired the best caterer and a string quartet to serenade her.

A wife in Cleveland kidnapped her husband from the office and took him to a friend's rustic cabin, where they camped out in sleeping bags around the fireplace and ate only what they could cook over the fire.

Two couples rented a historic house outside Atlanta for their newly married children. The couple was told to pack a bag for the night. At six o'clock a car arrived and took the couple for a romantic night in an antebellum mansion. The parents had added vases of fresh flowers, chilled champagne, and a box of chocolates.

If you can't get away from it all, pack an elaborate picnic hamper with china plates, cloth napkins, crystal, candles, and flowers and surprise the object of your affections. For dessert, have a special message written into a block of chocolate.

*In the dead of winter, what could be nicer than to celebrate Valentine's Day in a lush conservatory or greenhouse (right)? Guests have received an invitation attached to a small potted pink azalea tucked into a hatbox and left on the doorstep at the crack of dawn. Plants courtesy of Rohm's.* HIMMEL

*Have a dinner party to introduce several of your single friends and serve course after course so they must sit and talk for hours (right). A wine-tasting dinner is perfect because guests will want to discuss the merits of each wine.* HEYERT

*If you can't get completely away for a romantic dinner, erect a tent (left) for a private getaway.* HEYERT

of chocolates. Ask guests to come as one of the world's greatest lovers or assign single friends a character that they must come as. Men can be asked to come as Romeo, Hansel, Anthony, Tristan, Rhett, Clark, Roy, and so on. The women must come as Juliet, Gretel, Cleopatra, Isolde, Scarlett, Lois, Dale, and so on. They must find their mates at the party and sit together at dinner. Guests may also be asked to submit baby pictures of themselves. Each female is given a male picture or vice versa, and they must figure out whose picture they have. Once they find each other, they sit together at dinner.

Use all-white tablecloths and china and accent with bright red napkins. As a centerpiece, outline a heart shape using Hershey's Kisses and fill it with red votive candles and red tulips in clear containers, or make a giant heart-shaped cherry tart and surround it with candles.

## Mardi Gras

In New Orleans, Carnival is dancing in the streets, costumes, mirth, and joy for the whole family. Mardi Gras translates literally as "Fat Tuesday" and is celebrated primarily in those areas of the Western Hemisphere settled by French or Portuguese Roman Catholics. The most spectacular festival is Carnival in Rio. In the United States, Mobile has the oldest celebration and New Orleans has the largest. The Carnival season in New Orleans is celebrated from Twelfth Night (January 6) until Shrove Tuesday, the day before Ash Wednesday, that date, of course, varying with the church calendar.

The primary events, as the season is celebrated in New Orleans, are the private balls given by hundreds of clubs and organizations. They feature elaborate tableaux in which beautifully costumed people act out a play without words and accompanied by music. These are followed by several hours of dancing. Most balls are presided over by a king, who is a prominent member of the particular Carnival organization, and a queen, who is the college-age daughter of a long-time member of the club. After the balls there are elegant midnight suppers.

Throughout the season, the entire city becomes involved in parade watching and celebrating with friends at rounds of parties at which king cakes are traditionally served. These large brioche cakes, which are decorated with colored sugar in purple, gold, and green, contain a plastic baby. The person who gets the baby in a slice of cake must host the next party.

Carnival colors are purple, gold, and green, so no party at this season is complete without balloons, streamers, tablecloths, napkins, plates, and banners in these colors. Mardi Gras "doubloons" of aluminum in various colors and plastic beads, which are thrown to the crowds by float riders, are also used for decorating. Some people even decorate their Christmas trees (kept up until Ash Wednesday) with Mardi Gras beads and photographs of their family in costume.

Costumes and masks are de rigueur and are often very lavish. More important than expense, however, is creativeness. Whole families can be seen outfitted as crawfish or Goldilocks and the three bears; entire neighborhoods of people may dress as characters from the French Revolution.

You don't have to be in New Orleans to have your own Mardi Gras celebration. Blaine Kern, the master float designer who is known as "Mister Mardi Gras," suggests that for a Mardi Gras party you should do the following:

Decorate everything in the Mardi Gras colors.

Import Dixie beer if you can.

Serve Creole food: jambalaya, red beans and rice, shrimp Creole.

Put on New Orleans jazz, especially Dixieland, and "second line" (dance in a line, almost but not quite Conga style) around the neighborhood.

Doubloons, beads, masks, and any Mardi Gras decorations can be ordered from Blaine Kern Artists, P.O. Box 6307, New Orleans, Louisiana 70174.

## Easter

Because Easter signifies the coming of spring, it is symbolized by the egg, which signifies new life. Easter egg hunts are fun for small children, but not unless they are geared to different age groups. A ten-year-old is much more adept at finding eggs than a three-year-old. Allow at least six eggs per child. This means three to four dozen eggs for six children, six to eight dozen for twelve children.

Judy Paine, a creative hostess in New Orleans, likes to give a "Mad Hatter's Garden Party" for all ages on Easter afternoon. Invitations are

tucked into painted wooden Easter eggs. Her pathway is lined with giant lollipops made from garden stakes and balloons. The bushes are made into egg trees, decorated with a mass of silver, white, pink, and blue paper eggs. Oversized Easter baskets filled with spring flowers are color coded for each age group. The three- to four-year-olds look for yellow eggs, five to six for red, seven to eight for blue, and nine to ten for green. After the hunt, the kids turn in their eggs for candy and stuffed animals.

An hour into the party, Alice in Wonderland and the Mad Hatter magically appear to lead the children in a bunny hop through Judy's garden to a tiny enchanted cottage, where they have their tea while they listen to Easter stories told by Alice. All

*Make a wreath out of whatever is in your garden, even if it happens to be bare vines (left). Create decorations that will last for weeks and get your guests in the mood for spring. Wallpaper from Imperial Wallcoverings.* PROCTOR

*A Georgian Sheffield egg cruet (circa 1810) serves as the centerpiece for this Easter Sunday breakfast for two (top, right). The eggs have been painted with watercolors and names written in silver and gold markers. Lilies and alstroemeria have been placed in the egg server. Biedermeier birch tilt-top table, circa 1820; pair of Biedermeier chairs, circa 1830; French faience ornamental statue of a lamb; Meissen porcelain plates, circa 1850; English café au laît cups, circa 1870; George II silver-gilt knives, circa 1730; French Louis Philippe egg cups, circa 1840; sterling silver egg cutter, London, circa 1911; English hock glasses, circa 1830; Meissen knife and fork, circa 1755. All from Lucullus.* HIMMEL

*Fresh fish poached and served cold on a shaded deck (bottom, right) is an uncomplicated way to celebrate Easter. Never mind if you don't have a fish poacher large enough. Wrap the fish in cheesecloth and poach it on the top rack of the dishwasher (run without soap, of course).* BRONSON

the while the parents sit in the rose garden sipping tea as they listen to a string quartet.

In bad weather, have a "Goose That Laid the Golden Egg" supper on Easter evening. Light the house with hundreds of candles in brass candlesticks. The centerpiece on the dining table can be a moss-covered goose surrounded by dozens of foil-covered chocolate eggs. Food can be served in individual Easter baskets.

Since Easter often falls during spring break from school, it can be the ideal time to host a party to honor a debutante, a graduate, or a bride. One Lexington, Kentucky, hostess likes to have an Easter brunch for eight to ten young couples at her annual "Chicken House Party." She actually holds her party in an old chicken house, although the party need not be in such authentic surroundings. Her decorations are authentic, too, down to the straw on the floor and the country music. She borrows serving pieces and china with chicken shapes and motifs. The meal, of course, is egg drop or bird's nest soup, followed by fried chicken and floating island.

One Philadelphia hostess has a mannequin that she uses in the center of her table for each one of her parties. The night before Easter, she holds her annual "Bunny Party." Guests are sent copies of *Playboy* with the invitation substituted for the centerfold. The mannequin is dressed as a whimsical Playboy bunny, with blonde wig, bunny ears, furry high-heeled slippers, and hot pink long johns with a bunny emblem over the heart. The guests, of course, must come to the party dressed as bunnies.

*Create Easter decorations around the traditional colors of purple and yellow (below). Experiment with objects— purple bottles with yellow lemons, violets, and lemon drops.* SCHINZ

## Fourth of July

Planning a party near water—whether a pool, a lake, or the ocean—is a wonderful idea for the Fourth of July and other summer holidays. Invite all your favorite people, in all age groups, to an afternoon party, which can start at three o'clock for the sunbathers. For water sports enthusiasts, there can be water volleyball, diving contests, and races. At seven, have a barbecue and music, and plan for guests to take a midnight dip before they go home. Keep lots of drinks, cold fruit, and ice cream on hand before and after the meal.

Bee Longley likes to invite friends over on the Fourth of July for a game of three-hole putt-putt golf around the apartment building where she lives. She has lots of beer and soft drinks during

play and afterward there is champagne by the pool. Lucy Core, a native Texan and mother of writer-painter Philip Core, invites all ages for an Anthony Trollope croquet party every summer on the lawn near her carriage house apartment. Guests dressed as Lady Glencora and Phineas Finn happily drink mint-laced iced tea and nibble on lemon-curd-filled lady fingers.

Friends can get together for a costume tea party. Everyone comes as a figure from the American Revolution or, for Bastille Day, the French Revolution. The food is authentic, and fireworks are a must. Leisurely beach picnics, ice cream socials, and masked balls can add a bit of sparkle to any of the warm-weather holidays.

*The summer holiday colors of red, white, and blue are carried out (bottom, left) in white wicker, red Guatemalan shawls, and a blue glass sculpture by Claire Steinart Thorn of Boston. The table is set with blue Depression glass in the Royal Lace and Newport or "Hairpin" patterns (Hazel Atlas Company) from the collection of the Crescent City Depression Glass Society.* HIMMEL

*Even if getting away on a boat (left) must be scheduled like a business meeting, relax and give guests the freedom to sit quietly and enjoy the sea breeze, light meal, and company of good friends. Long Island caterer Alexandra Troy specializes in doing yachting picnics for those souls who are too busy to cook.* HAGIWARA

*Throw a party on the porch of your favorite country restaurant (right) and invite your friends from the area to come over for the day. Add your own tablecloths and flowers you have arranged yourself and ask the chef to prepare some of your favorite recipes. The Cook restaurant on Shelter Island, New York.* HARDIN

*Pull together everything you have in your house that is black or orange. Edit out everything but one orange object and use all your favorite black things. Now add some candles and apples, a few masks, and miniature pumpkins. Voilà! You have a great Halloween table decoration without buying a thing. Terra-cotta and black-glazed plates, cups, and bowls (by Loneoak) and basket from Platypus; flatware, black-and-white miniature chair, tray, vase, and sunglasses from Clodagh, Ross & Williams; twig napkin rings and green glass goblets from Wolfman Gold & Good. HIMMEL*

*At the David Payne penthouse (top, right), guests are treated to different kinds of pasta. At one table they may have black squid pasta; at another, an orange tomato pasta. Plants filled with twinkle lights give the feeling of being outdoors on a starlit night. HARDIN*

*On Halloween night this host and hostess invited five couples to dinner at Primavera (bottom, right). As a surprise they were taken to the wine cellar, which was lit only by the luminaria on the table. The meal was the restaurant's special grilled baby goat, while the decorations were the host's own favorite things. Plates from Gear; silver from Buccellati; glasses and pitcher from Wolfman Gold & Good. Courtesy New York magazine. HEYERT*

## Halloween

Halloween is a fun time for both kids and adults, with the season lasting from the weekend before until midnight Halloween night.

Trick-or-treating, unfortunately, has become hazardous in many areas of the country, so people are modifying the tradition. One group of mothers with preschool children make trick-or-treating "appointments" for their children. Those neighbors who don't want to be bothered can leave an envelope with a Halloween greeting for each child. One group of Oregon teenagers organizes a neighborhood treasure hunt. Their friends go from house to house looking for clues and at the last stop there is a party.

Young Tristan Bultman, born on Halloween, has a party with his friend Edward Haik to celebrate their birthdays. The guests arrive at Tristan's house at six o'clock for a barbecue. Each year the party activities remain the same, but the birthday boys think up new themes for the costumes. One year it was little green men from Mars, another it was cartoon characters, and another year it was super heroes.

Edward's and Tristan's parents, knowing they will be giving this Halloween fete every year, have invested in a stock of Halloween decorations. They have recycled all their old sheets into ghosts, which are hung all over the front porch. The eyes are made of black glitter, and the screaming mouths of red glitter. In the living room "fog" comes from pots of water and dry ice placed in each corner. Tapes of animal sounds play in the background, and the room is lit with black votive

candles. A mirrored wall is covered with masks, whose eyes and mouths glimmer from the reflections of the candles.

The backyard is alive with pumpkins—plastic pumpkin lanterns in the trees, pumpkin pinatas filled with party favors, and dozens of carved pumpkins housing candles around the perimeter of the garden. Low tables, made from doors on cinder blocks, are covered in bright orange sheets and hold clear fishbowls and toy dump trucks that are filled with candied corn, gummy worms, and popcorn. For before-dinner entertainment, there is a tent set up with a fortune teller, another with a face painter, and a third with a palm reader.

Dinner consists of barbecued sausage and hot dogs with chili served from a hollowed-out pumpkin. After the meal, the parents and children pile into cars and go to Edward's grandmother's house for trick-or-treating and dessert. Guests and their parents trick-or-treat on the private street for half an hour and then it is back to the house for carrot cake, pumpkin custard pie, and pumpkin-spice ice cream. By eight-thirty the party is over and the two birthday boys are left with all of their presents and their Halloween candy.

The Mission Hills Country Club ball in Kansas City is a popular adult alternative to "hitting the streets." Planner Linda Coburn says that costumes are mandatory because they get guests in the spirit. In her year as chairman, the guests entered the party through a cemetery of papier-mâché gravestones, spiderwebs made of thin string, skeleton heads, and lots of dry ice to make it foggy. There were two caskets. One had a cos-

tumed actor who popped out to scare people, and the other contained an inflatable skeleton holding the country club towel and golf clubs.

The ballroom was decorated with hundreds of orange and black helium balloons with black streamers hanging down. The tablecloths were black with orange overlays, or orange with black. Carved pumpkins lit by candles sat in the center of each table, and wax vampire teeth were used as napkin holders. Guests danced all night to the two bands, one of which played ballroom dance music and the other, rock and roll.

One Trenton hostess held a fabulous witches party at her family farm outside the city. Her invitation was a broom with a note attached: "A Bewitching Do for a Witch Like You." When guests arrived at the farm, all dressed in black witch costumes as specified by the invitation, they were taken by hay wagon to a barn with a giant bonfire in front. The tables were covered in black with square gold overlays, and at the center of each was a black cauldron with gold helium balloons attached. Hanging from above was a spinning mirrored dance ball. Light was provided by bonfires at the front and back doors of the barn, liquid candles in the cauldrons on the tables, and tiny clip-on spotlights aimed at long gold-lamé banners hanging from the hay lofts.

A combo dressed as red devils played such Halloween classics as "That Old Black Magic," "The Theme from Ghostbusters," "The Devil with the Blue Dress On," "It's Witchcraft," "Monster Mash," and more. At the stroke of midnight, to the strains of "Thriller," gold confetti

M*ariette Gomez designed a Hallow-een table for a meal in a tent in her backyard in the country. Tables were covered in kilim rugs from the Pillowry and topped with Napali masks from Himalayan Crafts and Tours and stir-rup drinking cups from Circa 1890 Antiques.* HIMMEL

drifted down upon the guests from the hay lofts, and flaming baked Alaskas proclaiming "Happy Halloween" were carried in. No one had trouble finding the hostess to tell her they had enjoyed the evening. As the good witch from the *Wizard of Oz*, she was dressed in white chiffon and had gold glitter all over her face.

## Thanksgiving

Thanksgiving is America's only national feast day. Happily, being a day of thanksgiving (and not spending), it hasn't been overly commercialized. Of course, there are those who just can't get too excited about Thanksgiving, viewing it as a pale imitation of Christmas. And there are diehard Southerners who think the holiday is "yankeefied" and refuse to make any fuss over it. Then there are the sports fans who would rather watch the football games on their midweek day off.

As a Thanksgiving Day host or hostess, you must decide on the tone of the celebration. If you and your guests would rather watch football in the afternoon, you could have an early brunch or an evening dinner. If you and your favorite lady or gentleman would rather have a private celebration, take a long weekend and go to a quiet inn, letting someone else do the cooking.

One of the nicest ideas for a celebration comes from a family in the Midwest who has made Thanksgiving a time to entertain "strays." They decided that they had a great deal to be thankful for and wanted to share it with others. Each member of the family makes a list of the people they'd like to invite, and a family meeting is held to de-

*P*aul Bott's opulent fall arrangement in an antique silver bowl sits on the sideboard (top, left), leaving the luncheon table bare save for a magnificent display of food. Tureen by Bardith; plates by Thaxton and Company; flatware, water glasses, salt cellars, shaker, decanter, and coasters by James Robinson; wine glasses by Baccarat; horse hunting cup by Tiffany & Company; place-card holders and Staffordshire dogs from James II Galleries; bowl and tray by Michael Feinberg of The Ghiordian Knot. HEYERT

*D*on't let your small living space prevent you from serving a Thanksgiving feast with all the trimmings. Improvise by arranging platters on stools, bookcases, stereo speakers, or any other surface (bottom, left). Putting everything within arm's reach is far easier than running back and forth from the kitchen. SCHINZ

*Fruit and dried wildflowers and grasses make an attractive autumn door decoration. For special occasions San Antonio floral designer Jimmy Hernandez wires fresh flowers into the grasses.* GREENE

183

cide. One year they invited a great-aunt they had never met. She had recently been widowed, so they sent her a plane ticket and asked her to come be an honorary "grandma." The family also likes to invite guests from foreign countries. By making the holiday meaningful to someone from another land, the family members have come to enjoy it more themselves.

Other families have learned to keep all ages busy on Thanksgiving making ornaments for their Christmas trees, writing letters to Santa, and addressing Christmas cards. Linda and Rob Bjork of Piedmont, California, make two complete Thanksgiving dinners. One they share with their family and the other they deliver to a needy family.

Several single friends in Louisville, Kentucky, have a house party. Guests arrive on Wednesday night to set the tables, arrange the flowers and decorations, and prepare the food. The Thanksgiving celebration begins at noon with cocktails—mimosas, Bloody Marys, screwdrivers—and some yummy hot hors d'oeuvres. The meal is served about one-thirty. At three, a large group invited for homemade ice cream and pecan pie arrives. Then it's time for sports, and everyone walks, runs, goes bike riding, or plays volleyball. Nighttime brings a video movie and homemade vegetable soup, hot spiced cider, and leftovers.

If it is the actual traditional meal that turns off you or your guests, then go for authenticity. At the original feast the Pilgrims and their guests dined on lobster, cod, eel, duck, clams, oysters, and lots of succotash, besides the turkey. The meal was washed down with Scotch whiskey,

Dutch gin, Dutch beer, and home-brewed red and white wine made from wild grapes. Your decorations could be Native American arts and crafts.

## Hanukkah

Margaret Buring is a master at creating authentic and meaningful Hanukkahs for her children and grandchildren. For days she, her daughter, her daughters-in-law, and her granddaughters make the traditional foods, such as potato latkes. She decorates a miniature pine tree with gold stars and cookies made in traditional Hanukkah shapes, all attached to the tree with blue bows. The house is lit with candlelight from the menorahs the family has collected from all over the world

On the first night of Hanukkah, she has a large party at which the children play games for prizes and everyone sings the traditional songs. On each subsequent night, one of the children hosts the family at his or her home. On the last night Margaret has a formal dinner for the adults at which they exchange their gifts.

## Christmas

The secret to a happy Christmas is participation. Share the season with others, especially children. Their enthusiasm can make Christmas a joy for everyone. A group of widows in Washington organizes an indoor picnic each year to which they invite their families and surrogate families. The extended family party is a special time for all involved. Singer Kenny Rogers and his wife, Marianne, like to have a matchmaking Christmas party for forty or fifty guests. This is a lovely gift to all their single pals. Some Bostonians organize a Christmas Eve slumber party. They trim the tree, sing carols, and make preparations for Christmas dinner together. When they awaken on Christmas morning, they open gifts together, then welcome several of their older neighbors who have been invited to share Christmas dinner.

Before the holiday, gather friends or family together to go to a nursery and pick out a tree. Invite people in to make ornaments or front door decorations, arrange Christmas greens, write Christmas cards, or make cookies and Christmas foods. Edith Carlson makes twenty varieties of Swedish cookies to use for decorating, to give away, and to eat with her granddaughters in her Victorian townhouse in Louisiana, Missouri. Video artist Janet Densmore keeps neighborhood children entertained making dozens of white fruitcakes while their moms go out shopping.

Christmas music, especially if it is sung by carolers or played by musicians, will set the mood for any gathering. At a recent party in an eighteenth-century house on Bayou St. John, the host hired a jazz musician to play popular Christmas tunes on the saxophone, while at an open house in Newport, the hostess had a string quartet playing Baroque Christmas carols.

Instead of spending too much money on gifts that are never used or played with, some families have decided to buy something that all of them can enjoy. One San Francisco family visits dozens of galleries in the Bay area between Thanksgiving and Christmas. They then vote to decide which piece of art they will buy for Christmas. Other families buy new bikes for everyone, water or snow skis, a motor or sail boat, or they take a trip to a favorite place. The key is family participation.

One Oregon arts patron and her family have a party each year for underprivileged children. First she finds out what present each child wants. Then she and her own children go on a shopping spree to buy all the gifts. The young guests arrive for what they think is just a hot chocolate and caroling party. After half an hour, several wonderful sleighs arrive to whisk the children off to a cabin in the woods, where there is an actress dressed as Mrs. Claus taking hot cookies from the oven. Elves appear who just happen to know what each child wants for Christmas.

Actress Lane Trippe likes to have an annual "Partridge in a Pear Tree Party" based on the old English folk song. Each guest must come as one of the twelve days and bring the appropriate food and accompanying tableau. For example, the guest told to come as the sixth day is to bring six geese a-laying. Since geese don't lay eggs until spring, that presents a challenge. One year a clever guest showed up with six pregnant friends dressed as geese, each bearing a goose liver pâté. As Lane says, "It's like a scavenger hunt. Guests have to come up with 'creative friends' to complete their tasks."

Hairdresser Albert Brown and his wife, Carolyn, have a Cajun Christmas party with a "Crawfish in a Fig Tree" theme. Each room in the house is decorated to be one of the twelve days of Christmas, but with Cajun style, so there are alligators, Spanish moss, red pepper garlands, and magnolia

*Zézé has created a permanent decoration that can be used year after year. A grapevine tree has been covered with fresh moss and festooned with dried roses and gold European ribbon-covered wire. Antiques from Yale Burge. Courtesy* House Beautiful *magazine, the Hearst Corporation.* SKOTT

*P*atsy and Marshall Steeves like to do holiday entertaining under the covered portal of their Mexican colonial-style home in south Texas. GREENE

188

Put twinkle lights on all of the trees and plants in your house or apartment.

Simmer spices on the stove to fill the house with the scent of cinnamon and nutmeg. Put baskets of apples around the house.

Fill an old-fashioned kerosene lamp with bayberry oil. Put it in your entrance hall and surround with holly and cinnamon sticks. (Never use holly or mistletoe where there are young children or pets; the berries are poisonous.)

Place big clay pots of chalk white narcissus all over the house and surround with a multitude of red votives or liquid candles in cranberry glasses.

Outline every picture, doorway, stair rail, and window with garlands of Christmas greens festooned with a gigantic bow of moiré or velvet ribbon.

Decorate each door in the house with a wreath or a fan shape made of wood and studded

with nails to hold fruit—cranberry- and clove-studded oranges, lemon leaf and apples, pine or spruce and lemons. Flowers, baby's breath, and bows can be added. In the Southwest, prickly pear cactus and red chilis are used to make unusual wreaths and garlands. In other parts of the country, crèche scenes can be part of a wreath, the figures wired into the greens.

Outside, bank undecorated Christmas trees with twinkle lights all around your house. They can be used around a tennis court to transform it into the ideal spot for a holiday dance.

To preserve a Christmas tree, mix one part Sprite with two parts water and add 1 tablespoon of chlorine bleach for the watering stand. Scotch pine lasts the longest and blue spruce is the most beautiful.

To wax greens, dip them in a mixture of one-half acrylic floor polish and one-half water. Hang upside down or lay on newspapers to dry.

*Designer Candy Davey has enhanced the stairways with garlands to echo the feeling of the architecture of this house , designed in the late nineteenth century by famed architect Thomas Sully. Known as the "wedding cake house," it was inspired by Henry Wadsworth Longfellow's house in Cambridge, Massachusetts.* HIMMEL

*San Antonio floral designer Jimmy Hernandez creates a simple holiday table wreath (far left) by using pads from a prickly pear cactus.* GREENE

leaf wreaths adorned with miniature bottles of Tabasco.

Christmas traditions are wonderful, but not if they are not enjoyed. Think about all the people who will be sharing your holiday plans. How would they like to spend the day? Maybe the little ones don't want to wait until eleven o'clock to open their gifts or until two to eat. Maybe the teenagers would rather be out skiing, skateboarding, or just hanging out with their pals. And you —do you really want to spend all Christmas Day cooking and cleaning the kitchen while everyone else is having fun? If every time you announce the next activity, half of your family begins to curl their lips, you know it is time for a change.

Cheryl Lentz and her husband, Dr. Rick Lentz, of Daytona Beach are carrying on a thirty-year family tradition, but with originality and style. At five-thirty on Christmas Eve, sixty out-of-town relatives and friends gather at the Lentz home to go en masse to church. They have received an invitation written on an ornament, which each year fits the theme of the party. One year it was a clear ball ornament tied with blue ribbon; another year it was a teddy bear with a plaid ribbon, and most recently a shell decorated with silver on a silver cord. They return home to one of Cheryl's fabulous theme feasts.

The small children have their own tables covered with surprise balls, bags of old-fashioned candy, tiny sleighs, and sparklers. A giant piñata is filled with individually wrapped gifts, specially chosen for each child and bearing each child's name.

*Designer Karen Luisana designed a cozy kitchen (top, left) in this North Carolina country house. Friends are invited to drop in on Boxing Day, December 26, for breakfast. Wallpaper from Millbrook Wallcoverings.* WHICKER

*Christmas need not be all holly and evergreens. Christmas in Santa Fe (bottom, left) has overtones of the Mexican and Indian cultures. Early American pewter, a Guatemalan sash, Indian baskets of peppers, Mexican terra-cotta churches, and cactus plants create the ambience for a southwestern celebration. Dried grape leaves painted with guests' names are used as place cards. The meal is served in terra-cotta saucers, with each course being served in individual saucers or seashells.* HIMMEL

*A southern Christmas circa 1740– 1770 was re-created in the Marlboro Room at Winterthur (right) for a special exhibition in 1982.* LIZA-NINA

For holiday candleholders, use old Christmas balls. Glue a washer on the bottom to keep the ball steady, add several inches of sand (use a funnel), and use for tall, thin tapers. Cover the top of the ball with holly, and mass the balls on mirrored squares.

On mantels or down the center of a table, arrange unscented Christmas greens or ivy in a serpentine pattern. (See page 189 for waxing greens.) Intersperse red flowers into the arrangement and add a row of your favorite brass, silver, crystal, or cut-glass candlesticks.

Mass small presents in varying sizes on a square of your favorite fabric in the center of the table. Use matching napkins tied with bows that match those on the presents.

Create giant papier-mâché turkeys, geese, pies, cakes, or cookies and mound them on platters to keep all of your guests hungry throughout the holiday season.

Build gingerbread houses of varying sizes and styles and use on tabletops and mantels.

Use a topiary braided ficus in the center of your table. Hang sugar plums and small candles in antique holders.

Mound together all of your treasured dolls and toys. They can be spruced up with Christmas aprons, starched collars, and bows. One hostess places a miniature carousel in the center of her table. At the doors to the dining room are two antique life-sized carousel horses holding sprigs of holly in their mouths.

Core a dozen apples and fit with tall red candles. Surround each apple with 6-inch cinnamon sticks tied with ribbons to a bed made from the lower boughs of the Christmas tree.

*Liza-Nina's favorite antique teddy bears (below, left) serve as the decoration for her entrance hall, filling her guests with warm memories of their childhood Christmases. On Christmas Day she seats her youngest guests at low tables, with the bears as dinner companions. LIZA-NINA*

*A traditional open house during the Christmas season (below, right) is a gracious way to keep up with those dear friends you seldom see. R. O'ROURKE*

Other families have opted to serve an elegant adult meal on Christmas Eve, after the children are asleep. A champagne and dessert party can follow for neighbors, family, and close friends. An invitation attached to a bell on a red silk cord might say, "Come with bells on when the children are asleep." The next morning the whole family has a hearty informal breakfast in their pajamas while they open their presents. After the wee family members wake up the adults—usually at dawn —they are kept at bay in their rooms where they open their stockings (which Santa has placed on their bedposts) while the breakfast is prepared.

Christmas dinner is in the dining room, but it is designed for the children. Lots of green and red balloons decorate the room, and the table is covered with red candles and candy canes. The food is all left over from the night before, but— miracle of miracles—there is a drumstick for every child! For dessert there is mile-high pie—a ten-inch-tall meringue and peppermint-stick ice cream pie. All the family helps to clean up, and by one-thirty, everyone is free to do whatever he or she pleases. The parents who want to take a nap can keep the little ones occupied by videotaping all the Christmas programs shown on television during the holiday season. Make a six-hour tape for children to watch on Christmas afternoon.

Folk art collectors Patsy and Marshall Steves of San Antonio carry on many of the traditions brought to this country by their ancestors, the Tobin family, two hundred years ago. The dishes served at their formal Christmas Eve dinner are all from original family recipes. At each place is a book of carols that the Steveses have made for their guests, and between courses they sing carols. When it's time for dessert, the lights are dimmed as the flaming plum pudding arrives and the family sings "Silent Night."

A recent stepparent in El Paso (a real turkey hater, too) decided that he didn't want to try to recreate the same Christmas his stepchildren had had with their father when they were younger. He realized that the chief thing he had in common with the children was their love for his wife, so he made Christmas a "Mom Appreciation Day." He and the children made Mexican Christmas decorations, chose the tree, bought the food, and prepared the meal—barbecued steaks and Mexican side dishes. After the meal, they all took Mom across the border for the rest of the holiday.

Another family with lots of members from all over the country has a tradition that always breaks the ice. On Christmas night when the family gathers for supper, everyone must wear whatever clothes they received as Christmas gifts. There are men dressed in hunting attire, children in animal pajamas, ladies in evening dresses and running shoes, and other family members in tennis outfits and house slippers. No one can be standoffish when dressed in jogging shorts and a pith helmet.

Being a gracious host or hostess doesn't mean you can't delegate responsibility. Ask others to make the dressing, salad, or dessert if you don't want to do it. You can even have the entire meal brought in by a caterer or a restaurant. Believe it or not, your family won't disown you. You can still supply the decorations and the spirit.

*In the mountains near Snowmass, Colorado, Santa takes groups of kids on a sleigh ride to a cabin in the woods, where hot cider awaits them.* SNOWMASS

# Chapter 7
# THE EVENTS OF A LIFETIME

Different generations look upon family gatherings in different ways. Grandparents and great-grandparents enjoy visiting with all of the younger family members and finding family traits in little ones. For them, a family gathering evokes memories as they watch a grandson gnaw on a drumstick the way his father did as a boy or help a mother and daughter set the table with the antique silver the grandmother received as a wedding gift. ☞ For the under-twenty set, family gatherings provide a wonderful means of gleaning information about their roots, worming family secrets out of intoxicated great-aunts, and getting in touch with family support structures. It can be a very happy time for togetherness. ♟ The age group in the middle, however, may not find these occasions so pleasant. They may be too close to family problems, and they have to do all the work as well. Will Joan tell Grandpa that she's dropped out of medical school to be a ski instructor? Will Aunt Mary make rude remarks to Joseph's foster child? What will Uncle Fred say when he sees your son's green crewcut and pierced ear? It may lessen the tension to include other people in the party—close family friends who are friends of all of the factions—perhaps an old neighbor who is now widowed or the family doctor and his seven children. ✗ Some families have grown to the point where meals involve a cast of dozens. A seated dinner for thirty-six may be an impossibility, yet excluding anyone

Luncheon Table Laid Under a Tent for Fêtes, *eighteenth-century Meissen tureen, and eighteenth-century English wine glasses are from Lucullus.*
*HIMMEL*

*196*

can create a family crisis. The best advice is to have a party where everyone can be involved. If seating is a problem, serve a buffet on the dining room table and let everyone sit at tables set up all over the house. If there are lots of small children, give them their own tables. Let them eat first and then put on the television or a videocassette or get an older child to read them stories while the adults enjoy their meal.

A wonderful activity at family parties is to have a "This Is Your Life" presentation for the oldest and the youngest family members. Get everyone involved in collecting stories and photographs. The athletic family can have a volleyball or softball game. Other families can do skits. Family members draw three partners and three records. They must do a musical incorporating the music they choose. It can be great fun seeing Aunt Ethel lip-sync "You Ain't Nothin' But a Hound Dog" to baby Lester while cousin Adolfo howls in the background. Charades is another good family activity in which all ages can participate.

As simple as it may sound, you don't have to give the party in your home unless you want to. Have a picnic in the park or take everyone to a movie or, better yet, help someone else have the party at their house.

## The Baby Shower

Although it is customary to have a baby shower before the baby is born, to help the parents get ready for the new arrival, it has always seemed more sensible to entertain the joyful parents after the event. That doesn't mean they can't be given gifts and assistance before the birth. Groups of friends can offer to help paint the nursery, make curtains, embroider crib sheets, make quilts, and any of these events can be turned into a party. Organizing baby equipment that can be borrowed is a great way to help. Babies outgrow newborn clothes in a matter of days, it seems, and most people have attics and cellars full of infant car seats, carriers, snuggies, and layettes they would love to lend to someone.

Mothers- and fathers-to-be also enjoy receiving books and records for their own enjoyment during the weeks before and after the arrival. One group of women in North Dakota organizes a "nap" brigade. Each afternoon, one of them comes over to sit with the new baby so Mom can have a nap. During the babysitting time, the friend bathes the baby and makes dinner for the couple.

Bev Reese likes to make a scrapbook on the day the baby is born. She includes the newspaper masthead, the horoscope, what was playing at the movies, fashion photographs, the sports news, recipes, and the international news. A few weeks later she has a party for the new parents and the baby. This "Coming-Out Party" is billed as the baby's introduction to society.

Bette Ewald prefers to have a "Birthday Party" for the baby on his one-month birthday. The difference is that the guests are asked to bring gifts for the new mother. She may receive gift certificates for a massage, babysitting, a facial, or a trip to the beauty shop. If the party is near Christmas, Bette also asks guests to help trim a tree for the baby's first Christmas.

*Heirloom treasures for the new baby are always appreciated. Flowers by Paul Bott of Twigs; lace cloth by Anichini; silver porringer by James Robinson.* HIMMEL

plastic baby toys, rubber bath animals, rattles, and such. Have a cake made in the shape of a cabbage with a tiny plastic baby on the top.

## The Christening or the Bris

Not only is the baby the center of attention at one of these ceremonies, but he is not held responsible for his actions. If he should feel like dozing off, no one will even comment.

This is not the time to invite everyone you know. It is for family and close friends. Guests can be invited by phone or by a handwritten note that gives the date and time of the event, the baby's name, and a few sentences explaining the activities. Will there be only a religious service or is the guest invited to stay for refreshments?

*Have a quiet place for the honoree to retreat from the excitement during the festivities. Designer Karen Luisana created this dressing room especially for the young master of the house. Wallpaper from Millbrook Wallcoverings.* PROCTOR

At other times she hosts "grandmother" showers for her friends with new grandbabies. Guests stock the grandmother's house with a high chair, a collapsible playpen, side guards for a bed, toys, and such. If the grandmother doesn't have the storage space, the guests draw up lists of all the equipment they have that the new grandmother can borrow when baby comes to visit.

If the guests at a shower don't know one another, break the ice by asking each of them to bring a baby picture of themselves to the party. Put all of the pictures in the center of the floor and let the guests sort out whose picture is whose.

Decorations for a shower can be clumps of pink and blue balloons tied together with one giant white bow and attached to baskets filled with

At a christening, the traditional decorations are white. The traditional foods include a white cake (angel food is divine), with the child's initials in blue or pink, caudle (hot egg nog punch), and champagne. The British have a custom that the bride saves the top tier of her wedding cake and serves it at the christening.

At other times a family may want to turn the occasion into a glorious reunion that celebrates the arrival of a new addition to its ranks. Five-month-old Veronica Pipes Swanson's christening became just that with relatives aged nine to ninety arriving in Naples, Florida, from all over the world. After a church service in the late afternoon, guests returned to a party on the beach. There was a jazz band, Cuban and Creole food, and activities for young family members. Each guest gave Veronica a gift to bring her luck—poems, silver dollars, antique family photographs, and mementoes of previous family parties.

A *bris* takes place on the eighth day after the birth of a Jewish boy. This circumcision ceremony may be performed at home or in the hospital. A Jewish daughter is formally named at services on the Sabbath after her birth, with a reception at the temple or at home. The first-born son may also have a *pidyon haben* ceremony. These ceremonies are generally followed by a reception at home at which traditional foods are served.

## The First Communion and Confirmation

Among Roman Catholics, the first communion takes place when a child is in first or second grade, and confirmation when the child reaches seventh or eighth grade. In some Protestant churches, confirmation or entry into adult membership takes place about the time a child is a freshman in high school. These ceremonies may be followed by a reception for the family and close friends at the church, home, a restaurant, or club. They are a time to honor the child, not a time for elaborate decorations or festivities. Make the day one that the youngster will remember. Each guest might say a few words or make a toast to the child's future.

## The Bar Mitzvah and Bas Mitzvah

The bar mitzvah or bas mitzvah is a very important rite of passage in every Jewish child's life. It is the mark of the religious coming-of-age for which the thirteen-year-old child must spend months studying. It is also a major social event for the parents and is celebrated with the same joie de vivre as a debutante ball. Many parents spend as much time planning for the party as the child spends preparing for the service. The religious service takes place at a synagogue, followed by a private party at a club, hotel ballroom, or restaurant. The guest list is made up of relatives and close friends, many from out of town.

Several years ago Naomi and Howard Bloom had a three-day extravaganza for their son, Jason. Reservations for guests were made in one of Dallas's finest hotels. In each room the Blooms placed champagne, large vases of candy and fruit, and an acrylic hat filled with maps, brochures, and a computer printout containing the names and addresses of all the hosts and hostesses, their hotel

*Gretchen Bellinger fabric is used as a table covering for a simple bar mitzvah dinner. Flowers by Paul Bott of Twigs; invitations by Crane.* HIMMEL

room numbers, and the schedule of events for the weekend.

The Blooms' friends not only hosted parties over the weekend event, but also stocked the hospitality suite on the morning of the bar mitzvah with flowers, freshly squeezed juice, and lox and bagels so the guests could be together. Limousines arrived at nine in the morning to take everyone to the ceremony.

After the service, reception, and luncheon and an afternoon of shopping and sightseeing, the guests were ready for the nighttime gala. Jason and his friends were treated to boat rides while the adults attended a cocktail party. At eight o'clock, an actress in outlandish attire came into the party carrying a large tape deck blasting rock and roll

and began calling for Jason. The horrified guests wondered if she was an uninvited guest. When she found the shocked Jason, she told him to follow her as she led the party through the hotel garden and up the fire exit to the ballroom. As the doors to the ballroom opened, guests heard the same music being played by a pianist in the foyer. On each side of the ballroom was an enormous slide show—one of Jason's bar mitzvah and the other of his father's.

The program began with traditional Jewish music. In place of the traditional candlelighting service, Howard and Naomi did a slide show about the history of the family. Then the entertainment began as actors impersonated everyone from Elvis and the Beatles to the current teen idols. After the show ended, the guests were led into the foyer where every conceivable dessert was arranged.

Debby and Dennis Barek from Great Neck, Long Island, planned a party around their son Jonathan's love of computers. At their luncheon they had computer centerpieces made of flowers and gave pocket calculators and computer robot watches as favors.

One couple wanted their son's bar mitzvah to be a special celebration that all the families who attended could enjoy together. On the first night of the weekend, the host and hostess took all of their out-of-town guests to a Broadway musical that the kids would enjoy. On Saturday after the service, everyone walked down Fifth Avenue to the family's club for an early supper dance. The club was decorated with giant five-foot-tall helium bal-

*Design a party around your assets. Invite guests to a black-and-white party that is planned down to the last detail, and you will make a lasting impression.* JEFFERY

loons. There was a room for the kids, complete with soda fountain, bite-sized hamburgers, and pizza. This room opened onto a central hall that became the dance floor, and on the other side was an elegant buffet for the adults. Music was planned so that all ages could dance together, and a photographer was on hand to take pictures of each family.

Some families are foregoing the conventional bar mitzvah and taking their children to Israel. Special meaning is given to the ceremony by having it in the Jewish homeland.

## The Debutante Party
Debutante parties are alive and well in most of the large communities in the United States, as just a quick glance at *Town & Country* or *W* will confirm. Beneath all of the hoopla, this is the traditional time when young ladies from prominent families take their places in society. It's a once-in-a-lifetime experience.

While all debutante parties don't have to be balls, there are some common requirements. The more elaborate the party, the more important it is to obtain the services of a social secretary or party planner. You must have a list of all the debutantes that includes the full name of each girl, her height, the names of her parents and grandparents, their telephone numbers and addresses, the school she attends, the dates of her school vacations, and a list of boys she'd like to have escort her and their addresses. Any good social secretary not only will have this information on her computer, but will know the dates and times of each girl's party.

The Christmas holidays are a popular time to have debutante balls. Designer Kyle Burton created a romantic Russian Winter Palace Ball in a Los Angeles hotel ballroom using sheets of Mylar, a forest of fifteen-foot flocked Christmas trees, and grand-scale arrangements of white lilies, lilacs, and sprayed branches. Gold chairs and stemware, mammoth ice carvings, and a few touches of Fabergé completed the magnificent illusion. FROGER

Paul Bott of Twigs in New York has created a setting of opulence and romance for this dance in a loft apartment. Lace cloths from Patrizia Anichini and pink fabrics from Gretchen Bellinger have been used to soften the bare windows and as coverings for the tables. Invitations and escort and dance cards by Crane; tea table and chair from Charlotte Moss & Company. HIMMEL

The typical debutante is in one of her first years at college. The round of parties she will attend lasts for a year, with most of them being crammed into school vacations. The most prestigious presentations during the year are given by social clubs that invite debutantes to be presented to their membership. One of the oldest and most exclusive is the St. Cecilia Society in Charleston, South Carolina. Established in 1762 to give concerts of fine music, it is notable today for two things—the restriction of membership to the sons of current members and the annual presentation of debutante daughters.

In other communities, the debutante tradition has evolved so that each girl performs some civic service along with attending the rounds of parties. Gretchen Jones of Tucson, Arizona, explains that in her area each debutante, attired in her debutante ball gown, serves as an usher at the symphony. In Columbus, Georgia, the ball at which the members of the Cotillion Club are presented benefits the Historic Columbus Foundation. Members of the prestigious Atlanta Debutante Club are presented at two balls, the Bal de Salut and the Harvest Ball, both at the elite Piedmont Driving Club, to benefit the Henrietta Egleston Children's Hospital. In addition, all the debutantes have parties during the summer season at which they make Christmas ornaments and gifts for the children at the hospital.

Perhaps the most sophisticated of all debutante balls in the United States were those given in New York and Boston prior to 1940. In New York the family of a debutante held the party in its own ballroom at home or in the Crystal Room at the Ritz. There was continuous music provided by two well-known orchestras and entertainment by leading Broadway performers. After breakfast at 2 A.M., guests went off to El Morocco and danced until dawn. In Boston during this period, all the important balls were given at home.

Today many debutantes go to great lengths to have sensational themes and decorations. Balls may be held in a tent, on a boat, or in the ballroom of a hotel or club. Every girl wants her party to stand out against the throng of parties. One debutante went so far as to have her name spelled out in lights on an erected marquee in the center of a ballroom, while another covered the walls of a restaurant with twenty-foot blowups of Marilyn Monroe's pictures and then had herself made up to look just like her.

Crystal Moffett had a "New York, New York" party in a hotel ballroom that was transformed into Manhattan. At the center of the room was a twenty-foot-tall revolving apple made from red carnations. The walls were covered from floor to ceiling with a lighted artist's rendition of the skyline. After strolling through a replica of Central Park complete with park benches, trees and streetlamps, the guests dined in ethnic "neighborhoods" from Little Italy to Chinatown.

Two Florida debutantes held a "Gatsby Ball" in a garden right on the water. The band was located on an island in the middle of the swimming pool and was surrounded by thousands of floating candles. The whole time the party was going on, the film *Great Gatsby* was being shown

*Simple gifts are often the nicest. The gift that delights the young bride and groom today could end up in the attic five years from now. For the centerpieces at a bridal shower, arrange flowers in hidden containers slipped into lovely boxes. Tablecloth and napkin from Anichini; china and flatware from Wolfman Gold & Good; champagne flutes by Baccarat; flowers and hatboxes from Twigs.* HIMMEL

on a three-story screen located on a boat several feet offshore. Hired actors dressed as the characters in the film mingled with the crowd, and 1920s Charleston music was played by a costumed orchestra. A seated dinner was served at midnight while a fireworks display lit up the sky overhead.

### The Bridal Shower

Let's examine bridal showers in the spirit in which they are given. The host is inviting the couple's friends to help them set up their new household. This is an admirable tradition in much the same spirit as the pioneer custom of helping new neighbors raise a barn. Showers are a great joy for the honoree, but the guests may not be too keen on attending, especially after the third one for the

same bride. It is the host's responsibility to keep competitiveness in check, to be certain the guest list is made up of people who aren't "overshowered," and to make the party fun. Send invitations that make the party irresistible. One hostess sends each guest an expensive-looking jewelry box tied with a white satin bow. Inside is a large piece of clear crystal rock candy set like a diamond with the invitation rolled around the ring.

The new trend is to have weekend or evening coed parties that aren't so gift centered. The hostess (never a member of the immediate family) should ask the couple what type of shower they want, the kinds of things they need, and any color scheme they prefer.

Lisa and Robert Bell of Los Angeles had couples over for a wine-tasting shower to fete some of their friends who were to be married. The Bells provided eight different wines to taste, and each guest brought wine for the couple to take home. Lisa and her husband prepared a myriad of foods to complement the wines they served. Guests were given a rating chart for the wines, and a case of the winning wine was later sent to the couple as an "after honeymoon" welcome-home gift.

A Minneapolis hostess gave a new couple a house shower. The invitation, which reproduced a picture of the house, read: "Bring a present to help Hayden and Chip keep house. To avoid gifts for the attic, bring gifts for the room with the mouse." The hostess assigned each guest a room by putting a mouse sticker in the appropriate place on the invitation.

Frequently the hostess doesn't know the

guests at all. In this case a personal note may be best for the invitation. For example:

Dear Anne:
Heather's great-aunt Jean and I are having a kitchen shower for her on Tuesday at ten at my houseboat, No. 37, at the marina. Her colors will be red and blue. She's desperate for pot holders, recipes for chicken, freezer containers, and Le Creuset saucepans.

This will give the guest some idea about what is needed in several price ranges. Of course, another alternative is for the guests to buy one gift jointly. The hostess may suggest that they contribute to a Cuisinart for the couple. They are told the name of the store and can contribute whatever they choose toward the purchase rather than bring a gift of their own. The amount of their contribution is between them and the store. The hostess then makes up the difference in the cost or uses the extra to buy accessories.

One Washington State hostess likes to give communal showers twice a year for the brides in her small community. This way the brides and their friends get to meet new people—"a gift in itself," says the hostess. On each table is a basket painted in a different bride's colors and filled with whisks, wooden spoons, homemade pot holders, and silk-screened dish towels with baby's breath tucked among the utensils. After the party each bride gets her basket as a favor.

Before the party the hostess asks each guest for a favorite recipe. She types them out and has them spiral-bound as a gift for the brides. She also

207

*IOU Shower:* Each guest donates a service—mowing the lawn, shoveling snow, manicure for the bride/haircut for the groom, washing the car, raking leaves, gardening, building a bookcase, dog-sitting while the bride and groom are on their honeymoon, an astrological chart, tickets to a play or concert, fresh flowers for their first dinner party, a trip to a weekend house.

*Spice of Life Shower:* Guests bring spices or whatever they think would spice up the life of the couple.

*Gadget Shower:* Guests must disguise their gifts and the bride has to give silent clues to the groom to guess what it is and vice versa.

*Trim the Tree Shower:* Each guest is asked to bring something to hang on the couple's first Christmas tree—anything from homemade ornaments to nice, crisp, newly minted legal tender.

*Library Shower:* Guests bring a favorite book they've read (or record they like) with personal inscriptions explaining why the couple would enjoy it. Other guests might want to chip in to buy a subscription to a book club or magazine (or video club membership).

*Garden Shower:* Anything from blooming plants and grass seed to croquet sets and mulch can be given. One couple reports having received four birdhouses and a weeding machine, but they used them all.

*Bar Shower:* Anything from expensive liqueurs to beer may be given, as well as glasses, bar tools, ice buckets, trays, and mixers. One couple

*Recreate a "kitchen of old" to add a sense of history to the foods served within its walls. Collect decorative as well as functional antique utensils for the bride and groom. An amusing idea is to ask guests to bring kitchen gadgets for "better or worse," for example, a rolling pin and a heart-shaped cookie cutter. SCHLVZ*

gave a shower in an old-fashioned neighborhood bar with a country-and-western jukebox and a floor littered with peanut shells.

*Pantry Shower:* The couple is given gourmet canned goods—tins of imported olive oil, vinegars, jams and jellies, exotic mustards, imported pasta, chocolate sauce, and caviar. The party can be held in a kitchen with lots of good food to taste.

*Porthault Linen Shower:* Betsy Bloomingdale likes to give this shower for friends. Each guest is asked to bring one napkin or towel, and the bride soon has a beautiful linen trousseau.

*Research the wedding cakes of the nineteenth century to find the most elaborate confections imaginable. All antiques from Lucullus.* HIMMEL

assigns the guests to teams of eight. Together they pool their resources to buy a gift for their bride. Instead of merely opening the gifts, the brides must guess what their gifts are, charades-style, with each guest providing a different clue. This breaks the ice before lunch.

Again, after years of trying different menus, the hostess has settled on do-it-yourself salads with fresh fruit, vegetables, sprouts, seeds, olives, grated cheese, and her own homemade dressings. For dessert she serves frozen yogurt.

After the meal the guests don silk-screened butcher's aprons bearing their names and go into the kitchen to make food for the couples' freezers. The hostess has all of the ingredients precooked for lasagna, which is then assembled. Another group puts on the vegetable soup and still another prepares chicken and dumplings.

The party is a happy event for both the guests and the brides. The brides treasure their custom-made recipes and freezer foods, and the guests can enjoy the new friends they've made.

## The Wedding . . . A Sensible Guide

Weddings are a time of great joy and tremendous tension. Each family wants to show the other who they are, with some family members being more visible than others (remember Spencer Tracy in *Father of the Bride*?). Some family members feel put upon, some feel left out or neglected, and others have such fun that they overlook the serious purpose of the event. Some weddings are such spectacles they would put P. T. Barnum to shame.

While it is up to the couple to make plans for the wedding, it is also their responsibility to take into account the means and expectations of those who will be paying for it. Of course, many working couples choose to pay for the whole thing themselves. If parents are participating, however, they should make it clear what the budget is before the plans get out of hand.

It is most thoughtful to consider relatives and old family friends who may not be able to participate in the wedding festivities. Visit them to announce the engagement and let them feel they are being included in the planning. After the ceremony, have some candid wedding pictures made up for them and send them wedding cake and favors.

*Lace and more lace create romantic tables for a quiet party for an older bride. Miniature braided topiary ficuses are used as tall centerpieces that won't block the guests' cross-table conversation. Orchids, roses, and sprayed white branches echo the flowers used in the bridal bouquet, and the pot is wrapped in the same material used in the bridesmaids' dresses. HIMMEL*

There are many excellent publications that explain all the details of the wedding—who does what, when, and who pays for it (see Recommended Reading). If their guidelines do not fit the various needs and economic realities of the families involved, set up the event so that everyone feels comfortable.

Second weddings, especially when there are children involved, should be structured so that all family members feel that they have a part in the ceremony. All of the daughters can be bridesmaids, the sons groomsmen. Another alternative is to have a quiet family wedding, the honeymoon, and then a large reception after you have settled in as a family.

Some couples have been together for a long time and the wedding is just the icing on an already perfect cake. Famed pianist Ronnie Kole and wife Gardner celebrated their wedding at their country home. Friends boated in for a round of wonderful parties and a musical country wedding, then everyone went into the city nearby where Ronnie and Gardner were king and queen of a large Mardi Gras ball.

### Parties Before the Wedding

If the conventional regime is followed, an engagement or announcement party is given by the bride's family or a close friend. It should occur before the engagement announcement appears in the newspaper. Whether a tea or coffee for the female friends or a coed dinner or cocktail party, it provides a nice way for the friends of the bride and groom to get to know one another.

Keep a master list of the wedding guests handy at all times so that you don't leave someone off the guest list for one of the other parties. A card file is a sensible idea. When gifts are received, they can be logged on the cards as well. In addition, make a list of the members of the wedding party and a bit about them to give out to everyone, especially out-of-town guests. Include phone numbers and addresses so that they can get rides to parties with one another. Also assign each out-of-town guest to a local "host" family who can help them while they are at the wedding.

It is a custom in many communities that the first shower be given by the maid or matron of honor or by a group of members of the wedding party. It is gracious for the bride to have a party for her attendants at which she gives each a gift. These are usually silver or gold items engraved with the person's initials and the date of the wedding. One popular gift is a silver picture frame. After the wedding, the bride may also give the attendants a photograph of herself with the attendants taken at the wedding.

The bachelor party is given by the groom or his friends. Under no circumstances should the bride's father, or anyone who will tell her what happened at the party, be invited to one of these raunchy events. Neither should the events be photographed, videotaped, or recorded. The classic bachelor party is characterized by heavy drinking and lewd, sophomoric behavior. It is the sensible bride and groom who choose to slip away from the crowd and celebrate their last night of "freedom" together. To be on the safe side, if the event

# WEDDING TRADITIONS

The toast dates from Elizabethan England when slices of toasted bread were placed in the bottom of a tankard of ale or wine to absorb the sediment at the bottom of the glass.

The tossing of the bouquet to unmarried women dates back to fourteenth-century France.

Rice is a symbol of fertility. Originally couples were showered with cereal grains in Rome, Persia, India, and Anglo-Saxon England.

Lilies of the valley symbolize a return to happiness; ivy, wedded bliss; orchids, beauty and refinement; orange blossoms, purity; roses, love; and fern, sincerity.

Greek brides carried long sprays of ivy to symbolize unbreakable love. Roman brides carried herbs to ensure their husbands' fidelity. It was the ancient Saracens who invented the modern tradition of carrying orange blossoms. The tree bears both blossoms and fruit, symbolizing conjugal bliss.

In an ancient ritual, bridesmaids carried bouquets of pungent herbs and sprigs of garlic to ward off evil spirits from the happy couple.

The multi-decorated wedding cake began as a thin loaf of bread which was broken over the bride's head at the close of the ceremony in ancient Rome. The wheat symbolizes fertility. The custom evolved so that in the Middle Ages it was considered good luck for the newlyweds to kiss over a stack of small cakes.

will be raucous, have it a week before the wedding so the groom will have time to recover.

One father of the groom who wanted to spare his son the humiliation (and hangover) of the conventional bachelor party rented a bus and took his son and the other men in the wedding party to the country. They spent the day drinking beer, water-skiing, playing tennis, fishing, and barbecuing. They were delivered back to their doorsteps by midnight with glowing suntans.

### The Rehearsal Dinner

The rehearsal dinner takes place the night before the wedding and is hosted by the family of the groom. It is for the entire wedding party and should also include out-of-town guests. If the groom's family is from out of town, they can bring a bit of home with them—food, decorations, or music. Since parties are difficult to arrange long distance, it is a good idea for the bride's family or a friend to offer to help with the logistics. Budget discussions are imperative.

One divorced father who lived in the Orient could not find anyplace to have his son's rehearsal dinner in the bride's home town except the church hall, which had a prohibition on liquor. He hired a party planner in the closest big city and had a tent, table, chairs, and music shipped in. Dinner was an elegant picnic supper served in Japanese lacquered boxes.

### The Wedding Ceremony

The time of the wedding is important. If out-of-town guests have a whole day to kill before the

*Elegance and imagination combine to make this meal into a glorious event (left). Gold ribbon streamers are tied to the nineteenth-century Dutch brass chandelier. At the end of each piece of ribbon is the name of the person the guest will dance with at the completion of the meal. Instead of a large centerpiece, alstroemeria and oncidium orchids are suspended from the chandelier in lipped Two's Company vases. Favors wrapped in gold lamé fabric are used at each place instead of a place card.*

*Lace tablecloth, assembled in 1870 with eighteenth- and nineteenth-century laces; French Belle Epoque oyster plates, circa 1890; nineteenth-century Worcester dinner plates; French Belle Epoque Baccarat stemware; American sterling silver candlesticks, San Francisco, 1920; Irish Georgian crystal compotes, Dublin, 1820; Sèvres gold and white porcelain, 1840; napkin rings, India, 1900; Napoleon III pearl-handled knives, circa 1860–1870; vermeil forks, George III, London, 1777. All from Lucullus.* HIMMEL

*Empty plates at a festive meal can be a bore (right). A piece of iridescent paper can be tied with silver ribbon, and a galax leaf and rose inserted. Guests may pin them on their lapels or dresses as the first course is served.* HIMMEL

event, the day will drag. The nicest thing anyone can do is offer to have a brunch on the day of the wedding. Margaret and Dick Punches not only have a day-of-the-wedding brunch for their friends who are getting married, but they send an arrangement of home-grown roses to each out-of-town guest's room as the invitation.

Remember, don't leave out the bride on this day; she will not want to sit home alone watching *The Donahue Show* while everyone else is at a party. Thanks to a nineteenth-century custom, the superstitious believe that the groom should not see the bride on the day of the wedding until the ceremony. If the groom holds this belief, then he should sit home and watch television and the bride should go to the party.

Weddings are a family time. Don't overlook the children who will be attending. At one rehearsal dinner, Bev Reese kept everyone's kids happy by giving each child a bag of activities before each seated meal. The bags contained mazes, puzzles, cards, crayons, and coloring books. At the rehearsal she borrowed a vat of Legos from the Sunday school and let the kids sit around in the church vestibule while the adults rehearsed.

There is one big wedding "don't" that all families must consider. While bridal consultants can be a great help in the planning of the wedding, most clergymen find their direction offensive during the religious part of the ceremony.

If the service will be terribly long and complicated, consider having a private service for the family, close friends, and out-of-town guests. The reception can be the time to have mobs of people.

### The Reception

Having the receiving line at the front door can cause unpleasant congestion as guests wait to enter the reception. Put the receiving line past the first bar. Assign one person the task of supplying food or drink to each member of the wedding party who is in line. (Holding a glass while standing in line, however, is not proper, so this must be done on the sly.)

The reception should reflect the interests of the bride and groom, as well as those of their parents. The party is not a success if the "old" people and the "young" people split off into separate areas. Following the reception there can be a wedding supper or dinner dance for the wedding party, close friends, family, and guests.

Many gracious newlyweds have a party after the honeymoon to say thank you to their families and those who have entertained for them. It is particularly thoughtful if they can find a way to use their wedding presents to serve the meal.

## The Surprise Party

There are some people who love surprises and others who would rather have teeth pulled than be the recipient of one. Just because a spouse, lover, or friend detests parties does not mean that he or she will instantly fall into the spirit if the party is a surprise. There are alternatives to a party, however. One group of friends in Minneapolis knew that the couple they wanted to surprise for their anniversary hated parties, so they organized a surprise gift instead. A scroll was sent to the couple that read: "Reserve the night of May 1. We'll take care of the kids. Signed, The Committee for the Preservation of a Perfect Marriage." A phone call the day of the event told the couple what to wear and to pack an overnight bag.

Thirty friends chipped in to give the couple a dream anniversary. At seven o'clock a chauffeur-driven limousine was sent to the couple's home to take them out for the evening. The neighbors came over to spend the night with the couple's children. The couple was taken to the ballet, then to a champagne supper, then to the candlelit honeymoon suite of an elegant hotel. The next morning they were given breakfast in bed and the driver was downstairs to take them home at ten.

For those who like them, surprise parties are a great thrill, especially when they are not held at the home of the celebrant. (Having to clean up a colossal mess is not a treat.) There are certain logistics worthy of a CIA agent that the host of the surprise party must master.

First, arrange for the celebrant to be engaged in something of a business or obligatory nature at the appropriate time. You may have the boss or a relative call and ask the unknowing celebrant to take a client or relative to an important meeting or dinner.

Second, have the party the day before the special day to catch the person off guard. Then ask a friend to help so that all of the arrangements can be made in another name with a phone number and address different from yours. Many a surprise is blown by a merchant who calls to reconfirm an order for birthday cake.

Third, have some surprise guests—friends from out of the past—to say "Surprise!" Invite an old coach or a favorite teacher from high school, the butcher or the hairdresser.

Fourth, have the party in an unexpected place that can be decorated beforehand. One wife called her husband at the office and said her car was at the shop and they wanted $3,000 to fix it. The husband stormed into the service station to berate the mechanic, who listened to the tirade and then said "Surprise!" as he lowered the car down from the hydraulic lift, decorated with Happy Birthday banners and balloons. The back of the garage area had been decorated in a Grand Prix theme, and a band and one hundred guests awaited the guest of honor.

Another man wanted to surprise his business partner on his birthday. He had someone call and say that he had an important package at the train station that had to be picked up by seven o'clock when the train left. Of course, the birthday man was the only one at the office. Once at the station, he was directed to a railroad car where there was

*Surprise a favorite friend with a profusion of flowers, gifts, or delectable foods. Three green Depression glass vases are presented in a decorative hatbox from Les Rubans. The flowers are straight from the garden—bamboo mixed with roses and azaleas. The glass is courtesy of the Crescent City Depression Glass Society. HIMMEL*

a gigantic box, much too big to carry. As he turned to leave, the box flew open and out popped a girl in a gorilla suit singing "Happy Birthday." Out of the back of the car came his friends, who feted him at an elegant railroad car dinner party.

Hilary Brookes, whose husband, Navy carrier pilot Jim Pollard, was born on December 27, gave a real surprise birthday party for Jim—on August 13. Jim's birthday being so close to Christmas meant that it always got lost in the holiday season and he had never had a real birthday party. Since Queen Elizabeth has an official birthday in June to take advantage of sunny weather for the outdoor pomp (her real birthday is in April), Hilary decided Jim must have an official birthday too. Conspiring with their friends, Hilary arranged an ostensible "let's-just-get-together-and-have-fun" party with a theme of "Weird Wines and Good Cheese." Happily, Jim went shopping to choose the unheard-of, inexpensive wines (from the Mississippi Delta to Australia and Moravia) and exotic cheeses, never dreaming all this was in his honor!

The decorations and cake had been hidden away when Hilary rushed home from the office at lunch, and her son, Eric, was stationed at the door to greet guests and stash their gifts in a convenient closet. On cue, one of the guests asked Jim to show him the beautiful rooftop view from their apartment building. Banners were hurried out of hiding and taped in place, gifts and cards quickly piled around the cake with lighted candles, and everyone donned party hats and grabbed noisemakers and streamers. The ensuing surprise was a textbook success—open mouth, wide eyes,

speechlessness turning into a huge grin, and chuckles of appreciation. Jim commented, "Best birthday party I ever had!"

## The Housewarming

Housewarmings are generally organized for people who are moving to a new location, even though it might be just next door. The idea is to fete the new homeowners with gifts and good wishes. This is not the time for a big bash attended by neighbors and friends who want a house tour. Unpacking boxes, entertaining the kids, organizing books or records, and sending over food will be appreciated much more.

Friends and family can hold a party for the new homeowners in one of their homes and might

*It is your first night in your new house. In essence you're beginning anew, mixing your treasured objects with new ones. Paul Bott of Twigs illustrates that the same flowers need not always look the same. At left, the same flowers are shown in five arrangements, each one in a different style and mood. Vases from Twigs; cheese and fruit tray from Wolfman Gold & Good.* HIMMEL

Plan an outside supper for friends in the garden of their new house on the day before they move in. Courtesy *House Beautiful* magazine, the Hearst Corporation. SCHINZ

217

even invite them to stay over during the move. Decorations can be made out of small packing boxes filled with vases of flowers and packing straw and baskets of useful items—picture hooks, pushpins, cleaning supplies, extension cords, electrical tape. Guests can be asked to bring a certain color towel for the bathroom or gadgets for the kitchen. When Judge Michael Coburn and his wife moved into their house in Kansas City, they found their friends had sneaked in and put gorgeous linens on the bed and soft music on the radio.

Another nice idea is to have a garden-warming party after the weather gets pleasant. Let the guests bring plants and flowers to be planted right at the party. A "Pink Flamingo Treasure Hunt" is another idea along this line. Sneak into the garden of the new homeowner and fill it with tacky garden statues. Under each put an IOU for a nice piece of lawn or patio furniture to be collected the next night at a party at your house.

A housewarming held for someone who has just purchased a weekend cottage or condominium is very helpful. You and your friends can collect pots and pans, linens, dishes, and other household necessities.

When Nancy Winton of Minneapolis found herself between San Francisco and Minneapolis with all her furniture in transit, she called on her friends for help. She threw a "Dire Straits/Fill Up My House with Furniture" housewarming! At the front door she had a guest book and Polaroid to record the pieces of furniture each friend was lending to her.

## The Anniversary Party

Anniversary parties are celebrated much more along the lines of a wedding than a birthday. At a formal anniversary party there is a receiving line. The honored couple stands nearest the entrance to greet their guests. They are followed by their children and their spouses (from the oldest to the youngest). If someone else is giving the party, that person or couple stands in the front of the line as host and hostess, with the anniversary couple next to them.

*Grover Mouton combined a cotton rug collected from a recent trip, wicker chairs from a childhood home, cushioned by soft down pillows, and fresh salad from the garden to create an intimate anniversary away from telephones and social schedules. FREEMAN*

218

At a formal party, the couple sits at the center of the head table surrounded by members of the original wedding party and their spouses, or by their children. The host and hostess sit at either end of a long table or facing the couple if the table is round. Wedding cake is the traditional dessert. Gifts are brought and opened at the party.

A few years after a couple has been married, it is nice to have a party for as many of the original wedding guests as you can gather. Show the wedding pictures and relive old times. This need not be a formal party and gifts are not necessary. It is very thoughtful to take a widow or widower out for a quiet dinner on an anniversary, although a large celebration is in poor taste.

Kay Wheatley Kerrigan of Tulsa and New Orleans decided that she wanted to host a whimsical anniversary party for all her married friends. She sent out an invitation that showed her in her wedding picture on the outside, and on the inside showed her in the same dress now but with a lampshade on her head. Guests were invited to come to a dinner wearing their wedding clothes and bringing their wedding photographs. On the day of the party, a florist delivered a wrist corsage and boutonniere to each couple.

At the party, Kay had a revolving five-foot-tall cardboard wedding cake and an accordion and kazoo trio performing traditional wedding music. After champagne and wedding hors d'oeuvres, the wedding cake erupted to reveal the maitre d' from a favorite eatery who escorted the surprised guests out to dinner via white wedding limousines.

*Collectors can treat each other to breakfast served on an assortment of new acquisitions received as gifts. The green Depression glass is in the Tea Room pattern (Indiana Glass Company) and the Block Optic pattern (Hocking Glass Company) from the Crescent City Depression Glass Society. The two-tiered cotton moiré tablecloth was designed by Pam Ryan of Les Rubans.* HIMMEL

*Three couples in this country community came up with the ultimate anniversary gift. They treated their friends to a Sunday in bed. Not only did they entertain the couple's children out of the house all day, but they delivered the London Sunday Times (no mean feat in rural Kentucky), bouquets of flowers from their gardens, a stack of novels, and breakfast in bed. The English Pink Luster tea set, circa 1810, was a cooperative gift, with each friend giving a different piece.* HIMMEL

## The Class Reunion

It can be rewarding to touch base with our past every twenty years or so. In a way it is a yardstick by which we can judge our successes and failures. There are happy thoughts: "Isn't it great that Barbie and Ken are still so happily married? We should see them more often." And negative ones: "I've got more hair than the captain of the football team!"

Reunions are not the time for those who have achieved success to gloat about it—at least not in public. Rather, they offer the chance to relive old times and reestablish friendships. Don't have an "in" crowd of successful adults in the spotlight and everyone else on the sidelines. Have lots of activities so that all the guests are in the limelight!

Before the event, print up a class directory. Include the names of classmates and their spouses, along with home and business addresses and phone numbers, hobbies, names and ages of kids, and where they are staying for the reunion.

*Recreate a wonderful theme or period in time through music and food. Guests can step out of the present and dress in outfits from the past. That poodle skirt from yesteryear can make a whimsical overlay for a table or a cover for the base of a plant or the Christmas tree—so take it out of the attic and keep it in your party closet. Five photographs: DAVIS*

This will give people something to talk about. Use yearbook pictures to make name tags.

One of the most thoughtful things you can do if you live in the town where the reunion is held is to have a prereunion party for several old classmates. That way you can catch up on the intervening years, meet everyone's spouses, and go to the party as a group.

Begin the festivities with an informal "transition" from adulthood back to school life. Have a volleyball, basketball, softball, or touch football game. Let everyone else form a decorations committee to get ready for the big party, which can be held at a favorite hangout or at least be catered by a similar establishment. Have a sock hop with the music of the era, but don't try to recreate the prom theme and decorations. That chickenwire top hat stuffed with Kleenex will look pathetic to the adult eye.

A master of ceremonies who is not a member of the class can keep things rolling. Ask a favorite

teacher, a deejay, or a class sponsor to introduce people by reading from the yearbook what their goals were then as opposed to what they are now. For example, "Back then, Joey wanted to join a rock band—now his goal is to keep his daughter from joining one." Forget about flashing "then" and "now" pictures up on a screen. Too many people find them embarrassing.

For the grand finale, arrange for the school band to march in playing the fight song, complete with cheerleaders. Award trophies to the person who knows the words to the school song, to the most bald (the Chrome Dome Award), to the couple married the longest (the Ma and Pa Kettle Award), to the classmate with the most kids, to the person who traveled the farthest, and so on.

## The Milestone Birthday

Each decade and half decade after about the age of twenty, there is a birthday just crying out to be celebrated. There are those people who do it in such a big way that getting older almost seems to be a luxury.

Sandra Pulitzer wanted to give a great party on her husband Arthur's fortieth birthday. He didn't want anyone to bring him a gift, so they decided to surprise the guests. She had one of his baby pictures blown up and wrote the invitation on the picture: "I'm 40, come celebrate with me." There was no name on the invitation, just the time and place, a funky neighborhood bar. No one knew until they arrived whose party it was.

Helene Waters got a group of her friends together and took out an ad in the *Kansas City Star*. In it was a large picture of one of her friends with the caption: "In two days it will be Mary Francis' birthday and we want to celebrate. See tomorrow's paper for details." Needless to say, Mary Francis was surprised to see herself in the paper and wondered who had placed the ad.

The next day she was told that on her birthday, at the exact time of her birth, she was to go to the house nearest her favorite restaurant that sported a red mailbox and a snowman. She was thrilled and looked forward to her birthday for two days.

One New York decorator wanted to have a meaningful celebration for her husband's fortieth birthday. Since they had been married in Japan, she took over a Japanese restaurant for the party. She had her husband's name written in Japanese characters on rice paper as the party "logo." Guests received their invitations in take-out food containers, and inside each was a motorized sushi toy with the party information attached. The director of a Japanese flower-arranging school was hired to do the flowers, and an artist-chef constructed a seven-foot cake in the shape of a giant piece of sushi.

This hostess doesn't believe in surprise parties because she feels that the honoree will enjoy the party more if he is involved in the planning. She did, however, have one big surprise for her husband. She hired a film crew to make a four-minute film about his life, dubbed in Japanese with English subtitles.

When the guests arrived, they were greeted by two geishas, one male and one female, who bowed and gave each man a black and white happy coat with the birthday boy's Japanese name on the back. Everyone immediately relaxed and settled back for their seven-course Japanese banquet. After dinner, there were authentic Japanese dancers and a Sumo wrestling demonstration.

Lynne White knew that her husband, Hunter, and two of her best friends were planning her birthday party. She just didn't know any of the details. They created decorations around her interest in gardening. A trellis of palms and lights was created at the entrance to their club. Flowering trees of varying heights were used as the centerpiece on each table, creating the illusion of walking into a garden. Her friends dressed as flowers from her garden and serenaded her with song and dance.

M*ake the event memorable by choosing the perfect gift and filling a trunk with all the goodies to create a birthday celebration right on the spot.* JEFFERY

There are times when the person you want to honor lives in a nursing home and cannot leave to have a celebration in your home or a restaurant. If your friend or relative is game and the administration of the nursing home agrees, have a party right on the premises. (As an alternative or in addition, have everyone the person knows send birthday cards so there is a shower of them for a week before the event.)

To make the party special, send invitations to everyone in the nursing home who will be attending the party so they have something to look forward to. Give all the guests a little gift—perhaps a small potted plant or a picture frame, a silk-screened hand towel or a pillowcase.

Many times the room for the party is the same recreation room where the residents spend most of their waking hours. You must transform the space into a new environment. Decorate with lots of brightly colored helium balloons—oversized red hearts, pale blue ovals, and silver circles —things that will show up well. Tie large clusters together with streamers hanging down. Dimming the lights may cause confusion, so introduce new lighting effects, such as a few red bulbs near the food area. After the party, tie a balloon to everyone's bed or wheelchair.

Ask the dietician or nurse what type of food the guests can have. Maybe you can serve a variety of bite-sized hors d'oeuvres suited to the guests' different diet restrictions and, of course, their preferences. Nearly everyone can have cake and ice cream or you can make a giant Jell-O mold. Play to your audience and be certain to have plenty of food for everyone. Nonalcoholic champagne is a sparkling alternative to punch, but if the guests would prefer punch made from ginger ale and sherbet, by all means serve it.

Find out the type of music the guests like. You might play records of big-band swing music or hire an accordionist to play polkas. Another possibility is to have a mime troupe or a choir perform—nothing rowdy or long. The party should last no longer than an hour.

Cherished gifts to the birthday person include a soft afghan for the bed, photo albums of family pictures with captions and special messages from each family member, a videotape or cassette recording of birthday wishes from friends and family, a bottle of sherry, Scotch, or bourbon, fancy chocolates or hard mints, a jogging suit that can be worn instead of pajamas for lounging, a lighted magnifying mirror, a gift certificate for a weekly massage or visit from the beautician or barber, or an IOU from you to take her or him shopping once a week or to do the shopping yourself.

An alternative is to give a gift to the nursing home in the name of the birthday person—a book for the library or a plant for the garden.

*Food should be simple, colorful, and appealing. Fresh fruit sorbets served with or without fresh fruit toppings are a refreshing change of pace from ice cream. A carved ice basket is not only a festive touch but also a definite change from institutional food service.* BEADLE

To invite guests to Ann Burka's birthday party in New Orleans, her friends hired a composer to write a special song and had it recorded. The night of the party, Ann arrived to find a red carpet rolled out to the street, klieg lights blazing, and wet cement prepared for her footprints. She was the star for the night. Inside, pictures of her when she had been homecoming queen at college were blown up and displayed in every room.

Susie Ringer of Wysata, Minnesota, had to do something special for her husband John's thirty-fifth birthday since it fell on Friday the thirteenth. She had a "Magical Mystery Tour" and told guests to come in 1960s attire. A parade of decorated hay wagons and tractors took the party down the old Luce railroad line to a pumpkin patch, where several special pumpkins were hidden. Guests had to find the decorated pumpkins in the dark, as well as the largest, smallest, longest, and fattest. Afterward, everyone went to a local honky-tonk for chili and dancing.

## The Funeral and Memorial

There are very few people who want to be the guest of honor at one of these events, but sooner or later everyone will be. Either you can plan your own now or leave it to your friends and family. Whatever you say you want, those who do the planning generally will try to adhere to your wishes. There was the lady in California who was buried in her Mercedes, the man in Connecticut who was buried with a telephone and Hershey bars, and an Oakland man who had an antique horse-drawn hearse, a procession of a dozen white Rolls-Royces, and pallbearers in tuxedos. Other people request cocktail parties instead of funerals, have jazz processions to the cemetery, or stipulate in their wills that the whole family must take a cruise, at the expense of the estate, to scatter their ashes. Some people even make a video to be shown at their funeral in which they deliver comforting messages to all of their friends.

A funeral is often a sad time when tradition and ritual can aid in the process of saying farewell to a special person. In almost all cases it is those most bereaved—the spouse, the children, or close friends—who will be called upon to play host to all of the other mourners. Just because you might not feel up to making an effort to have a nice service, don't think others won't notice and make comments—they will. Unfortunately, funerals can't be put off until you feel like having them, and you don't get to try again if the first one is a disaster.

While people in different parts of the country and those from different backgrounds may have their own funeral customs, they have one thing in common: those in mourning like to get together to share their sense of loss. No one wants to drive nine hours to a funeral and find themselves sitting in a hotel room watching game shows before a ten-minute graveside service at which the minister didn't even know the deceased.

Being "in charge" and the chief mourner does have a few positive aspects. When someone close dies, there is usually a sense of numbness and a certain therapeutic value in doing mundane things, be it polishing silver or writing thank-you

notes. Many friends will want to help, and there is plenty for them to do. Let them be on the battle lines answering the phone and the doorbell, making tea and coffee, taking children to a movie, and manning the kitchen. Ask some friends to call out-of-town friends and relatives. Have someone else log each floral arrangement in a book with the name of the florist (in case you have questions when you get ready to write the thank-you letter), the name of the sender, and a description. Have the person in charge of the kitchen make a list of who brings which food and what container it comes in. Others should keep lists of who calls and should be able to judge whom you do and don't feel like seeing.

It is often more convenient to have the actual service at a place of worship or the funeral home. After the service, many guests will want to get together in a personal setting. You can go to your home, a friend's house, or even a restaurant or private club (you, as host, will pick up the tab unless someone offers beforehand).

At home you are not having a cocktail party, but a reunion of friends and relatives who share a common experience. If ever there was a time for lackluster catered finger sandwiches, sherry, and pound cake, this is it. The occasion is a solemn one; there need not be any decorations or fanfare. Food and beverages should be unobtrusive. It is not improper to simply offer Perrier water. Dozens of coffee and tea cups may be a hassle to wash. Remember that the more there is to eat and drink, the longer people will stay. Death brings out people's insecurities; their instincts about what to say

and do seem to fail them. Ask friends to play hostess if you and other family members want to retreat early.

Have a death announcement printed to send to out-of-town acquaintances, magazines, charity solicitations, and so on. It can simply be a 3-by-4¾-inch black-bordered white card that reads:

In Memoriam
Henry Louis Mencken
January 29, 1956

Every donation letter, floral piece, mass card (known in the trade as "spiritual bouquets"), and culinary contribution brought to your home demands a thank-you note written in black ink on a plain white note card, which may have your name engraved in black. If you have many of these to do, you may want to obtain printed acknowledgment cards from your funeral home so the sender knows his or her remembrance has been received. A note from you must then follow within three months.

### The Obituary

If you don't give the necessary information to a newspaper, the obituary doesn't have a chance, unless the deceased person was famous, in which case the paper probably has an obituary on file. In most cases you must supply the name and age of the deceased (no nicknames) and who the relatives are, from closest family members to most distant. The newspaper will also want to know the cause of death and then will describe it as a short illness, a lengthy illness, or an accident. You may ask that the obituary state that "in lieu of flowers, donations may be made to . . ."

Classified obituary notices are different from news stories. They are classified ads that appear in a special section of the paper. In some cities they are free, and in others there is a fee. Many times a paper will accept them only from a funeral home, thereby diminishing the chance of a lawsuit arising from misinformation in a death notice. The role of obituaries is to let people know that a person has died. It is a good idea to run them in out-of-town papers where the deceased was known, as well as in local papers.

### The Service

Decide on a type of service appropriate to the deceased, yet fulfilling to those who will attend. You will have succeeded when people say afterward: "That was so beautiful. Aunt Hermione would have appreciated it very much."

The least expensive way to do the service is to arrange for it yourself. Prepare and record all the legal documents, arrange for the permits, contact a member of the clergy, and contract with a cemetery or crematory for disposal of the body. The body may be given to a research institution or various parts to organ banks. Some areas have burial or cremation societies to handle such details (they can be found in the telephone directory).

Generally, the next least expensive way to do a service is to have the funeral home remove the body and have it cremated (caskets are not necessary, although some type of container is) or buried directly. The procedures and charges vary and will cost between $500 and $1500, depending on the area of the country.

The third and most common way is to avail yourself of the services of a reputable funeral home. This does not mean that you have to have a funeral. It means that they will arrange a service fitting your requirements. The single greatest expense in a funeral is for the professional services of staff. They are paid on a twenty-four-hour day basis to ensure a prompt response to your call. They can do anything from arranging for a symphony to perform to placing calls to your friends to inform them of the death. If you do not know a minister, priest, or rabbi, they can find one, or they can cut through the complicated red tape if you need to ship the body out of the state or the country for burial.

Choose a funeral home that has a good reputation or has been recommended by a friend or relative. In many areas of the country there are firms belonging to the National Selected Morticians, a professional group with the highest standing in the industry. There are many fine firms, however, that do not belong. Remember, just because a funeral home is small and unpretentious does not mean it will be less expensive than the grand old established one. Do not hesitate to ask for and compare prices.

The secret is to know what you want and ask the right questions. Top-of-the-line caskets are made of bronze, copper, American black walnut, or mahogany. Cloth-covered caskets are usually the least expensive. If your funeral home doesn't have a casket you like, it can order almost anything, in a short period of time. After your meeting with the funeral director, go home and think about your options before making any final plans. Do you want the funeral at home? Will the casket fit through the front door? Where will people park? How many people will your house hold? Do you want an open casket? Flowers?

Even if you don't want a member of the clergy, have someone be the leader of the service to hold it together. Poetry can be substituted for prayers. If the deceased was very old or incapacitated for a long time, you might ask friends to tell stories about when he or she was young and active. If friends do speak, ask them to keep it short. Too many speakers can result in a service dragging on. Ask those close to the deceased, not close relatives, to be pallbearers.

Think the event through from start to finish. Will any of the participants have trouble finding the location of the service? If so, send cars to pick them up. What will happen if it rains or snows? Have a contingency plan. If you aren't using a funeral home, where can people call for information about the service? If the deceased will be cremated, do you plan to inter the remains? If you are scattering ashes, what do you do with the container when you've finished?

Hiring cars and drivers for the family is a good idea because mourners do not tend to have their minds on the road. Any time there is heavy traffic and a distance of more than five miles from the church or funeral home to the cemetery, have two police officers on motorcycles as an escort. In some cities this is free; in others there is a fee.

Graveside services are planned in conjunction with the burial and may be held after a regular service or by themselves. There is a short service, and then the mourners leave before the actual burial. If you like, each mourner can say something brief about the deceased and then throw a fresh flower into the grave.

A memorial service takes place after the fact, after burial or cremation. Every service needs a beginning, a middle, and an end. For example, a prayer or a poem can be read, music can be played, a tree can be planted or ashes scattered, another prayer, poem, or eulogy, music, and the final prayer. At one memorial service champagne was passed at the end and a toast was made to the deceased. Afterward everyone walked down the hill and had a picnic. At another service a park bench was dedicated and afterward participants decided to sponsor a yearly poetry reading in the park to commemorate the deceased's birthday.

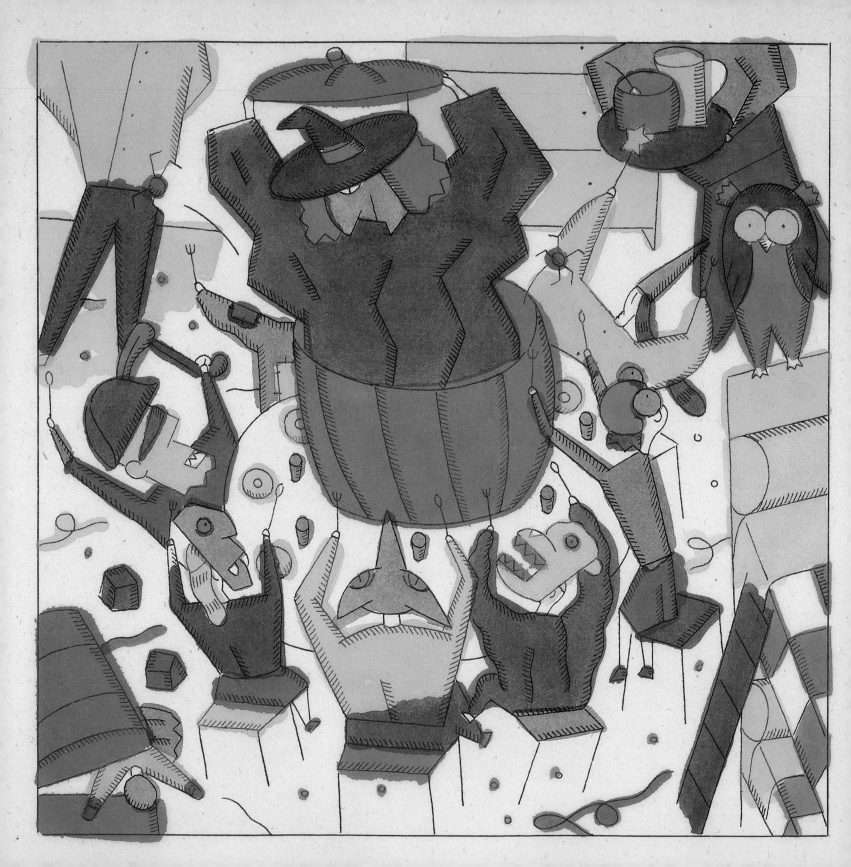

# *Chapter 8*
# HAVING A BALL
# WITH KIDS

any adults look forward to entertaining kids with about the same enthusiasm they would have for preparing a seven-course dinner for Attila the Hun and his band of marauders. "Why is it that children today come into the world expecting to have the same active social life as an adult?" they moan. It's a pity that these adults look at any event involving young people as being a nightmare. Believe it or not, some parents, grandparents, aunts, uncles, and godparents enjoy entertaining children so much, they have not only birthday parties for them, but Christmas, Halloween, August Doldrums, Easter, Back-to-School, and Valentine's Day parties as well. 🐝 The mental attitude of the adults has a great deal to do with the success of any children's gathering. Children are quick to get into the spirit of an event. The whole family can get involved in helping the child plan an event, decide on the desired theme, decorations, and location. For weeks before the event, you and your child, and maybe a friend or two, can work on the party list, the invitations, the decorations, and the activities. Right before the party, the child can help with the refreshments and getting the location ready. Not only does this activity make the child feel involved and build expectation for the event, but it also teaches your little Scott or Jennifer to be a good host or hostess. 🫖 If you plan to entertain at home, think about the spaces that will work best for your child to entertain in. Plan the

*Children tend to get more into the spirit of the festivities when they can dress as a favorite character. Entertainment should be so enticing that the children lose themselves in the spirit.*
STONE

number of guests, the food, and activities accordingly. Don't make the mistake of having a party in the backyard without planning a space to move to in case of an unexpected rainstorm; otherwise you'll find hordes of sopping kids and drenched decorations in your formal living room. Once decorated, garages, galleries, studios, hallways, basements, porches, and attics can be fabulous places to have a party, as are shelters and bandstands in public parks. Also keep in mind that things run more smoothly if there is a separate place for eating, away from the other party activities.

An alternative is to entertain away from home. Hamburger and chicken franchises, pizza parlors, ice cream parlors, and such places as pizza/theater restaurants have made kids' parties into a business. They handle the food and the mess and you pay for it.

Building expectation for a children's party is very important. Clever invitations and a few decorations can make the difference between hanging out after school and an "event." Cathy Burka and her seven-year-old daughter, Aden, go all out. For one slumber party, Cathy and Aden made tiny baby doll pillows for each of her friends and wrote the invitation right on the pillow. It was a BYOSB (Bring Your Own Sleeping Bag) party. For a party they gave at a miniature golf course, they printed the invitations directly onto golf balls.

## Parties for the Under-Six Set
From the time that a child is about two, the planning of a party can be a joyful activity in which both of you can participate. Parties are a wonderful way for you to show your child that he or she is a special person. So what if the child is too young to remember the party? Take lots of photographs or make videotapes. All of the family will enjoy reliving the event, year after year.

Spending a great deal of money on elaborate decorations and favors does not ensure the success of a party for this very young age group. At one party for a four-year-old, the formal dining room was transformed at great expense into a land of ice and snow—silver icicles were hung from the ceiling; lighted murals were attached to the walls. The entertainment consisted of watching the birthday boy open his gifts. Within fifteen minutes the other children became bored and began pulling down the silver icicles, which proved to be more popular than the motorized robots given as party favors. The birthday cake was baked Alaska, which the children hated because of all the liqueur poured over it. Most of them went home in tears, and the mother of the birthday child took to her bed. It seems that one of the disappointed children told her that he'd had more fun at the birthday party he attended the day before: "Andrew's mom let us run around the backyard and slide on sheets of plastic while she squirted us with the hose, and she gave us neat food—pizza!"

The number of children at a party is also important. The rule of thumb is two children for the two-year-old, three for the three-year-old, four for the four-year-old, and so on. Today, with many children beginning some sort of day care or play group by the age of two, the children themselves may have other ideas. Many a two-year-old

*Give one-year-olds the foods they enjoy, the people they love, and the pleasure of making a mess. Marvelously yummy strawberry shortcake served right in your child's favorite "chair" is the perfect way to commemorate one year of life. STONE*

will rattle off the names of six or seven "best" friends, and it would be a shame not to let them all come to a party. Just be prepared and keep the party simple. You need not add the children of your friends. As one five-year-old said to her mother, "Mommie, this party is wonderful—but who are all of these people?"

A famed professional party giver and author of *Jeremy's Birthday Party Book* Jeremy Sage likes to give parties only for childen aged four to ten (they listen better). His advice is that the birthday boy or girl get special treatment, such as being first in line (with siblings always second) for everything. "Warm, friendly greetings are crucial," says Jeremy. "I make certain that they know I'm their friend and that they are going to have lots of fun, that they won't be scared, and that they can always come to me if there is a problem. Then I stage the party and they stay so busy that they are never bored." At his parties kids are entertained by enormous electric trains, laser and light shows, magic, bubble machines, kid food, robots, and participatory game shows, and everyone gets a party favor.

An alternative to home or restaurant parties is to arrange to take your child and a few friends to see a fire station; a cookie, soft drink, or candy factory; or a special movie or show. Afterward, go to your child's favorite spot for refreshments.

Keep parties simple and short for this age group. Let the party be over before the children are tired or bored. An hour to an hour and a half is plenty of time for the under-six group. A lot of confusion and noise will frighten the children.

235

Children can be taught early to respond to invitations by having a part of the invitation that they can tear off, color, and return to the host.

Oversized picture postcards or posters of animals, rock stars, airplanes, or sports figures are perfect for theme parties.

Let your child do a drawing and have it photocopied on brightly colored paper. Fold the sheet and seal it with stickers in the theme of the party.

Cut a pair of miniature Oshkosh overalls out of denim and decorate with a marker and real tiny buttons. Write the invitation on a miniature bandanna stuck in the pocket.

Cut a mirror shape out of cardboard. In the center put a round piece of reflective Mylar (or use a real mirror from the dime store). Write the invitation on it using a china marker.

Make a cone out of paper and top it with a balloon that has the party information on it.

Roll a scroll between two candy canes.

Write the invitation on cardboard and cut it out so that the child can put it together like a puzzle. Blank puzzles can be bought at any school or party supply store.

Make a cassette recording of a story you can make up about the party. For example: "Hi, Valerie Jane, this is Tippy the Turtle. All of the turtles who live in the lagoon in the park are so excited because we know a secret! Next Saturday, a very special little boy named Joey who comes to visit us is going to bring all of his friends to have a picnic in the park to meet us. They're going to have fried chicken and blueberry muffins. Joey said that if we were all very good he'd give us some bites. He wants you to come to the picnic too. Get your mom to bring you to the second picnic shelter near the lagoon at 11:30 A.M. Joey's mom will bring you home at 1 P.M." (Obviously, this can be made more sophisticated for older kids.)

Attach a note to a panty hose egg with a tiny stuffed animal inside.

Attach the invitation to a kite, paper airplane, or paper doll.

Attach the invitation to a small bowl with a tiny turtle, some tadpoles, or goldfish.

Send a snapshot of your child holding up a sign saying: "Come to a party at my house—Saturday at 3:00 P.M. Bring a swimsuit."

Decorate the cardboard tubes that come from paper towels, tin foil, bathroom tissue, wrapping paper. They can be used to hold a scroll.

Attach the invitation to a soldier or space man made from a clothespin.

Write the invitation directly on an origami paper figure.

*Words to the wise:* Be sure to let parents know whether or not they are wanted or needed to stay. ("Just drop Elvis off and we'll deliver him at about 5 at your house" or "Please come with Pauline.") Don't send invitations to school unless you are inviting the whole class.

One of the worst mistakes is to have entertainment that lasts too long—a magician who loses his audience halfway through his act, a fire engine ride that lasts so long that the children go to sleep, or a pony ride that children have to wait to go on. Have plenty of things to do so that none of the children are waiting to have fun.

Remember that many youngsters are at their best in the morning or after nap time. Also be considerate of meal times unless you plan to serve lunch or dinner to the little tykes. The ideal party time seems to be about three-thirty to five on Saturday or Sunday afternoon. Some parents schedule a party on Saturday and list Sunday as the rain date.

The only way to be certain that your house can withstand the onslaught of a horde of little darlings is to pretend to be one yourself. Crawl around on all fours and survey the scene from that level. Just because your little Clementine has never tried to drink the furniture polish doesn't mean that Dwayne Detterling Northrope IV won't make a beeline for it the second your back is turned. Kids seem to be attracted to keys—could they possibly lock themselves in the bathroom or steal the key to your eighteenth-century Dutch secretary? Are there any tables, beds, or chairs with sharp corners? Are there any hanging tablecloths that a child could pull off? What about unprotected electric sockets and trailing cords? Are there any cleaning products, medicines, or makeup within their reach?

Balloons and paper streamers are a great deal more appealing to children than your hand-painted silk wallpaper, so use them to cover anything and everything that might get damaged. Painter's drop cloths can be used to cover the floors. Just in case, keep a good supply of sponges and paper towels close by to mop up spills and packaged wet cloths for sticky fingers and dirty mouths.

The ideal table for children of this age can be made with an old door placed on four cinder blocks. The children can sit on the floor or the ground around it.

Party theme paper plates, napkins, and cups are cute but expensive, and young children don't seem to notice them. In the long run, if you plan to entertain for your children more than once, it will to be less expensive to invest in brightly colored plastic plates that can be used over and over again.

An alternative is to put each child's food in a lunch box or bag, which your child can decorate with stickers prior to the party. Tuck a prize inside and tie with a ribbon. Always use huge, brightly colored napkins and drinking cups that aren't hard to hold or easy to knock over. Drinks packaged in individual boxes or foil bags are a sensible choice.

It's a good idea to have a few party helpers, either teenagers or favorite adults, who come in costume. These "play pals" can be responsible for keeping games moving along—so that you don't have to take the role of boss. For children up to four years, it is good to have one responsible "big" person for every three children. That way if a child has to go to the bathroom, be cleaned up after a

*Designer Candy Davey has created a decoration filled with Christmas toys to welcome young guests to a family caroling brunch the week before Christmas. After the brunch all the guests will reassemble at a nursing home to entertain and serve a Christmas tea party.* HIMMEL

## DECORATIONS AND CENTERPIECES

Decorate the front door so that it says "Here's the Party!" Use a cluster of balloons, a hat, a poster, some streamers, a picture of a birthday cake. (Remember that helium-filled balloons, unless filled with an expensive substance called Hi-Float, will last only three to four hours, so they can't be inflated too far ahead of time.)

Create a walkway of balloons by tying them to garden stakes. At the end of the pathway have a giant bouquet of balloons on which you have written the name of each guest.

Create banners out of felt or let your child make a banner on a computer.

Cover the table with butcher's paper. At each place draw a circle with a guest's name printed over it. Provide lots of water-soluble

markers and crayons and let the children draw their own place mats. For older children, draw out a city with streets, airport, lakes, and parks, which they can color. Have baskets of miniature trees, planes, boats, and cars.

Use toys as centerpieces. Serve food out of the back of a toy dump truck; pile the table with Legos that can be played with; construct a train track using wooden or plastic trains.

Put hats on a few wig stands—cowboy, pirate, sailor, police—to use as a centerpiece.

Decorate a potted plant with pieces of candy and tiny toys and use as a centerpiece.

Hang kites in trees, on the front door, and from the ceiling. Some can be free-floating if attached to clumps of helium balloons. Give all away as favors at the end of the party.

*Cookie baking, both for eating and decorating (facing page), is a ritual that the entire family can enjoy. Try making salt and flour dough ornaments that can be painted with acrylic paint, tied with ribbon, and used year round as decorations. This is an ideal way for young and old alike to put their imaginations to work. Courtesy* Health *magazine.* HAGIWARA

*Hunter Heumann (top, left) waits patiently for his teddy bear birthday party to begin. His mother, Annie, has draped a portion of the garage with fabric. Each child will get a bear balloon with his or her bear's name on it and a painted toy box filled with popcorn. Balloons from Ballunacy; children's furniture, moon, star, and clouds by Bev Church; painted gum ball machine, toy box, and pennant from Happi Names.* HIMMEL

*A children's table (bottom, left), whether set up for their own party or for the kids at a family party, should be filled with things to see and play with. White butcher's paper has been clipped to a tabletop and marked off in a tac-tac-toe pattern with red shoelaces. Colorful paper plates and cups are mixed and matched with plastic cutlery and masses of toys. All toys from Little Rickie.* HIMMEL

Be prepared for rain if you don't want to move an outside party inside. Ryan Littlewood and his friends donned plastic garbage bags and plasticized hats and kept right on playing in the rain. CUTRONE

Play pal Christine Martzell paints Adam's face at his buddy Patrick's birthday party. LECORGNE

bath in punch, or is trying to escape into the neighbor's garden, there is someone to handle the situation without leaving the others unattended.

The parents of the other children, however, seldom make good party helpers. It is best to discourage a lot of them from staying for the party because they inhibit the activity of their children and they expect to be entertained. Inevitably, you'll be walking into the party with a lighted birthday cake and some dad will say, "Isabelle, when you have a minute, could you get me a beer?" Or "I don't think my little Mimi is having much fun. Do you think she could help Johnny open his presents?" If you know that all of the parents will stay, invited or not, plan the activities so that the children keep the adults too busy to cause any trouble.

Parties should be joyful, but when any group of small children gets together, there will be the inevitable confrontations over toys, the piece of birthday cake with the most icing, or whatever. By ignoring the fighting, you merely encourage more problems. Be cheerful and firm, but let them know that if it continues you will take the object or food away from both of them. Children like to know what their limits are. Another way to keep the peace is to be sure that all of the children win a prize—be it for the most freckles, the cleanest plate, the curliest hair. Let the favor be a special reward just for him or her, not a trophy for a competition. Prizes for games, such as pin the tail on the donkey or a wheelbarrow race, can cause hard feelings because there can be only one winner. Don't let any activity become too competitive.

The Crooked House at Storyland (left), in City Park in New Orleans, is a favorite spot for Foster Cronin, Tristan Bultman, Gwyther Bultman, their babysitter/pal Ford Church. Easter baskets by Annie Heumann of Rohm's line the path to the "bunny Hutch." Bunny pajamas by Suzo. HIMMEL

Party designers Gayle Cohen and Michael Aprato of Opus II (right) have a bewitching assortment of food and hot spiced punch, large character decorations, and plenty of rock 'n' roll to keep children happy indoors. FROGER

The same old activities won't seem like the same old activities if party helpers dress as the honoree's favorite characters (left). Cinderella helps Jackie and Toni White blow out their candles while Rachael Allen and Fran Taormina wait patiently for cake and ice cream. LECORGNE

Invite a few friends in on Halloween (right) to have pumpkin bread and hot cocoa after a night of trick or treating. Designer Gail L. McAllister of Panache in High Point, North Carolina, has used J. Yang wallpaper and matching fabric from Carefree Wallcoverings. WHICKER

241

A bit of sadness can occur when the party is over and your child feels let down. It sometimes works well if he or she can have one special friend stay on after the party to "help."

### Presents

Presents can be a problem at the birthday parties of young children. The gift-wrapped packages are ripped open and no one knows who gave what. Often pieces of a toy are lost or broken before the party is even over. There are several solutions to this problem. Some parents give a party together for two or three children. Each of the children has a family party with presents on his or her actual birthday. The big party then takes place up to a month after the real birthdays. Instead of gifts, the guests are asked to bring a few coins to put in a basket and the money is used to adopt an animal at the zoo in the name of the honorees. This is fun for the kids because they get to go to the zoo to deliver the money and choose their animal. (Many zoos around the country have a party once a year for all of the kids who adopt animals.) Another thing that guests can be asked to bring is a selection of Lego pieces in the age-appropriate size. All of the pieces are put in a basket and divided among the honorees after the guests have departed.

If presents are brought to a party, try to put them aside so that you and your child can open them after the party, or ask the guests to tell you what they brought as they arrive. It is a good idea to begin instilling in your children early that they should thank people who give them gifts. It also

helps them to remember who gave them what. They may draw a picture to enclose in the note, cut a picture out of a magazine, or send a snapshot of the guest at the party. For friends in town, they can make their thank-yous by telephone.

### Themes

The wonderful thing about children is that their interests keep changing. One week they are passionate about Kermit the Frog, the next it is He-Man, and the following year they may have forgotten both. Try to coordinate the theme of the party with your child's current interest—a cartoon character, a certain story, a movie, or a song.

*Prima Donna's Delight:* Have a party for your little ballerina at the ballet school or in the garage.

*Judy Paine and her family spend hours designing colorful gift-wrapped boxes. They use fabrics of all types, from moiré to tulle, and various yarns and dozens of accessories. Julie Johnson and Henry and Darcy Lowen Pulitzer enjoy this series, whose designs were inspired by the art in a favorite children's book. HIMMEL*

*Keep youngsters constantly entertained with activities that last no more than five minutes apiece. Grover and his human companion, Christiane Martzell, read a story while Spiderman (Margaret LeCorgne) listens. Party produced by Confetti Corner of New Orleans. CUTRONE*

*With the right planning, even a small apartment can be converted into a magical environment for a child (below). One day each year create a space where your child and a few friends can enjoy such forbidden treats as fingerpaint and glitter. Clear everything out of a room and cover the floor with layers of plastic, newspaper, and drop cloths. On the walls pin up old sheets or drop cloths on which the kids can paint directly. Just be certain to stress that "Make a Mess Day" is a treat that comes but once a year.* STONE

*Anita Walker created an impromptu party for her children and their friends as an after-school treat on the fifth rainy day in a row (facing page). She invited a friend for each of her three children and set out the makings for cookies, cocoa, and sandwiches in the kitchen. The children spent the afternoon feeding and entertaining the bears, while Anita took it easy.* HIMMEL

All of her friends can be invited to wear their favorite dancing outfits. Have a "teacher" do a short ballet or disco demonstration, then let the kids join in. Videotape the little performers and let everyone watch the replay.

*Make a Mess:* Have vats of homemade finger paint, butcher's paper, clay, shaving cream and food coloring, rolling pins and cookie cutters, troughs of soap bubbles and strawberry cartons to pull through the solution, golf tees to hammer into plastic foam, and a few bales of hay to jump on. Ask the children to wear swimsuits and bring a towel. Before they go home, let them dance through the sprinkler. Give water guns as favors.

*Mothers and Babies:* Invite each little girl to dress up like a mommy and bring her baby. Have a teenage girl dress up like a fairy godmother to tell each baby's fortune or tell short stories. Save old cartons, boxes, and jars and set up a grocery store for the "mommies." Use play money, and give each a basket to hold her "purchases." Have a clothes shop full of dime-store earrings, women's dresses, and shoes in which to play "dress up" and let the teenage helper do makeup on each child. Take Polaroid pictures of each mommy with her baby. Put them in frames as favors.

*Rubber Ducky, You're the One:* Rent or borrow four or five plastic wading pools and fill them with several inches of water, some bubble bath, and rubber toys and balls. Have a plastic laundry hamper filled with water balloons for games. Let the children paint their bodies with finger paint or body paint. Give each child a beach ball, plastic pail, or rubber ducky as a favor.

*Toddler Road Rally:* Round up a riding toy for each child and take the group to a safe expanse of roadway (perhaps a parking lot unused on weekends). You can design a special driving course for them with helium balloons attached to cardboard boxes. A hill is even more popular and far easier.

*Art Gallery:* Have an art show for your child and a few friends. Attach the art with magnets to appliances, attach sheets from the ceiling and pin the art to them, or just string a piece of ribbon across a room and use clothespins to hold the art. At the end of the party, parents can be invited to view the show. During the party provide the children with markers, stickers, blunt scissors, old magazines, colored construction paper, stencils, crayons, and paste. The invitation can be a mock poster that says:

(*Your child's name*) Gallery
cordially invites you to a preview showing
Saturday, November 5
16 Van Gogh Lane
RSVP: 555-8969

When the parents arrive, serve cake squares and ginger ale in plastic wineglasses. Give each child a blue ribbon on his or her work.

*Impromptu Rainy Day Fun:* Invite several children over on a miserable day. Tell them to come as their favorite cartoon character and to bring their favorite stuffed animal, a pillow, and a blanket. Spread them out on the floor and let them watch rented movies of cartoons or just the regular fare of morning or afternoon cartoons. Provide

coloring books and crayons so they can color their favorite cartoons.

*Teddy Bears' Picnic:* Invite each child's teddy bear to a party by written invitation and ask him to bring his favorite human companion. When the children arrive, have high chairs for each bear as well as place cards and mats with each bear's name. Provide scraps of fabric and ribbon for decorating the bears. Take lots of photographs.

*The Whole World Loves a Clown:* Plan the party with your child's help, but as a surprise to the child, ask all of the guests to arrive dressed like clowns—even you and the adult helpers can don clown attire. Fill the party spaces with balloons and hire jugglers and magicians to provide short audience-participation entertainment.

*Noah's Ark/Carpentry:* Send each child a small hammer with an animal shape attached as an invitation (these can be mailed in an 8-by-10-inch envelope). Each child is asked to bring the hammer and an adult helper. Have stacks of scrap lumber, nails, markers, and animal stencils.

*Letter to Santa:* Invite a few children over at any time of the year to start their letters to Santa. Provide large sheets of paper, lots of toy catalogs, some paste, and blunt scissors. Let the children cut out the things they want and paste them on the letter.

*Sidewalk Parade:* Have all the kids decorate their tricycles, wagons, and Big Wheels and dress themselves in any costume. Let them make drums out of oatmeal and salt boxes, and shakers out of soft drink cans (place a few dried beans inside and tape over the hole). The children send invitations

*No matter what food is served at a party, children can find a way to make a mess with it—after all, that is part of the enjoyment. Serve gooey food last so it will be worn home and not smeared all over your house.* STONE

to all the neighbors, announcing the parade time. They throw flower petals and birdseed at their audience. This event can even be used by children as a way to raise money for a special donation to a library, school, or park.

*Menus*

Children in groups tend not to eat very much. They seem to wear more food home than they actually put in their stomachs. Keep in mind which foods and drinks will cause the least trouble after being ground into the floor or hidden behind a potted palm for a few months. Orange juice, grape juice, and cola drinks all stain; apple juice and lemon sodas don't.

One problem you certainly want to prevent is a child choking. To lessen the possibility, do not serve nuts, raisins, hard candy, or popcorn, which can get stuck in a child's throat. Also avoid candy on a stick. If a child should fall on the candy, it could be deadly.

Bite-sized things seem to make the biggest hit—mini pizzas, pizza rolls, fried chicken wings or drumsticks, chicken nuggets, potato puffs and french fries, tiny hamburgers made on biscuits, squares of cheese and pineapple chunks, fish sticks, fried cheese bits, fruit roll-ups.

Little ones do adore Jell-O and you'll win the hearts of all the kids if you whip up some layered Jell-O concoction in a cute mold. If you want to really dazzle them, add tiny marshmallows and some cherries.

Hors d'oeuvres can be made from those sweet, colored breakfast cereals like Count Chocula, Lucky Charms, Strawberry Shortcake. Just empty them into clear plastic bowls and let the little tykes grab a handful.

Make peanut butter and jelly rolls by removing crusts from bread and rolling the slices out so they are thin and mashed. Spread a small amount of peanut butter and jelly on each and roll up. Little fingers can't get to the peanut butter, and the rolls can be eaten in three bites.

Let the guests make magic pudding. Give each child a baby food jar filled with milk and add three tablespoons of instant pudding. Put the lids on tightly and let the children shake, shake, shake to music. Voilà—pudding!

Iced cake for toddlers can be a great mess. Make thin, uniced sheet cakes that can be decorated with toy cowboys, space men, or dolls or can be cut into simple shapes like boats, letters, or blocks. The colored icings that come in tubes can be used to do simple decorations.

An alternative is to make cupcakes and arrange them to spell out the age or name of the child. Put a candle in each one, and you have a very splashy presentation. Make enough so that each child can take a cupcake and candle home. Small amounts of cake batter can also be baked in flat-bottomed ice cream cones. Once baked, these cakes can be decorated with colored sugar.

Make pudding parfaits by layering butterscotch and vanilla pudding in clear plastic cups. Top with whipped cream or artificial topping, a cherry, and a candle.

Be sure to feed the kids at the end of the party so the "sugar rush" will hit at home!

*P*lan parties in locations that kids love. Groups of children can get together and build a "club house" to serve as the scene of parties and activities for years to come. One group of fathers in Washington state got together in 1956 and surprised their children with a "Swiss Family Robinson" tree house. More than thirty years later the tree house is still being used by appreciative grandchildren. STONE

## Parties for the Seven-to-Twelve Set

By the time they are seven, children have very definite ideas about what kind of party they want. Don't be disappointed if they want to have a party at the same pizza parlor where all of their friends have theirs. Peer pressure is heavy at this age. They are old enough to get really involved with the party and can make it come alive with their imaginative ideas.

### Themes

*Long John Silver Day:* Rent a boat if one is available. If not, create one. Ask all of the children to dress as pirates. Provide each one with an eye patch, a cardboard sword, and a bandanna to wrap around their necks. Divide the children into teams with an older child as leader and organize a treasure hunt to find the dessert. Fill a treasure box with bags of chocolate coins to be given out as favors.

*Old-Fashioned Ice Cream Social:* Invite the children to come in old clothes and bring big appetites. Have several ice cream freezers on hand making ice cream when the children arrive. While waiting for the ice cream to get ready, give each child a sheet of rolled-out cookie dough, an assortment of cookie cutters, and some colored sprinkles. When everything is made, you can have a great feast. Set out all sorts of ice cream toppings so the children can make their own sundaes. Remember to keep the portions small.

*Horror Film Festival:* Either take the children to see a double feature at a theater or rent two movies to show at home. Turn out all the lights

Kids love slumber parties more than almost any other kind of party. The older they are, the easier it is to manage the parties. At the six-to-eight level, you can expect at least one child to get scared and want to go home and others to try keeping everyone awake all night. As hosts of the party, the adults must be accessible to the young guests at all hours of the day and night. If there are siblings, they will be much happier out of the house or staying away from the party.

Don't let the party begin too early. From noon one day until noon the next is much too long. Let the party begin at five or six in the evening. Have an hour of well-structured games and physical activities, then dinner, which can be pizza, hamburgers, or hot dogs. After the meal, take the children to a movie or sports event, which requires them to sit down and focus their attention.

The minute you get home, get the kids to bed. Let everyone sleep in one room—mattresses or sleeping bags on the floor are fine—otherwise they will argue about who sleeps where. Put a nightlight in the room, preferably adjacent to the bathroom, a cup of water for each child, and an individual bedcover that will satisfy both the warm- and cold-natured. To get them to sleep, read them a story or play a taped story they will want to listen to. If there is one troublemaker, remove him or her from the group until the others are fast asleep.

In the morning have an activity. The kids usually will be up between six and seven, but no parent wants to fetch their children that early. Let them make waffles or pancakes and then watch cartoons or play games.

The nine-to-eleven age group, while easier to handle, does have a few problems. Let the kids know what activities have been planned before they come. This builds anticipation and weeds out those who don't like the plans. Most boys are sports minded and will be happy to skateboard, go to a wrestling match, or play football or baseball. Girls can be into sports too, but cruising the mall, shopping, and cooking are also popular.

The party can begin in the early afternoon. The major activity should occur before dinnertime and can be followed by a snack. You can let the kids make cookies, cakes, or brownies to eat later for dessert. Before dinner they can watch a movie or play pinball, Ping-Pong or other games.

After dinner have another major activity. This can be miniature golf, a movie, bowling, skating. When they get home, serve the dessert they made earlier in the afternoon. After a half-hour transition period, they must go to their room for "quiet" time. This is when they can tell ghost stories.

Party hazards for this age group include lost orthodontic appliances and glasses, marathon phone calls, and arguments or fights. The children need to be monitored, but from a distance.

*Slumber parties are as much a part of growing up as are skinned knees, loose teeth, and that longed-for first date. Sleeping bags, pillow fights, popcorn, and ghost stories are essential components. Plan to have a happy but sleepy child the next day, and take lots of pictures of the party in action.* STONE

*Hire some older dancers to come perform for the party, and encourage the younger guests to join in. Let them choose their favorite songs, and don't be disappointed if they all want to hear the same ones over and over again—it's their party!* PSIHOYOS

and spread blankets on the floor. Between the movies serve the food, Dracula punch, and a red velvet cake.

*Cheerleader Party:* Ask a high school cheerleader to come and teach cheers to the kids. Give out pom-poms as favors. Use banners, bull horns, and pennants from the favorite team.

*Skateboard Extravaganza:* Take the kids and their skateboards to a vacant lot with two or three "boom boxes" tuned to the same channel. Have races, trick competitions, and obstacle courses and award prizes. As favors, give stickers for decorating their skateboards.

*String Party:* String along the guests by having a ball of different colored yarn for every person invited. Tie a present at one end and the guest's name on the other. Wrap the ball up and over the furniture in the room until you've used up all the balls of yarn and the room looks like a spiderweb of color. It takes at least half an hour to unwind the yarn and makes for a jolly mess.

*Scavenger Camp-out:* Each guest must pack to go on a campout in a state park. Besides their regular gear, they'll need to bring the following in order to "buy" dinner: half a Ping-Pong ball, 3 inches of electrical tape on a ruler, a Christmas

card with a reindeer on it, a baby's bootie, a year-book from the 1960s, and a coffee mug. Organize the guests into two teams to put on skits for each other. They must build the plots around their scavenged items.

### Entertainment

This is a wonderful age group for miniature golf, bowling, skating, swimming, movies, hay rides, and slumber parties. They will already be into rock and roll, so loud music and disco lights can keep them happy. Cans of colored hair spray and theatrical makeup will produce lots of giggles, and girls can have fun decorating their own sweat-shirts with paints, rhinestones, and glitter.

This age group also enjoys going to sports events—ice hockey, basketball, tennis tourna-ments—and if you can pull strings so they can meet the sports stars, they will be in heaven.

### Menus

Children at this age are not adventurous eaters. They will like burgers and pizzas and oc-casionally you can pass off something like spa-ghetti, lasagna, chili, or Tex-Mex food. A good activity is to have some of your child's pals over to cook the day before the party. They can make dips, cakes, even homemade ice cream. Have plenty of sodas and munchies on hand. The idea is to make the foods they eat regularly look more appealing, not to have particularly exciting food.

Make a giant sugar cookie on a round pizza pan. Let the children decorate it with candy, marshmallows, and colored sprinkles.

P*laying dress-up with real makeup and experimenting with current hair-styles can be a thrill for pre-teenage girls. Adults or older girls who play beautician are essential to the success of the party.* STONE

250

## Teenage Parties

Teenagers love to hang around, talk, play records, eat popcorn, go to movies, go to sports events, and hang out some more. What differentiates hanging out from parties is planning. The best parties are planned before another event. Have the kids over from five to seven o'clock for swimming and a barbecue before a school game or on Sunday for brunch before they watch the Super Bowl. The guest list has a lot to do with the success of a party. Try to encourage your child to have one or two kids who like to be the "life of the party," the class clowns who make everyone laugh.

### Themes

One of the special events favored by girls is the "Sweet Sixteen" party. Sometimes four or five girls have one together at a club or in a hotel ballroom. Since this is usually the first time a girl hosts her own dancing party, she will care very much whether or not it is successful. Everything must sparkle.

Choose a theme and design a great invitation that will make the kids want to come. You could have a "Fort Lauderdale Spring Break" or "Miami Vice" party so the boys can wear Hawaiian shirts or sport coats with T-shirts and the girls can wear flowered semiformal attire. Create an exciting entranceway with masses of palms pushed together, archways of lights, paper flowers, lots of color and pizzazz. Your daughter and her friends can even make the invitations and the decorations themselves. Flowers are not important, but lots of balloons add to the party spirit, as do banners and enormous blowups of pictures of movie stars or rock idols.

A great way to get teenagers to interact is to have them eat at tables with place cards. Try to anchor each table with a couple who goes out frequently, then put together their male and female friends. Plan food that the group likes, not fancified chicken and flaming Kahlua crepes. Some parents have found that teenagers don't eat the food, so they plan strictly a dance party, with the honorees leading the first dance. A deejay playing recorded music or acting as master of ceremonies with a band will keep the party rolling. If the kids aren't dancing, get them started with a dance contest. For this age group a party from seven to ten o'clock is fine.

Dinner parties and progressive dinners are a nice change of pace for teenagers. Organize teams that are responsible for different courses of a meal. The teammates' names can be drawn out of a hat. The teams can then draw out of a hat the names of the dishes they have to cook. A Minnesota host-

## ENTERTAINING A SICK CHILD

No matter how old, a child who is sick on a birthday or special event has a lonely time. One mother whose child had to spend several months in the hospital invited two of her child's friends to visit every two days. She had pizza and malts sent up to the room. After the parties that the child missed, the kids brought decorations or favors to their sick friend, as well as photographs or videotapes.

Throughout the child's illness, his classmates made large posters to stick on the walls of his room. Some were blowups of friends; others were original artwork. One friend had a party and the kids made a dozen silk-screened pillowcases for the hospital bed. Another friend brought a "garden" of tiny potted plants that her friend could watch grow. Other friends organized an album of Polaroid photographs and notes from their classmates. The mother's friends kept the room stocked with huge silver balloons.

If the young child is sick at home, let him have an alarm clock set to go off at lunchtime, when a brother or sister comes home from school. This will make the time seem to go faster. Make "happy" bags filled with individually wrapped gifts. An old beach backrest will make the bed more comfortable, as will a large bedside table, such as a card table.

ess tells of the time her daughter and two football tackles had to make an authentic English plum pudding with hard sauce. They had to go to the library to do some research, then shop for the ingredients. The plum pudding took two weeks to make, but the group ended up fast friends.

Elizabeth Oudt likes to organize a convertible parade party. Friends are invited to meet in the park at dusk to decorate convertibles. Then they parade from one teenage hangout to another.

A group of kids in Philadelphia like to have a "Blind Taste Test" party. The hosts blindfold all the guests and let them taste things such as the white of a hard-boiled egg, a beet, a little bit of an artichoke heart, or a single baked bean. The winner is the one who correctly identifies the most items.

Sports are a lot of fun. Organize teams for broom hockey and baseball. Those not inclined to play can be cheerleaders or make a video of the event. This can be a fun alternative to a conventional birthday party. For refreshments, rent a crushed ice machine and let the kids make their own snowballs.

Another activity that can keep the teenagers busy for days is a film festival. They organize into groups to make their own video movies. Then they have an "Academy Awards Banquet" to screen the films and give out awards. John Mark Church has a "Virgin Daiquiri Bumper Pool and Movie" party. The kids set up a bar and make nonalcoholic drinks from fresh fruit and ice, decorated with fruit and paper umbrellas. They barbecue, watch a horror film, and play bumper pool.

*Make nonalcoholic drinks so appealing that teenagers give up all thoughts of imitating adult drinking habits. Drinking Coke floats on the beach after surfing or volleyball is much more fun than sitting in dark, smoke-filled rooms. SCHINZ*

*Annie Sarpy and John Mark Church decorate his prized MG for a car parade and a progressive dinner party before the big game. The theme of their car is "Spring to Life." HIMMEL*

Bonnie Reese, a perky sixteen-year-old from Austin, Texas, says her favorite party is a surprise breakfast. It must be organized by a few friends and all of the mothers in order to ensure its success. At 6:30 A.M. the first guest is surprised by the hostesses, who wake them up and make them come as they are dressed to the waiting cars. By 7:30 A.M. all the guests have been awakened, surprised, and taken to a large downtown hotel for a breakfast party in their sleeping attire. She recommends doing this the day of a big game, a dance, a graduation, or someone's birthday.

### Pitfalls of the Age Group

Parties and social functions are a big part of the teenage years. Many parents become nervous wrecks the minute their child reaches thirteen—will he get involved with drugs, will she drink, will he be popular, will she be too popular? While kids hate supervision, they do respond well to a little bit of help. Remember all the insecurities associated with being a teenager.

When you chaperone, you should be available, keep the food replenished, and keep an eye on things from a distance. Never walk around with a drink in your hand; this sets a bad example for the party. Act nonchalantly and inconspicuously, but be handy. If the party is large, try to have a favorite teacher to help chaperone. Stand at the front door to greet the kids. Once they've met you, they are less inclined to misbehave.

Some kids cruise through their teenage years effortlessly. They do everything well; they are attractive and have lots of nice friends. Then there

are the late bloomers, those kids who are too shy, too tall, too fat, too thin, too bookish, too immature to be caught up in the world of dating, going steady, and the glow of constant recognition. Those kids can have fun and should be told that they are special too. The night of the big dance to which your son or daughter isn't invited, let them have their pals over. Take them to a sports event, a movie, or out to dinner—do what they want to do. Let your daughter, who might not have a date, invite her friends over before a party. Hire someone or ask a friend to come over and do their hair and makeup. The girls can go to the party together and then come home and have a stay-up-and-talk-all-night slumber party. Never let your child stay home alone and sulk.

Unfortunately, drugs and alcohol are easily available in most parts of the country, and kids still think it is all right to get behind the wheel of a car when they are in no condition to drive. Experts estimate that 3.3 million American youths between the ages of fourteen and seventeen are alcoholics or problem drinkers; 25 percent of our nation's alcoholics are seventeen or younger. Teenagers generally don't drink alone, but will when they get together in groups. Doing something forbidden is a thrill.

Some parents swear by a contract that is signed by them and their teenagers. Designed by SADD (Students Against Drunk Driving), it is an agreement stating that if a youngster is too drunk

*While many kids adore sports, they seem to have trouble organizing events. Divide the children into teams for a bicycle scavenger hunt, which can be an all-day activity. Ask different parents to provide the food for lunch, tea, and supper.* STONE

to drive, a parent will come and pick him or her up, no questions asked. Other parents don't even want to discuss drinking and drugs—the subjects are strictly forbidden. Then there are parents who know drinking will go on and want to control it. They allow their teenagers to have 3.2 percent beer, wine spritzers, mimosas, or other drinks containing little alcohol. One person in the crowd is the designated driver, and he or she agrees not to drink at all that night. These parents reason that they would rather have the crowd hanging around their houses and drinking moderately than racing around the streets in cars. When there are out-of-town games, big concerts, or prom nights, either one parent drives a group of kids or they get together and hire a car and driver.

Gate-crashers are another problem in the teen years. A party can become an open invitation —Melissa, who is invited, asks Eldridge, who isn't, to be her date. Eldridge, who doesn't want to be her date, comes anyway and brings his date, Cissy, her twin, Prissy, and the sister's date, Malcolm. To be on the safe side, Melissa also invites Tom, Dick, and Harry just to be certain she has someone to dance with. According to teenage rules, these extra party goers are not gate-crashers; they might give the party some life. Gate-crashers are people whom no one has invited to the party. If they behave, they may stay; if not, ask them to leave. If they don't, you'll have to call the police and that will be the end of the party.

# Chapter 9
## BUSINESS ENTERTAINING

*S*ooner or later it happens to every new wife. Your darling husband invites the boss, a client, or a colleague home for dinner. It doesn't matter that you've just moved into a new apartment or have to be away on business the day of the event. You know how important it is to make a good impression and that you'll be largely responsible for making it. It's enough to give anyone the hives. ♣ For many, this is the first introduction to business entertaining—entertaining with a purpose

beyond just getting together with friends for a good time or hosting the family gathering. Whether you are entertaining your daughter's prospective headmistress or your husband's client, if guests are in your home for any reason other than your altruistic desire to show them a good time, then you are entertaining in order to achieve something —whether it's a favorable impression on the boss or funding for the community opera. Determine what your goal is, the image you wish to portray, and structure the event accordingly. Experts advise that no matter what, keep the evening short and sweet. Cater to your guest, but never lose sight of who you are. ◈ Business entertaining can be done during the working day or during leisure hours. "Let's review the figures over lunch" has the advantage of not invading leisure time. Many "go-getters" use the power breakfast to get a jump on the day. Others agree with Reinaldo Herrera, who says, "Power breakfasts are for exceedingly second-rate tycoons. The

*The proper invitation extols success, style, and savvy. Those in the know who entertain during the business day often include an engraved card with the telephone number of the place where they will be having lunch, which their busy guests can leave with their secretaries. Flowers by Paul Bott of Twigs; invitations by Crane.* HIMMEL

only civilized place for breakfast is alone in your home, and preferably in your bed."

"Let's review the figures over dinner" means entertaining during leisure time. A restaurant is still an appropriate neutral spot for the working dinner, but if you invite a business guest into your home, you have made the event a personal extension of yourself.

## The Boss or Superior

Many managers do not expect or even like to socialize with subordinates. If all the other attorneys in the law firm have had the senior partners over, however, you are probably expected to as well.

Keep in mind that the evening will go much better if you are at ease. You don't need to blow the budget on a new dress, a butler, or matching silver. The boss will not care whether or not you serve caviar, and you certainly don't want to give the impression that you are too good for the job. Be yourself. Let the end result of the evening be the boss's impression that you are very nice. After all, you don't want to become best friends or move into his or her social set. You want to enhance your relationship at the office.

Unless there is marvelous chemistry between the boss and his spouse and you and yours, it is a good idea to have one or two other couples to bridge the gap. Don't, however, have more than four or five extra guests. If you invite others from your office, be certain they won't steal the show. If you invite a dignitary or prospective client who could benefit the boss, be sure you don't imply "See what important people I know? I really don't

need your crummy job!" but rather "I thought it might be nice for Lee Iacocca to get to meet you and your spouse." It's helpful to have guests with interests in common with the boss or his wife. If you don't know what her interests are, look for clues—maybe his office is filled with her paintings or pottery or pictures of her on the golf course.

Plan the menu around the boss. Try to find out what type of food he orders at lunch. Is he a gourmet, a weight watcher, or a meat-and-potatoes type? If need be, have a try-out dinner for friends a few nights before. Be certain to create a menu easily made in advance so that your final preparations are minimal. In a pinch, ask your family, your husband's family, a caterer, anyone, to prepare something you will feel comfortable serving.

Entertainment is unnecessary, and so is any unnecessary distraction. If there are young or unruly kids in your home, farm them out to a friend's house for the night or at the least have a sitter for them. Whatever you do, don't produce your little Celeste playing the oboe, the slides of your backpacking honeymoon in the Ozarks, or your collection of unexploded Civil War cartridges. Let the boss be in the spotlight and encourage him to talk about his interests and experiences. The same holds true of the boss's spouse. Let her "entertain" you with the details of her recent campaign for city council or her ongoing battle against mealybugs. No matter what, you and your guests should act interested.

If you are very at ease and know the boss well, you can really put your imagination to good

*An important client or associate may be impressed by your ability to pull off a multicourse dinner with precision. This conference table has been transformed into gracious dining service with the addition of a scalloped tablecloth from Anichini. The menu should not be overly heavy or ambitious, and the pace should never lag. Busy guests do not want to feel trapped at the table. Alhambra pattern china from Bernadaud; silver from James Robinson; stemware from Baccarat; centerpiece by Paul Bott of Twigs. HIMMEL*

*When architect Grover Mouton entertains European clients in his native Louisiana, he makes an effort to show them picturesque, untouched corners of the Cajun country. His wife, Bitsie, produces an elaborate picnic to enjoy along the route. FREEMAN*

use. The wives of two rising executives in an advertising firm decided to throw a surprise "This Is Your Life" party for their husbands' boss—who was big on the "corporation as family" philosophy. They enlisted the boss's wife and his secretary in the project, and the evening was a great success. Maybe it was coincidence, but within a year both of their husbands were promoted.

### The Client

The ultimate goal here is to leave the client feeling inclined to repay your kindness by furthering your business relationship. To achieve this, plan the evening around the specific client, catering to his or her interests.

The evening should be fun but not raucous. Serve a Japanese meal on the floor or take the guest somewhere out of the ordinary—your boat or your club—or have people over who are interesting to meet, be it Willard Scott's dentist or Miss America's mother's hairdresser. In Cleveland one banker always takes clients to his favorite elegant eatery. After the meal a flaming baked Alaska is presented to the guest with the name of the client's company spelled in meringue on the side.

You may find a style so workable and successful that people will want to become your clients so they can share in it. After thirty years of entertaining collectors, artist Fritz Bultman and his wife, Jeanne, concluded that weekend lunches worked best for them. They invite four to six people, all professionals who are busy during the week. Guests at one luncheon included a Harvard psychiatrist and his social scientist wife, both of

whom traveled constantly; a well-known writer from New York; an ex-model turned fashion editor; and a midwestern museum director.

"Our guests at these parties rarely know one another before the lunch," explains Jeanne, "and one can feel the lightning flashes among these highly competitive people. To harness and focus this energy, I get everyone to the table quickly and have it laden with simple, fresh, gorgeous food. Sparks are generated by a good meal. Strangers meet, hesitate, converse in banalities. Once they start eating, however, the tone of the conversation goes straight up the chart. Eating reduces inhibitions and people feel each other out. After the meal guests wander into the studio to see new work and they are in the mood to buy!"

W*hen Charles and Kent Davis, African art dealers, entertain special clients, Kent likes to use objects similar to ones collected by the client. In this case she has used three Bozo marionettes from Mali, and on the mantel are two royal weapons from the Baule tribe. HIMMEL*

S*upper in the store for clients (right) can be planned around good food and company, with guests sitting at the table for hours, immersed in conversation. Favorite objects are placed on the nineteenth-century fruitwood farm table—English ironstone plates, Japanese bronze candlesticks, and a George Febres alligator egg, from the collection of Marjorie and Walter Davis. All antique objects from Lucullus. HIMMEL*

*A greenhouse can be a welcome addition to an office. It offers a quiet meeting and eating space away from business-day interruptions. Designer T. Whitcomb Iglehart specified that fresh flowering plants be on hand year round to provide a springtime feel to this Connecticut space.* BUSSOLINI

*Give the client or associate from out of town a memorable glimpse of your city. On your list should be the most beautiful view, the best food, and guests that any out-of-towner would be thrilled to meet. Courtesy* Working Woman *magazine.* JEFFERY

## The Associate or Colleague

If you are entertaining an associate or colleague, your goal is simply to enjoy yourself—and maybe get some extra information—with friends from work. The food and entertainment would be the same as for any social gathering. A problem can arise with disinterested spouses forced to endure gatherings where the primary topic of conversation is coronary bypass operations or balance sheets. If the group is small, see that everyone meets everyone else early on and launch them into other topics of conversation if you can.

After years of tedious company-client dinners, the husbands and wives of a group of architects decided to take the curse off the evenings. Now they all get in the kitchen and prepare the dinner—the clients' spouses get involved too—or they organize a croquet or volleyball tournament, play Trivial Pursuit, or rent a great movie for the VCR. As a result, the business part of the evening is now shorter because it's hard to work when everyone else is having such fun.

## Associates from Out of Town

Business travelers love to return home and brag about the great time they had while away. If your home isn't particularly thrilling, ask a friend with an exceptional house, garden, or view to have you and your guests over for cocktails—a penthouse overlooking the city at sunset is certainly memorable. Go to a restaurant the guests have heard about and where you are known so you can ask the staff to pamper them. Make them feel they are on the inside track in your city.

Coffee served at the office need not be a dreadfully pedestrian affair characterized by coffee-stained paper napkins. In this stark room (left) with Robert Gordy lithograph, black Italian leather sofas, and glass coffee table, the addition of a few pieces of antique silver gives just the right touch of opulence, while one orchid blossom on each cup sets the tone of elegance tempered with gracious attention to detail.

The table was custom-made by New Orleans craftsman Jim Drury; the silver is American and English Victorian. HIMMEL

If meetings must be held at breakfast (facing page, top), make a splash with plenty of good caviar, champagne, and lots of coffee. Don't, however, expect to get much business done. HIMMEL

A seventeenth-century painting by Jacob Huysman dominates the boardroom of the Windsor Court Hotel (facing page, bottom). The formal style of the room lends dignity to the most mundane meeting. HIMMEL

### The Potential Investor or Contributor

A social event geared toward an investor or contributor is not a fund-raiser, even though you are "fattening him up for the kill." When Sara Dunbar entertains for her ballet company, "the goal of the evening is to leave the guest glowing from the attention he or she has received and convinced of the worthiness of your company or cause." If you go all out, be sure you don't intimidate your guest or give the illusion that you're doing so well that you don't really need support. Cater to your audience. You want the investor to feel comfortable, flattered, and at ease.

Other guests should be stimulating and of equal or superior importance. You might even host a small dinner for a noted person and invite the contributor as a guest: "Margaret Thatcher has been asking to meet you. They'll be in for the weekend and we'd love for you and Barbie to come for brunch."

The food should be tempting and well served. After all, who wants to give $9 million to a host who can't even provide a well-thought-out meal to his guests? Stay cool and collected, no matter what happens.

"Parties for politicians in Washington are extremely conservative," says Barbara Boggs of Washington, Incorporated, a party-planning service. "The idea is to say that the politician is solid, level-headed, and not given to excess. What impresses the guests is the importance of the other guests, not the food. And parties should never, ever have a theme. They must be gracious, simple, and elegant."

### Boards of Directors and Trustees

Boards and trustees, especially those who give their time on a voluntary basis, deserve a bit of pampering. If you're in charge, try to arrange for something other than the usual banquet in a hotel or restaurant. One museum director hosts an elegant trustees' picnic on the museum grounds, including tables on the lawn set with her own crystal and china. The chairman of another board hosts a dinner at home, usually formal, to thank board members for their hard work. Often this is the only opportunity members have to socialize, since meetings are taken up with business.

Even if it's only a luncheon, you can still offer something special for the board. At a corporate board luncheon held in a Philadelphia club, the guests were seated when an embarrassed CEO announced there had been a snafu in the kitchen and the meal would have to be brought in from outside. Drinks were served to the startled members, and ten minutes later an army of waiters burst in carrying trays of fast-food containers. Each dismayed guest opened up his container, only to find a miniature of the magnificent sculpture being installed at the company's headquarters. The real meal followed immediately.

Entrepreneur and developer Roger Ogden feels that business should be business and pleasure should be pleasure. After a week of serious meetings, he often invites friends to join him at his Gulf Coast hideaway where they can relax and the subject of business is taboo. Guests are on their own to sail, water-ski, or go deep-sea fishing. That's real pampering.

## The Office Party

Even the words *office party* can bring on snickers and images of pot-bellied accountants wearing lamp shades and buxom secretaries squirming on the bosses' laps. In reality, both sexes may indeed find themselves having to resist the advances of intoxicated co-workers, most typically at Christmas parties.

Office parties can actually be very pleasant, especially if they are not held at the office. People are a little more restrained in unfamiliar surroundings. The executive wives at one firm get together each year and give a party at one of their homes, usually a cocktail buffet on a weeknight, with or without spouses. The food is lovely and plentiful and liquor takes a back seat to the eating, so it becomes more of a reception than an orgy.

An insurance executive in Omaha defused the rowdy atmosphere at his on-premises Christmas parties by switching to brunch in a chic restaurant for his two hundred employees, followed by dancing into the early afternoon.

You can transform the office party into an "event" held at a club, hotel, or restaurant. Send out engraved invitations. Engage a prominent speaker from the world of business. At the reception for the employees and their spouses, be sure the speaker-guest is accessible. Invite city and state officials so the employees can meet them too. Limit the party to two hours. A small dinner for the speaker and upper echelon can be given after the reception.

Outdoor events in summer or fall allow whole families to attend. A barbecue or picnic can

*Porter, Wright, Morris & Arthur, a law firm in Columbus, Ohio, commissioned architect Warren Platner to create a space that not only functioned as offices for the partners, but could be enjoyed by organizations throughout the community. On the ground floor Platner designed a garden atrium surrounded by conference dining rooms. In one of the conference dining rooms that opens onto the atrium (below), Platner designed a table inlaid with figured mahogany, cherry, rosewood, and bird's-eye maple, and a wall panel that repeats the pattern of the marquetry in the table. The wire chairs are Knoll International, designed by Platner.* ARDILES-ARCE

follow a corporate run or baseball game, a greased pig-catching contest, wheelbarrow races, a pie-eating contest, and sack races. Burrus Investment Group's corporate picnic is tied to a "big brother" project. Employees adopt orphans for the day, take them shopping for athletic shoes and jeans, then off to a barbecue and baseball game, after which they go to an ice cream parlor for dessert.

Company picnics are gaining in popularity as a way to entertain employees and sometimes clients. Everyone is invited to come to a country place at noon on a Saturday. Many companies provide buses from the office to the site.

There may be tractors pulling hay wagons for hayrides, horses for riding in the woods, and pony carts for the youngsters. Lunch is a barbecue —chicken, hamburgers, ribs. In order to get dessert, employees must compete in teams in cake walks, three-legged races, and equally ridiculous competitions. Afterward there is a big baseball game, complete with cheerleaders; the hosts provide the pom-poms and bull horns.

Later, guests can retire under the trees for a nap while they listen to a concert. In the evening there may be a dance with music provided by a country and western band. Light soups, quiche, and marinated vegetables are good choices for supper. Before going home, guests can enjoy fireworks or a refreshing swim.

## Conventions and Sales Meetings

Conventions have become so enormous that there are companies that do nothing but plan conventions for companies and professional groups from year to year. Wherever the gathering is held, meetings, accommodations, sightseeing, and entertainment must all be coordinated. You're not likely to be planning a convention alone, but a few gracious touches make the event more memorable.

Merrill Lynch took over the Newport Country Club during a convention. They set up beautiful green and white tents for luncheons and dinners, held golf and tennis tournaments with winners invited to play with celebrities, and had sailing races for relaxation between the meetings.

A group of motel franchise owners from all over the country rented the *Mississippi Queen* riverboat for a conference. At each port, a different franchise owner hosted a party. In Natchez, a bus took everyone sightseeing and antiques shopping, then to a mint julep party in an antebellum home. In New Orleans, after dinner at Antoine's, a mock Mardi Gras parade led the group through the French Quarter to a Dixieland concert in the courtyard of a historic house.

## Groundbreakings and Grand Openings

Building-site parties can be deadly dull. Who really enjoys looking at mud or getting coated with dust? One Atlanta producer of groundbreakings says that it is crucial to create excitement if you want to get press coverage. He advises that ten to eleven is generally a good time for them. Have as many important people in attendance as you can get—prominent business leaders, the financiers, the architects, politicians. If the invitation looks good, people will want to come.

For a corporate-office groundbreaking in

Large-scale business entertaining is a serious and integral part of many corporations. Many businesses feel that giving lavish parties for employees, stockholders, or clients is a vital means of building morale and increasing corporate pride.

Dan McCall is one of the nation's premier corporate events planners. Once he has an assignment, he spends hours meeting with corporate executives going over guest lists to determine the mindset of the crowd he will be entertaining, their likes and dislikes. He uses this information to create an event that will be memorable—and accomplish the corporate goal.

There are certain constants. Food must be simple, elegant, and plentiful; he recommends prawns, lobster, milk-fed veal, lamb, and beef. The decorations must be colossal and the lighting spectacular; special effects must change the mood every sixty minutes to keep guests from getting bored; entertainment and music must be knockout.

McCall recently staged a six-hour extravaganza for the executives of a corporation in San Francisco. Guests entered a room with food tables connected by balloon rainbows arching twenty feet in the air. Colored lights played endlessly over the clear balloons to create the rainbow effect. After cocktails, guests moved into a silver-wrapped ballroom for dinner. Each table was topped with mirrors and tall arrangements of exotic flowers on mirrored pedestals. The walls were flooded with dramatic lighting.

After dinner the guests returned to the first room, which was now filled with liquid smoke and dimmed lighting. Once the guests were inside, the soft music and lights went dead. Suddenly the room was ablaze with remote-controlled spotlights and the deejay played Dire Straits' "Money for Nothing." As the dance moved on, a pyrotechnician set off an inside fireworks display and a ceiling of balloons dropped on the guests to the music of the Pointer Sisters. The remote spotlights dazzled the crowd as they moved in the exciting environment.

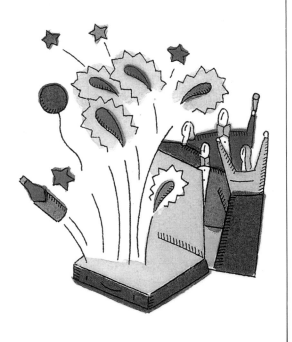

March, one Detroit party planner used the building's green granite to hook into St. Patrick's Day. Guests were greeted by leprechauns and given hard hats painted faux green granite. Champagne cocktails had a touch of green food coloring added to the sugar cubes and the food was green too—watercress sandwiches, oysters Rockefeller, and snow peas filled with artichoke mousse.

You can also have a picnic at the building site. Give each guest a lunch box attractively imprinted with the name of the project. Serve drinks, coffee, and dessert from moving carts. During the meal you might have live music followed by the architect's presentation of the project. The whole event will take less than an hour and guests will leave feeling relaxed and fed.

When the old Jax Brewery on the Mississippi River was reopened as a shopping complex, the public was invited to bring family snapshots for a time capsule. This idea generated a lot of public interest, drawing people to the shopping center to see the plaque bearing their names. In other communities businesses have buried time capsules containing children's artwork or relics of the town.

Hot-air balloon races, skywriters, fireworks, free gifts, and music are all effective ways to generate enthusiasm for a grand opening. Actors can be hired to dress as a company mascot, or celebrity lookalikes can mingle with the crowd. A current trend coordinates grand openings with gala charity events.

A Southern antiques gallery gave a really well-thought-out opening, comprising an elegant black-tie cocktail party and dinner for out-of-town

clients. After cocktails in the shop, the visitors were put into limousines with bottles of chilled champagne and hors d'oeuvres, and were told they were being taken to dinner via a moonlight tour of the city's landmarks. They soon found themselves back at the gallery, which had been transformed into a dining room complete with special lighting effects and sumptuous table settings.

The party-planning firm of Capricho staged the elaborate grand opening of the World Financial Center in New York, using the theme "High Finance." Ticker tape imprinted with the center's name was incorporated into the 5,000 invitations, used instead of ribbon to wrap favors, draped over the tables, and woven into the immense floral arrangements. At the close of the dedication ceremony, Governor Cuomo and Mayor Koch sounded a gong copied from the one used to open and close trading on the New York Stock Exchange. On cue, dozens of employees up on the balconies, dressed as NYSE floor pages, rained thousands of feet of ticker tape into the atrium.

269

Coordinate decorations and food with the theme of the book you are introducing. The presentation needs to be well thought out so the book remains the "star" of the evening. Flowers by Paul Bott of Twigs; wooden plate from Wolfman Gold & Good. *HIMMEL*

### The Book Party

The guests here are usually book reviewers, opinion makers, friends of the author and publisher, and, if you're lucky, bookshop owners. The idea is to make everyone want to buy the book or tell others to—as many others as possible. Since the guests have been to dozens of these functions, a massive cocktail party alone won't make much of an impression. You have to really get their attention, find a special way to say, "We're behind this book, we believe in it, you'll want to be too."

Begin with outstanding invitations, preferably something they might pin to their office walls (where even more people can see it): a poster of the jacket or a print of an illustration, for instance. Then to be sure the guests focus on the book, create a magical environment keyed to it. Have the party in a museum, on a boat, in an airplane hangar—anywhere unusual but related.

Decorate the space to fit the book—hang giant banners or posters from the ceiling and use spotlights or other dramatic lighting on them. Even if you're not allowed to do anything to the interior, you can do something to carry out the theme. To introduce a book on weddings at a convention in New Orleans, Crown Publishers rented a museum house, tied mammoth white bows to the balcony, and had a gospel choir serenading the guests.

Have the author, illustrator, or photographer or any other contributors circulating freely. They and you, the publishing company or other sponsors, should wear something identifying you—chef hats (for a cookbook), flowers in lapels, name tags. A receiving line can help, but only if most guests will be arriving at once. Give everyone who comes a token as a reminder—a button, a bookmark, a fan—imprinted with a quote from the book or its title.

Another must is delicious food—a combination of gorgeous buffet tables, widely spaced for good traffic flow, and lots of waiters passing food. Have enough bars and never serve cheap liquor.

End the party on an up note. Have a marching band, a balloon drop, fireworks.

### The Gallery Opening

Gallery openings often seem like opportunities for any passerby to come in and have a few glasses of free wine. This brings in a crowd but won't make reviewers or collectors feel special.

Some artists have two openings. One is for important contacts—by invitation only. There may be a buffet and good liquor for serious collectors, the press, and friends. There might even be a string quartet or jazz combo. The idea is to make the guests see the art as important—just as they are. Then comes the public opening, the day the show starts officially.

Private parties are a good way for friends and key collectors to be with the artist away from the limelight. Hollywood costume designer Nolan Miller and his wife, Sandy Stream, gave a spectacular garden dinner for Erté, which they created with designer David Jones. Erté bronzes were at the center of each table, and the seating arrangements gave guests the feeling that they were in the thick of the action.

*Meetings are much more successful when they can be held away from the office, with its routine interruptions. David Burrus often holds casual business meetings on the secluded side deck of his boat house. As an incentive to conclude the business quickly, he treats associates to a trip on his yacht after the meeting. HIMMEL*

## Election Night Party

Election night parties are the most interesting to host as no one knows (theoretically, at least) until they are almost over who is going to win. While the party must in no way be grand (the politician cannot appear to be blowing hard-raised contributions on a splash), it must be gracious. It is a way of saying thank you.

The party can't begin until the polls close. Many people will have worked twelve to fifteen hours on election day, not to mention the long weeks before. Be aware that they will be exhausted and emotionally drained by the time they arrive.

Your room may be fairly large, so have plenty of television sets with smaller conversational groupings so that the first guests don't get lost in an enormous space. Have a bar in each area (it can be help-yourself) and provide plenty of food to munch on.

The press corps covering the election will be as tired as you are. Treat them graciously by providing a place where they can relax when they aren't "on." Even if the candidate loses, good relations with the press are crucial to success if he or she ever runs again.

## Awards and Installations

Awards and installations, whether for clubs or corporations, usually take place at banquets with a speaker and master of ceremonies. Generally, there is a cocktail hour, then a seated dinner followed by the awards or the installation of officers. Somehow this format doesn't work. One person tends to drone on and on for hours while the

others sit glancing at their wristwatches. It works well to present awards and install officers during half an hour of cocktails. People will talk for a lot less time when they are hungry. Then dinner is served and the event is over, preferably in no more than two hours. Otherwise, recognize all the honored people at the same time and hand them their awards privately.

## Employee Incentives

These can be very quiet or very public. The hands-down favorite seems to be a nice fat check, but even this can be done with style if you include it with a modest but special gift. If your secretary loves African violets, wrap a big basket of different shades of violets with a giant bow and enclose the check in a card. A pipe smoker might appreciate several specially blended tobaccos with his check.

Another popular gift is the all-expenses-paid trip. One woman whose husband was stationed abroad received a round-trip ticket from her boss, including a three-day stopover in Paris on the way. Another boss gives her employees trips to Disney World with their families.

Incentive awards, unlike gifts, are for a job well done, usually in sales. Salespeople compete on a point system, and winners get bonuses, cash prizes, trips, or other rewards. Some of these can be quite spectacular. Lesa and John Oudt and Ann and John Koerner, owners of Barq's Root Beer, give a fabulous weekend party each year for the most successful distributors of their beverages. One year it was a trip to Acapulco.

The first night there was a party by the pool where everyone met one another. Mexican drinks and snacks were accompanied by a mariachi band. To break the ice, everyone took turns trying to break several piñatas. Afterward there was a dinner featuring filet mignon and flaming desserts.

The next day everyone chose from golf or tennis tournaments, shopping, sightseeing, or just sunbathing. That night each Barq's representative took three couples out to dinner at a fine restaurant. After dinner everyone met back at the hotel for a trip to see the famous cliff divers—who just happened to be wearing capes emblazoned with the Barq's logo—plunge into the sea. Then it was on to a special disco reserved just for them.

They went to a bull fight the next afternoon and that night was the awards night. An unnoticed sixty-foot metal structure suddenly came alive after dark with lights flashing "Barq's," followed by fireworks spelling out "Barq's Has Sparks." The weekend was a hit, partly because the owners-hosts spent their time enjoying the company of their guests and being part of the activities.

## Promotions

Promotions have to be handled with kid gloves. The new vice president should be feted without offending those who were passed over. Dwell on the positive—the future of the company and the bright future ahead for everyone. A banquet with the new executive sitting to the right of the boss at the head table might be a little strong, whereas a cocktail reception to introduce him or her to the employees is a nice way to honor the person. Another alternative is to have the president or a board

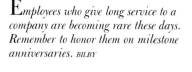

*Employees who give long service to a company are becoming rare these days. Remember to honor them on milestone anniversaries. BILBY*

*At a retirement dinner given after a large reception, company executives presented the employee with a specially commissioned portrait sculpture by artist Margot Datz from Martha's Vineyard. HIMMEL*

of directors take the new VP to lunch. This way, none of the rejected have to go along and act pleased.

## Retirement

When an employee retires, it is important to let the person know that his or her contribution to the company has meant a great deal. This is a milestone in the person's life, and it might not be as welcome as you think. A banquet, luncheon, or cocktail buffet would be appropriate; a party in a house might be too personal.

Work up a witty history of the company, highlighting the honoree's contribution. Here's an example:

> In 1951 Hortense became Mr. Peevey's secretary and held down the fort while he had those three-hour noon "sales meetings." During her time in the office, Mr. Peevey's sales went up 15 percent, Mr. Peevey did an authentic belly dance at the office party, Mr. Peevey left the firm, and Hortense took over his job. By 1955 Hortense was the sales manager but still had time to make her famous doughnuts every Monday morning to get us all to the office for her sales conferences. That was the year we broke into Minnesota . . .

The gold watch of yesteryear has given way to pearls, diamond rings, engraved silver trays, and VCRs, but in a pinch almost anyone would be happy to have a Rolex.

275

# *Chapter 10*
# ENTERTAINING FOR A CAUSE

*E*very day, we are bombarded by pleas for money—on television and radio, in magazines and newspapers, and in our mailboxes. Not to mention those people who call during dinner to sell light bulbs for some worthy cause, and the friends who gave money for your charity and wish the courtesy repaid. If you join the fund-raising ranks, you must start by recognizing what you're up against: the myriad of worthy causes, from

curing illnesses to beautifying the town to reelecting the mayor, all vying for the same dollar as your organization. ☛ The art of raising money for worthy causes has really become not only a business but a science, with market studies, donor profiles, and full-time professionals on the staffs of many museums, colleges, and foundations. Their efforts, in turn, are supported by thousands of hours of volunteer time. 🍷 The pros handle day-to-day solicitations; volunteers are more likely to handle the charity function—anything from bake sales to silent auctions to huge balls, which can often be the biggest moneymakers of the year. This is where you can offer contributors something besides the feeling of a duty done—something to eat, look at, listen to, take home, take part in—in other words, enjoyment. 🍸 How well you conceive, plan, staff, manage, and—more than anything—"design" your affair will have everything to do with how much you bring in and how you are received when you go back to the same contributors next year.

*Famed New York florist Renny has transformed this palatial but stark lobby area into an opulent environment for a party by turning each table into an individual island of color. A profusion of branches and dark vases surrounded by low candles creates a warm glow.* AARON

## The Nuts and Bolts of the Charity Event

Whether you are raising $500 or $5 million, the rules are the same. Here they are, along with some of the many ways you can use them to raise the money for that new wing on the hospital.

### Center Attention on the Cause

John Funt, the director of display at Tiffany's and one of the country's premier party designers, advises that it is crucial for the event to be geared to the charity but never upstage the serious purpose of the event. Seasoned charity event supporters say that when they get an invitation, they look at the cause first, the names of the chairman and committee second, the uniqueness of the event third, and lastly the quality of the presentation.

Rachel Oestricher Haspel, director of the Wallenberg Foundation, started in 1981 with only $5,000, and raised $500,000 on her first effort because she had a cause that important people cared about. The foundation's purpose is to research and honor Swedish World War II hero Raoul Wallenberg and fund associated scholarships, archives, and exhibits.

Rachel had hoped to persuade 300 people to attend her party in aid of the foundation; 1,200 accepted. "Our event [an elegant dinner with food flown in from Sweden] was spectacular, but it happened because of the strong commitment to the cause by each of the committee members," says Rachel. "New Yorkers lined up to come to a dinner whose guests included Henry Kissinger, Daniel Patrick Moynihan, Peter Jennings, Max von Sydow, and Bebe Anderson."

### Establish Your Financial Goals

Figure out the amount of money you need to clear after the expenses of the event.

The Tax Reform Act of 1986, should it continue in its present form, will make fund-raising even more difficult than before. Organization dues, for instance, will be only 80 percent deductible, as opposed to the former 100 percent. Tax-exempt entities will have to file taxes quarterly, increasing administrative costs and decreasing the amount of money available each quarter, and full

*Preview parties in a museum or gallery can be a lovely way to stir up public interest in a show and can also be a viable way of raising funds.* MESSER

deduction of charitable expenses is continued for those who itemize but is eliminated for those who do not.

Also, with rising costs, the percentage your organization raises must increase by about 10 to 15 percent each year. Either the event has to accommodate more people or it has to be so enticing that people will pay more money to attend. Bill Blass advises that if you sold your tables for $10,000 last year, they should sell for $20,000 this year. All of this will help you make up a schedule of what you need to bring in, for example:

    \_\_\_\_ patrons * (each responsible for filling a table of 10)

    \_\_\_\_ "A" guests (attending dinner and dance)

    \_\_\_\_ "B" guests (attending dance only)†

### Schedule Adequate Time

Determine the amount of time you have to raise the money. Look for a date you can link to your cause, such as Valentine's Day for an event to benefit the American Heart Association.

The amount of time you have will also establish the nature of the event you can manage. Typ-

---

* The group of people taking the most expensive individual sponsorship. Their names typically appear on the general invitation, along with committee members' names.

† The trend is to have a cheaper category for people under thirty who can get into the party later in the evening. This might bring in extra money and also get a new group interested in your cause.

---

ical "lead times" and number of volunteers for large-scale (over 250 guests) events are:

| Event | Lead Time | Number of Volunteers |
|---|---|---|
| Fashion show at a big hotel/ affiliated with store who handles details | 6 months– 1 year | 15 committee heads 50–60 volunteers |
| Auction | 9 months– 1 year | 8–10 committee members 40–60 volunteers |
| Luncheon with speaker | 6 months– 1 year | 10–15 committee heads 30 volunteers |
| Cocktail reception | 6 months– 1 year | 5–10 committee heads 20–30 volunteers |
| Dance only | 1 year | 5–10 committee heads 50–100 volunteers |
| Dinner dance/ Ball | 1 year | 20–30 committee heads 100–125 volunteers |

Note: If inviting movie stars/important speakers/lecturers, invite at least one year in advance.

Don't set a final date for the event until you have assembled all your support (see "Get Goods and Services Donated"). That way you'll stay flexible up to the last minute so that if someone offers a free yacht or dance band for the fourteenth instead of the seventh, you'll be able to accept it.

### Choose the Committee with Care

Choose a chairman and, in turn, a committee who are committed to working for the cause and whose names will draw support in the community. In many communities an honorary chairman and advisory committee are necessary because their names will show broad community support for the cause. Their primary function is to generate good public relations. Having important business people on the committee with whom guests will want to mingle certainly won't hurt ticket sales either.

Veteran fund-raisers say that every committee member should be able to ensure the sale of at least ten patron tickets, whether personally or through friends. The ideal committee is made up of one person who has a printing contact, one or more with media connections, one who has clout with whatever facility is wanted for the function, someone who has a connection with a liquor distributor, and others who can get the decorations and favors either underwritten or donated (interior designers, artists, and dress designers or buyers are a must).

Never have more than one chairman unless the work can be divided equally and quite separately. For example, one chairman could actually plan and put on the event and the other deal solely with corporate sponsorship and patrons. Beverly Anderson, who recently chaired a successful fund-raiser for the American Film Institute, states that the ideal co-chairman is a business professional who has a good backup staff willing to donate their services to keep up with correspondence and other details.

David Tardo and Larry Hill, owners of Churchill Caterers in New Orleans, advise that, no matter what size the committee, there must be only one person handling logistics. Otherwise, the consequences can be disastrous. The chairman of the liquor committee and the chairman of the patron party committee, for example, might both assume that the chairman of the food committee has told the caterer to provide 100 extra pounds of ice for a last-minute donation of hundreds of oysters on the half shell. When one person is responsible for keeping track of everything—a "command central" you can reach twenty-four hours a day—things run much more smoothly.

### Decide on the Event

Choose an event based on its ability to raise the target sum of money with the largest amount underwritten. An event that brings in $1 million has accomplished nothing if it costs $999,999 to put on. For the same yield, you could have washed your neighbor's dog. Plan an event around something you can get free. If one of the committee members will be opening a new restaurant or club in a few months, or is connected to someone who will, have your fund-raiser as a preview.

### Benefit the Benefactor

Make the benefit to the patron so great that everyone will want to give an extra hundred or thousand dollars to be patrons instead of regular contributors. Some people will gladly pay $5,000 per couple to go to a "drop-dead" patrons-only party at the city's most gorgeous house, especially

*Dim the lights in a large space and create visual interest by spotlighting large decorations and art.* MESSER

282

if they will get to view Bill Blass's new fall line, meet him and several other celebrities, get a signed Robert Motherwell lithograph, and have a chance to win a cruise on the *QE II*.

It is important to have some kind of patron party before a fund-raising event, even if it is simply a reception or a cocktail party. Some organizations like to have exclusive affairs a few nights in advance. Other groups have them an hour before the main event so patrons get preferred parking and a preview of the decorations.

Make the benefit so appealing to corporate sponsors and underwriters who might give up $25,000 that you can't be turned down. Of course, the cause must be compelling, but you must also get businesses the publicity they want by mentioning their names prominently in all press releases and other literature. Offer them plenty of free tickets so their people can mingle with the movers and shakers in your community.

Committee members should make personal calls on all the businesses and foundations that are important possible contributors. If two or three people make the call, the corporate representative will find it much more difficult to say no, especially if an important member of the committee takes him or her out to lunch. Whether or not a business ultimately becomes a sponsor, it can't hurt to familiarize it with your cause. You will be laying groundwork for the future.

### Get Goods and Services Donated

Think of every possible in-kind contribution you can—food, liquor, wine, flowers, tablecloths, decorations, door prizes, printing, even entertainment. An art school could make banners, a wine distributor launch a new brand into your market, a department store offer favors. Don't be afraid to think big—the worst anyone can say is no!

Sometimes you can "piggy back" on the grand opening of a corporate venture. The group supplies the glitzy guests, who pay to preview a new shopping complex, and the developer gets lots of media attention, as do the new merchants who supply all the food, drinks, and other goodies. Or you might get the promoter of a rock concert to support a food bank by asking that a can of food accompany each ticket as admission to the event. Do keep to a minimum the fund-raisers in which your organization participates, though. One cooperative venture with another charity and one of your own is about all the public can bear. Oversolicitation causes donor burnout.

### Solicit Patrons and Send Out Invitations

While you are arranging everything else, pay particular attention to the invitation list. Update the one you have (the average life is only about two years), or create a good list from directories of prominent people: the Junior League, the Council of Jewish Women, museums and other cultural memberships, parents of children in private schools. You can obtain a list of foundations and corporations from the chamber of commerce.

Then, once you have lined up as many goods-and-services contributions as possible and set the date, send out a splashy "save the date" card to the people on the invitation list as a teaser.

*The Patron Letter.* Three to four months before the event, this letter goes out to about 20 percent of the list, people carefully chosen because of their known standing in the community, support in the past, or personal connection to committee members.

To get attention, the presentation should be a bit extravagant—a rolled scroll or poster in a mailing tube—and sent via first class mail or hand delivered. Entrepreneur Louis Roussell III sent a tape-recorded message with a celebrity's voice to bring attention to his fund-raiser. The letter should explain clearly who benefits from the money to be raised by the event, exactly how the money will be used (will it go to pay the phone bill of the organization or will it be used to buy a new CAT scan machine for the local hospital?), where and when the patron party and the event will be held, the deadline for responding in order to be listed on the main invitation and program, and tax-deductible information. It is crucial to the success of the patron letter that each one have a personal note from a committee member. This tells the recipient of the letter that someone on the committee will know if they respond and cares that they attend. Beware: postal regulations prohibit any handwritten material sent under a bulk mail permit.

When the patron responses come in, the names must be pulled from the master invitation list and thank-you notes sent immediately. The list of patrons is then compiled for inclusion on the main invitation to the fund-raising event.

*The Main Invitation.* What it looks like is

important—don't think it isn't. An invitation run off on photocopy paper, even if it offers a trip to Paris for two for $250, is unlikely to have any takers.

Robert Armstrong III and the Gala Committee of the Museum of Fine Arts Council in Boston use innovative and catchy invitations designed to entice flocks of contributors to their event. They have concluded that fantastic invitations ensure that even those who don't go to the event will remember the cause.

The invitation should go out six to eight weeks in advance. If it goes out too soon, people will put it aside and forget about it. In the invita-

*Make your invitation memorable. The pop-up from the Hokus Pokus Cinderella Ball in Tulsa and the invitation from the gala committee of the Museum of Fine Arts in Boston are some of the best.* HIMMEL

tion there must be a return card and envelope listing all of the categories for contributions. It is all right to list patron prices on the invitation—maybe a few more people will want to become patrons, go to the party, and get their names on the program.

A general rule of thumb is that for a first event there will be only a 10 percent return on invitations. This means that if you send 2,000 invitations, 200 people will attend. If the response to the invitation is low, the committee can form a phone bank to call people they know. This, however, is a sign of desperation. It is far more effective to ask a few friends to host "before the event" parties. The idea is that guests will want to buy tickets to the fund-raiser so they can enjoy the rest of the evening with their friends. After all, who wants to get all dressed up and then go home at nine o'clock?

Gregory Fudge of the Luden Foundation and Isaac Tigrett of the Hard Rock Cafe wanted to do a benefit for the Children's Art and Ideas Committee of Dallas, but they had only two weeks to do it. They organized a private party to be held before a polo match between an English team (Oxford) and a Texas team. Their friends were invited to Isaac's penthouse apartment where they got to see such rock memorabilia as smashed guitars from The Who's world tour, John Lennon's leather jacket, an outfit from Elvis, and lots of items from the Hard Rock Cafe. As a special treat, Stewart Copeland of The Police entertained. The next day all their friends supported the cause and bought tickets to the benefit match and dinner.

### Publicize Relentlessly

Put posters up in local shops; get someone on your committee to be on a local talk show or do a newspaper interview about the cause and the event. Do public service announcements on television and radio. These ten- to thirty-second spots can be run when the stations have some leftover air time between regular paid commercials. Unless you have real clout, they might run at 3:00 A.M., but every little bit helps. Pamper the TV station or newspaper staffs with flowers or food to get them to cover your event far enough in advance to help sell tickets. Press releases generally end up in the trash, but what reporter can resist a hot-air balloon or a plane skywriting the name of the event? Don't forget to ask all of the media people to come to the event.

Ask local advertisers to plug your cause in their ads. You might even get the state legislature, mayor, or town council to proclaim an official "Save the Oak on Elm Street Day" in honor of your cause.

*Parties in tents by very definition demand exotic decoration. Los Angeles party designer Donna Paitchell of Summit Productions and designers Tom Pierce, Russ Porterfield, and Rick Smith of Tom Pierce Productions created a kingdom of light and flowers by utilizing mirrors, Lucite pedestals, and glass tubes with arrangements of orchids, gerberas, and exotic Hawaiian flowers. Tabletop mirrors reflect the glow of the lighted ceilings. To redefine the space, they erected floor-to-ceiling white trellises espaliered with night-blooming jasmine. FROGER*

Celebrities are veritable magnets when it comes to getting publicity for an event. Marcia Mitchell, former associate director of the American Film Institute, says, "Even when we do a fund-raiser in Los Angeles, where our patrons mingle with celebrities all the time, they still buy tickets for parties with movie stars." In Palm Beach, one hostess has patrons lined up to go to the Red Cross ball because ambassadors and dignitaries from all over the world are guests.

Before you proceed, however, you should be aware of some possible pitfalls. Here are the more common problems and solutions from people with experience.

*The No-Show.* Anyone from a local politician to a movie star can have a last-minute scheduling conflict and fail to show up. Many times a dignitary will try to get a replacement, but it is often too late to find a fill-in. One organization had to refund thousands of dollars worth of tickets when their tennis tournament celebrity failed to appear.

If at the last minute you find that a celebrity can't attend and it's too late to get a replacement, keep the news to yourself until the event is underway. Guests have had fun anticipating the festivities, so why disappoint them before you have to? Wait until everyone is having a good time before you announce that Greta Garbo's plane is in a holding pattern over Newark.

*The High Risk.* One international party planner warns that many celebrities, especially the newly famous, can be a problem because they simply don't know how to behave or have no discretion about who they bring with them.

First, tell the celebrity exactly what he or she is expected to do, how long to plan to be on hand, and what your organization will pay in terms of expenses. One fledgling ballet company in a small town found itself near bankruptcy when its guest artist charged hundreds of dollars in phone calls and then walked off the stage ten minutes into the performance.

*The Hidden Costs.* You should talk not only to the celebrity but also to his or her business manager or agent to find out if there are any hidden costs. For example, does the celebrity travel with an entourage? Who is responsible for them? What type of security will they need? Does the celebrity have any dietary requirements or special wants and needs?

Celebrities who give their time to fund-raising work hard. They must shake hands with a multitude of strangers, dance with lines of adoring fans, sign countless autographs, and spend hours in interviews. Pamper them. Have a car and driver pick them up at the airport, give them a tour of the city (just enough to get their bearings), and give them the home phone numbers of people on the committee they can call at any hour if they have questions. Allow them time to themselves between events and a spot where they can slip off to eat away from the crowds.

*More than 6,000 people drag them-selves out of bed at daybreak to watch forty-five pilots from all over America compete in the Snowmass Balloon Fest, the highest-altitude balloon race in the world. The annual event is an inter-nationally known fund-raiser for the Pitkin County Air Rescue and Moun-tain Rescue groups. SNOWMASS*

## The Main Event

The fun in fund-raising comes with the event—the memorable occasion mounted with all of the *vivre* your organization can muster. From city to city, event to event, the mood and style of the fund-raiser will vary, but the same gracious spirit prevails.

In Aspen, Colorado, a community with about four thousand permanent residents, more than a hundred charities vie for contributions at the height of the season. Christine AuBale Gerschel is one of the many Aspen Foundation committee members who have turned its yearly spring fund-raiser from a $35,000 event into a $1.3 million event in just six years. The secret has been pooling the resources of the twenty or so organizations the foundation benefits, having *the* party to be seen at, and offering the best benefits to the patrons.

Peggy Fisher, a long-time patron of the arts in Tulsa, says the formula that works best for the Tulsa Philharmonic is to offer prospective patrons several events. One year patrons could go to a fashion show dinner with a top designer in Sep-tember, an informal murder mystery dinner at Halloween, and a gala ball in December. (Those in the $5,000 category went to all three events; for $1,500 a couple attended the fashion show and the ball; in the $400-per-couple category, the ball only.)

From Sarasota to Seattle, Savannah to Sau-salito, the personalities of those who create the events leave an indelible stamp. In Chicago, Abra Prentice Wilkin says that many organizations write thank-you parties into their budgets as a special

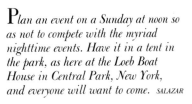

Plan an event on a Sunday at noon so as not to compete with the myriad nighttime events. Have it in a tent in the park, as here at the Loeb Boat House in Central Park, New York, and everyone will want to come. SALAZAR

treat for those who have contributed the most time and money to help make the event a success. In Aspen the board of trustees of the Aspen Art Museum placed a large ad in the local paper to thank the chairman and committee members of Les Dames d'Aspen who "Put On the Ritz" to raise money for their cause.

### The Ball

The charity ball is an American institution. The guests are dressed to kill, the themes and decorations are creative. and first-rate entertainment is a must. In smaller communities, some dress boutiques exist almost entirely on the money they make selling gowns to the women who attend these functions.

The ball must be such a good party that guests will want to return year after year and patrons stand in line to contribute. When people have paid substantially to attend and gotten all dressed up, they expect only the best, from liquor and food to door prizes. Committees must be highly skilled in order to pull off a spectacular event and keep the costs to a minimum.

The Cattle Baron's Ball for the American Cancer Society in Dallas is so successful that it clears between $700,000 and $800,000 a year. Fifteen hundred guests pay between $300 and $1,200 a plate for this outdoor extravaganza. The year that Melinda Wynn was chairman, she managed to get Southfork Ranch for the party and had friends fly in the entire cast of *Dallas* from Hollywood. At a specified time, the actors and actresses arrived in a procession of helicopters from Caro-

Some organizations actually let people who say they'd pay not to go to a ball put their money where their mouths are. Two months before the normal time for the ball, they send invitations, complete with categories for contributions, a specified financial goal, and a list of raffle prizes (trips to Europe, fur coats—the invitation is the entry). If the goal is met, there are no personal solicitations or ball. As an added incentive, those who contribute are given a thank-you party—which they don't have to attend.

At Christmas time, the patrons receive a silver horn tree ornament with a note such as: "Go blow your horn! We met our goal. You didn't have to buy a dress or be our guest. Please remember us next year."

*Treat patrons to a night of home-cooked ethnic fare unavailable in any restaurant. Provide exotic flowers, live music, and clever favors. Souvenirs, wines, and hard-to-find foods from the country you are spotlighting may be located by contacting the appropriate national airline or consulate. Travel agents may also be able to help.* HARDIN

line and Buddy Schoellopf's Pumpkin Air. All this while Johnny Cash sang and guests mingled with the chiefs of the Navajo and Apache nations, America's native royalty.

Pat Buckley, chairman of the prestigious Metropolitan Costume Institute Benefit in New York, always has a sellout. According to John Funt, the event's designer, the cause is important and popular in itself. "We try to design such creative centerpieces and costumes, and drape and light the space so dramatically, that guests feel they have walked into a fabulous 'New World' every year. After the ball, the committee sells everything it can, apart from the few things that are reusable from year to year."

At the Museum of Modern Art, the same basic guidelines are used to create totally different moods and illusions. At one recent gala, guests stepped into the 1960s from a Cadillac convertible at the entrance into rooms with live vignettes: actresses sitting at dressing tables making up for the prom; others doing the twist and practicing with Hula Hoops.

### The Gourmet Gala

The March of Dimes Celebrity Cooking Contest in Dallas is a very popular fund-raiser that has been a sellout in the four years it has been produced. In 1986 eleven hundred people paid between $250 and $1,000 a plate for the event, which, after expenses, cleared $400,000. Deborah Thomas explains, "Local members of the American Society of Interior Designers create a series of working kitchens in a hotel ballroom for contes-

tants to use. The night of the event, patrons and guests get a special tour of the kitchens and a taste of the entries, after which they are treated to a dinner, awards presentation, and dancing."

The black-tie Zoo-to-Do, held each spring in New Orleans' zoological gardens, is a fund-raising trendsetter. Dozens of the city's best restaurants each do a special food table, and competition is fierce. Thirty-five hundred guests (who pay between $150 and $1,200 per plate) roam from table to table sampling delicacies, many created especially for the party. New Orleanians fight for tickets, and those who don't get them have been known to sulk on the levee outside, where they can at least hear the music, usually a sixties group like the Temptations or the Four Seasons. The event enriches the zoo by about $600,000 each year.

Many cities have a local chefs' association that will lend its support to a charity. They can offer cooking contests, prepare gourmet feasts, or give cooking classes or tastings. Perhaps they could judge a community-wide cooking contest for which each entrant pays a fee and patrons pay to come to a dinner prepared by the winners.

### The Festival

Food and music festivals are marvelous family entertainment. Louisiana has made them a specialty. There are strawberry, crawfish, alligator, gumbo, and oyster festivals, to name but a few. The largest music and food festival in the world is the New Orleans Jazz and Heritage Fair, a $2 million event put on by a foundation that raises money for music scholarships and a not-for-profit

jazz radio station. The foundation contracts with a music producer to put on the events—two weekends of nonstop music on five stages and hundreds of food and crafts booths. The sales of beer and soft drinks, silk-screened posters, and T-shirts make almost as much as the admission.

Glenn Bernbaum of Mortimer's Restaurant recently co-hosted a French Street Fair at his Manhattan eatery, which earned $200,000 for the Cornell Medical Center Laboratory for AIDS research. He had Seventy-fifth Street tented for the gala to add to the festival atmosphere. Inside, the restaurant was transformed into a cabaret with entertainment by Mortimer's Prime Time Players, Julie Wilson, Frank Owens, Bobby Short, Peter Duchin, Peter Allen, and other noted performers.

Ethnic groups have long raised money by serving the foods of their countries to the public, especially at street festivals like the famous Feast of San Gennaro in New York's Little Italy. Some groups transform church halls into the "old country," with native music, dancing, costumes, and food. These events are especially popular for families who like to give their children exposure to another culture.

### Fashion Shows

The simple luncheon fashion show of a few years ago is being eclipsed by fashion show/tea parties held in museums, gardens, and concert halls. Free of the constraints of a sit-down meal, they can be held almost anywhere. Several years ago the New Orleans Museum of Art planned a fashion tea with Saks Fifth Avenue for the day

*Gourmets will clamor to buy tickets to an event where they can enjoy an array of delicacies and wines chosen by a celebrity chef, food writer, or food and wine authority. At the "cellar in the sky" at Windows on the World (facing page, top), guests are treated to a princely selection of wines while they overlook New York Harbor and the East River. Architect Warren Platner has designed framing projectors in the ceiling that project a dappled sunlight effect and reflect a pattern of grape leaves onto the tables below. On another wall of the same space (facing page, bottom) there is a repeat of tulips with a gold leaf border.* GEORGES

*Convince a shopping center to do a promotional fund-raiser for your cause. If you can get a radio station to coordinate music played on the air with your fireworks display (right), everyone in the area will know about your cause by the end of the evening.* BILBY

before its Odyssey Ball. The idea was to appeal to those who wanted to attend a less expensive event or who did not want to go out in the evening. The tea was served in the spectacular surroundings of Muriel Francis's art collection at the museum, and her personal collection of vintage Chanel, Dior, and Charles James clothes was modeled along with clothes by English designer Murray Arbeid, a favorite of Princess Diana.

Tips to remember: The show should never last more than forty-five minutes. The master of ceremonies must do more than merely describe the clothes, which the audience can see for themselves, and the models (even if they *are* committee members) must have personality and look as if they are enjoying the experience. Music is another must—it brings the event to life.

### The Theme Dinner

The New York Public Library's "Night of 100 Dinners" has set a new style for fund-raising dinners. Contributors choose among theme dinners offered in the homes of one hundred notable people. Themes in the past have included "Three Wise Men in the Kitchen"; "Top Hat, White Tie and Tails"; "A Literary Evening in Fifteenth-Century Italy"; "Junk Food on the China Seas"; "Extra, Extra, Eat All About It"; and "An Aphrodisiac Feast." Each host chef decides how many people he or she can accommodate, and each guest pays a flat $250 to attend.

In Corona del Mar, California, the American Field Service raises money for its exchange program by having a progressive dinner in the homes of families hosting foreign-exchange students. The meal is planned around the national dishes of each student. At the first home are Greek appetizers and Greek wine; at the second there is Thai food as a main course; and at the last home is an array of Austrian pastries. The students and their American host families are at the door to greet guests and have prepared the food as well. Not only does the event raise money for the cause, it lets the public meet the students their dollars support.

### The House or Garden Tour

House tours are especially popular around the holiday season when decorations are up. All you need are six to eight homes reasonably close together, with owners who are willing to do elaborate decorations and won't mind having strangers troop through their homes. Even a small organization with twenty to thirty members can pull off this event with ease. Other popular themes are historic houses, contemporary architectural gems, or expertly decorated houses (any can be combined with a lecture series). If security might be a problem, you can still have private tours, for which each member of the organization is responsible for sales of tickets to close friends.

One of the National Wildflower Research Center's most popular fund-raisers is an all-day tour of wildflower habitats followed by a supper party at the LBJ Ranch outside Austin. Maline McCalla decorates Austin city buses that are used for the tour with Mexican paper flowers and banners saying "Wildflower Special." Guests receive personalized lunch boxes, and in the evening they dine at the ranch, where the tables are covered with baskets of wildflowers.

The Philadelphia Open House to benefit the Friends of Independence National Historic Park is a trendsetter on many fronts. The organization acts as an umbrella to help promote neighborhood and architectural preservation all over Philadelphia and the surrounding areas. Last year they co-sponsored twenty-eight different tours in eighteen areas with neighborhood associations, historical societies, and the Junior League. Each year the patron's party is held in a building in need of attention. Guests pay fifty dollars to attend a lavish cocktail party, with half the money going to the sponsoring neighborhood group and half going to the Friends of Independence National Historic Park.

The hospital auxiliary of Hotel Dieu in New Orleans has a three-day tour of an historic house at Christmas time. Local party planners, decorators, and floral designers decorate rooms with their creations. Patrons of the event are treated to a first look and opportunity to purchase the decorations at a gala Victorian tea party held the afternoon before the home is opened to the public.

### The Show House

The Kips Bay Show House to benefit the Kips Bay Boy's Club is probably the best-known show house in America. Leading interior designers each decorate a different room, from the bare walls, in a large house, and the public pays to stream through and have a look at the latest trends. The event attracts the best New York has to offer, from decorators and patrons to all-out media coverage. Everyone gets behind it.

Because of all that's involved in doing a show house, you need between 300 and 400 volunteers willing to devote a year to the project, plus another 30 people who will work night and day on it. In addition, a paid consultant is a must for the first few years.

First, the house must be lined up. It must have an accessible location, be architecturally important, and be completely available to the orga-

*At the Hotel Dieu Christmas house tour and tea, guests were treated to tabletop decorations created by different local designers. Heirloom family china and Bohemian glass have been combined with a traditional nineteenth-century lace cloth and napkin. To add contemporary glitter, the cloth has been laid over gold lamé and the napkin tied with an array of festive ribbons.*
HIMMEL

nization for six months. It must also be the right size. A too-large house with huge rooms is not attractive to decorators, who must bear the cost of everything that goes into the rooms.

The decorators are chosen by a review committee, which must then match each of them to a room. The decorators benefit by having the opportunity to show their best work to large numbers of potential clients and very possibly selling the items they've used.

At most show house extravaganzas, patrons for the event are invited to two parties. The first is an elegant bash in the undecorated house (sometimes called the "Bare Bones Party"), with lots of good food, outrageous decorations, and dancing. The second party, a "Gala Preview," is a sumptuous black-tie benefit in the newly decorated spaces. Patrons are given the opportunity to bid on the furnishings before the event is opened to the public.

The public pays between $4.50 and $10.00 a head to take a guided tour of the house. It should be open seven days a week for a month. The organization can generate additional revenue by selling advertising for the program, by having a boutique selling specially commissioned crafts, and by running a tearoom for refreshments.

A show house can easily clear $250,000 after expenses, although very few organizations have the energy to do more than one every three years.

### Film Premieres, Lectures, Performances

Any time a cause can attract a *big* name, media attention, and "you can only see it here" entertainment, it has a winner. Barbra Streisand did her first live concert in twenty years and people paid $5,000 a couple to attend. Democratic candidates in California received $1.5 million from her efforts.

The American Film Institute has turned the film premiere into a successful fund-raiser. Several years ago it secured permission to premiere *The Right Stuff* in Washington, D.C., months before its release to the public. The day began with a patrons' luncheon on the banks of the Potomac and formation flying led by Chuck Yeager. On the night of the gala, guests walked into the theater at the Kennedy Center past a military honor guard. On the steps of the theater stood seven men, feet apart, hands behind their backs, dressed as America's first astronauts.

After the film, guests moved on to an airplane hangar at National Airport, which was decorated in black and silver and had an authentic space capsule suspended overhead and, in the center of the floor, a replica of the plane in which Yeager broke the sound barrier. The tables were topped with Mylar, and in the center of each was a mobile made of balloons and silver airplanes. The AFI staff were dressed in white flight suits with "The Right Stuff" stenciled on the back. On the runway outside, a dancing area was marked off by vintage fighter planes parked in a V formation.

On a far smaller scale but equally successful is the Antique Forum put on each fall in Natchez, Mississippi, by the Pilgrimage Garden Club to raise money for historic preservation. Participants, limited to 250, come from all over the country and

B*lowups of African sunsets and sunrises and mosquito net-draped ceilings and chandeliers set the mood for the premiere of* Out of Africa, *held in the Century Plaza Hotel ballroom to benefit St. John Hospital in Los Angeles.*
FROGER

pay several hundred dollars for three days of lectures given by nationally known authorities on antiques. Twice as many must be turned away each year. Those who attend are treated to parties in private antebellum homes and are generally given the red-carpet treatment.

Some institutions, especially universities, put on highly successful debates and lecture series with famous speakers. The most popular draws are the current President, a former President, a past or present Secretary of State, a liberal or conservative intellectual, a feminist or minority leader, a best-selling author, a noted economist, a network newscaster, or a syndicated columnist. Phoenix native Erma Bombeck donates her time each year to a highly successful luncheon to benefit the Arizona Kidney Foundation. The popular columnist's lecture is eagerly anticipated from year to year.

Performing arts groups can combine the need to sell tickets with the need to raise money. They can offer patrons high-priced tickets (mostly tax-deductible) to a special performance, such as opening night or a premiere. The patrons attend a cocktail buffet before the performance, receive a box seat, and then go to a post-performance supper or dessert party for the cast.

Other organizations that want to center a fund-raiser around a performance or concert can get national touring companies—from the circus to a Broadway show—to sell them a block of tickets to a performance, which they can resell at gala prices in conjunction with a party that is held before or after the event.

### The Awards Gala and Roast

Organizations will frequently select a nationally known figure to receive an award, thus attracting media attention. Amistad Research Center, the largest black and minority archive in America, recently gave its Fine Arts Award to artist Jacob Lawrence. People from the arts community flocked to meet Lawrence, who coincidentally had appeared on the *Today* show a week earlier.

Other organizations pick a person or group to honor as the best dressed, the most supportive of local civic causes, the father of the year, or the like. A panel of judges within the organization reviews the nominations, which are usually made by past recipients of the award. Those chosen are then asked to give the organization mailing lists of any groups in which they are active. Let's say the panel chooses ten people, one of whom is a young attorney who works with the ACLU, Junior Achievement, the Boy Scouts of America, and Big Brothers. Another is a journalist who is president of the Council of Jewish Women and is active in the League of Women Voters, the Education Task Force of the Chamber of Commerce, and the Opera Guild. These two individuals will bring in diverse groups of friends and co-workers, besides proud family members who will buy a table.

The Princess Grace Foundation, which raises money to assist gifted young people in the performing arts, holds a big gala each year in a different American city. Its recent party in Dallas attracted people from all over the country who paid $15,000 a person, or $750 in a lesser category, to be guests of the royal family of Monaco.

Other draws included master of ceremonies Robert Wagner and headliner Frank Sinatra, honorary chairman Nancy Reagan, and a gala committee including dozens of well-known people. In each major city in America, there was also a notable gala chairman who hosted a pre-party for a smaller sum as a preview of the big event.

The same idea can be carried out on a smaller scale. David Stickelber, trustee of the Kansas City Museum of Art, invited twenty-four people for dinner to hear professional lecturer and friend Betsy Bloomingdale. He charged $500 per person and it was a sellout. Such an event costs less to put on than a ball, and there need not be additional entertainment or elaborate decorations.

The "roast" testimonial dinner is sure to draw a crowd who would enjoy an irreverent, good-natured poke at their favorite politician, newscaster, sports figure, or business and civic leader.

### The Fund-Raising Trip

Louisiana Governor Edwin Edwards was able to raise $6 million through a luxurious six-day combination political fund-raiser and corporate delegation to Paris, Monaco, and Brussels. Participants paid $10,000 each to fly across the Atlantic on two 747s and attend dinner parties at Versailles, Maxim's, the Lido, Tour d'Argent, and other elegant restaurants. They attended special fashion shows at Revillon and took trips to Monte Carlo. Those taking part got to mix with movers and shakers from the States, as well as make important contacts for their firms in France.

Many organizations sponsor tours to other

301

parts of the world or simply to another city to see a play. The group and a travel agent do the planning, and usually an authority on art, music, or architecture from the organization and a travel agent accompany the group. Organizations rarely are able to make more than several thousand dollars on the trip, yet it is a perfect opportunity for people with a shared interest to see the world.

### Sports Events and Games

Celebrity tennis and golf tournaments, polo matches, ski races, horse shows, sailboat races, and other sporting events are good ways to get a great deal of publicity for your cause as well as raise money. The Dinah Shore Golf Tournament is purported to be the most successful of all. Patrons are typically asked to pay several thousand dollars to participate in a sport with celebrities and hobnob with them afterward. In Palm Beach, people paid $10,000 a plate to dine with Prince Charles and Princess Diana after they watched him play in a polo match.

If there is a race track or sports arena in your area, you can arrange to have a race or game dedicated to a cause. Your group sells tickets to the clubhouse, where contributors can eat and watch the race or game. This event will attract a different crowd than a charity ball and is a good means of entertaining.

For those who like high school or college sports, have a pregame fund-raiser. Use school buses to take everyone to a football game without the hassle of driving, and at the game, provide seat cushions, lots of food and drink, pom-poms, and

After a day of fishing or sailing for trophies, invite all the participants to an old-fashioned seafood boil, complete with country and western music for dancing. The event will draw a crowd different from the one that goes to the ball. BILBY

noisemakers. Have an after-the-game sock hop and no one will ever remember they were at a fund-raiser.

As trite as they may seem, charity bingo games do raise a lot of money, provided the operators are above board, and casino nights have gained widespread popularity in fund-raising. They can be organized around a theme like "Roaring Twenties Speakeasy," with drinks served in tea cups, Prohibition style, and the ladies given jeweled and feathered headbands and long pearls as favors. At the "Lark in the Park," a fund-raiser for City Park in New Orleans, there is a casino where guests dressed in twenties attire gamble for trips, antiques, life-sized dollhouses, objets d'art, and hundreds of other donated prizes.

The Quick Fix: Raising a Few Thousand

### The Picnic Basket Benefit

Martha Hopkins Burson of Denver does a lot of fund-raising for her children's schools and suggests that one of the most effective means of raising money is to have a picnic basket raffle/dinner party at someone's home. Each couple makes an elegant and unique picnic for two complete with wine, appetizers, main course, salad, and dessert. The baskets are auctioned off with the bidding starting at twenty-five dollars for each basket.

### Ice Cream Social and Tree Planting

Politicians are embracing this idea as an easy way to solicit money from small contributors. Not only is it a nice change of pace from the "rubber chicken" circuit dinner, it also attracts media attention. The most effective way to stage an old-fashioned ice cream social is with a local ice cream and soft drink distributor making in-kind contributions to the cause. Each contributing family pays fifty dollars for which a tree is planted in a public park with a plaque bearing their name. Their immediate reward is to get all the ice cream they can eat. Balloons and a banjo player can add to the spirit of the occasion.

### The Film Festival

In the summer, an outdoor film festival can feature vintage films shown afterward and moonlight picnics. Patrons can pay a flat fee for the series or pay to see each. These are a popular chaperoned entertainment for young teenagers.

### The Lemonade Stand

A lemonade stand can garner a surprising amount of publicity for a popular cause if the stand is well decorated and in a good location. Allison, Darryl David, Brandon, and Ryan Berger spent all one summer standing on the street corner with their friends from the neighborhood selling lemonade by the glass to passersby, all to benefit the public library. They were given spots on each of the local television newscasts, stations which increased public awareness of the plight of the library system and attracted additional donations.

### Festive Feast

A gourmet committee can be formed to cook donated food, which is then prepared for immediate freezing or serving. Contributors are invited to a "Festive Feasts" sale, generally before the holiday season, where they are served tea while making their purchases of gourmet food. It is a good idea to attach a list of ingredients to items if the recipe is not included. Unsold food can be donated to a charity serving the hungry.

### The Novelty Event

Zany antics can attract attention and money for a cause, as long as they are not so silly that they detract from the serious purpose of the organization. A real crowd pleaser is the "Jell-O Jump" at which patrons pay for the privilege of seeing local luminaries or friends slide into a giant vat of green Jell-O (which is made in large garbage cans and kept cold in a hotel meat locker). A group of good-natured celebrities is asked to par-

*Not only do lemonade stands raise money, they are also a viable way to give children the chance to participate in helping a cause they care about. Adults can keep a watchful eye from a distance, but too much hovering can deter customers from stopping. Those in the know suggest locations near tennis courts, baseball diamonds, and parks.* STONE

Bachelor Raffle
Christmas Greens Sale
Book Fair
Silk-screened T-shirts, Aprons, and Sheets
Garage Sale
Spring Plant and Bulb Sale
Recycled Can or Paper Pickup
Car and Dog Washing Service
Pledge Stunt to attempt a mention in the
    *Guinness Book of World Records*
Swear Box
Community Pothole Fill
Cookbooks
Limited-Edition Posters and Books
Donations of Christmas tree ornaments or
    Easter eggs in the names of others
Bingo
Raffles
Marathons, Walk-a-thons, or Pet Walk-a-thons

ticipate. After people pay an entrance fee to watch the event, the celebrities are auctioned off to the crowd. When they are sold, they jump—unless they want to double the bid and save themselves.

Other organizations like to put local celebrities in jail until they can raise bail (usually between $500 and $2,000.) The "prisoners" get on the phone and call their friends to get the money. One small-town YMCA put all of the town's elected officials in jail. The sheriff raised $2,000 in half an hour and was the first out of jail. To reward him, the organization treated him to a roast the following month.

At "Celebrity Waiter Breakfasts," local celebrities serve as waiters and donate their tips to a favorite cause. The participants dress up in outrageous costumes and try to do such a good job that they will get big tips. The event costs thirty-five dollars a plate. At each table a heart-shaped balloon bearing the waiter's name is attached to a hat into which the diners can throw money. Women dressed as sexy cigarette girls sell samples of perfume and cigarettes for five dollars apiece.

Cyril Laan and Tommy Coleman were going to take off on a transatlantic voyage in a helium balloon. The Friends of City Park in New Orleans hooked up with them and staged a tailgate launch party in the park. Media coverage was phenomenal. The organization got people to pledge money for each mile the balloonists traveled and bet on how long they would stay in the air. The organization spent $1,000 on a large mailing and a band and cleared $10,000 after the event. (After a successful fifteen-hour flight, the two pilots realized they were aimed directly at Cuba; they threw a line to a passing shrimp boat, who thought they were a UFO, and got towed back to shore.)

### The Telethon and Pledge-a-Thon

There is probably not a person in this country who is not familiar with the Labor Day Muscular Dystrophy telethon. It is the prototype followed by all the others—top celebrities and good entertainment keep the viewers' interest. It is an excellent way to alert large numbers of people to the role and goals of an organization.

Public radio and television stations must raise money and usually do so by means of a "pledge-a-thon," but they are so unpopular with the public that some progressive stations promise not to have them if people will just send in enough money. They do, however, make the public aware of a station's need for financial support.

### The Sale and the Auction

Antiques shows with dealers from all over the country buying booths and the public paying to attend can be very successful if they are properly promoted. For example, the Theta Show in Houston and the Winter Antiques Show in New York are world renowned. Professional organizers and a noted antiques authority who can serve as chairman are vitally important. It seems to take about five years of having the event annually before it is established and realizes a significant profit.

Other groups have auctions at which donated items are auctioned off by a professional auctioneer. At smaller auctions, guests can pay a fee to attend and then bid silently on items. Parents groups can organize a "service" auction: one couple may donate a month of French tutoring, another provide a gourmet dinner party, another a babysitting service.

Shirley Kritzik, a savvy fund-raising committee member for the Milwaukee Ballet and several hospitals, says she finds that people in her area are attracted to big-ticket items such as cars and boats. "People want to bid on things they can't ordinarily buy," says Shirley. At a recent auction, a trip was made available for a father and son to fly to the Super Bowl on the same plane with the football team, eat with them, and stay in the same hotel. They even got box seats at the game. Another man in Saratoga Springs offered to send his private plane to pick up a couple, let them stay in his house, and attend the races as his guest.

### The Follies

Follies are a terrific means for members of an organization or a community to get to know one another. In Omaha the Jewish community does one that even out-of-towners fly in to see. It is the perfect fund-raiser for a school because kids love to see their parents and teachers make fools of themselves and the talented ones adore having an audience. Follies take hours of preparation, with committees that sell tickets, print programs, and sell ads; volunteers who make the sets and costumes; as well as all those who actually put on the production. Don't even attempt this activity unless you can enlist the help of a professionally trained director.

*Guests should leave your party feeling they have been treated to the most festive of occasions. Chef Tom Cowman has spotlighted the desserts and garnished each with fresh flowers at this Pennsylvania fund-raiser for a political candidate.* BILBY

# COCKTAIL SAVVY

## *THE WELL-STOCKED BAR*

To be well stocked, a contemporary bar should reflect the new eclecticism in drinking habits. Only twenty years ago, a modest supply of Scotch, bourbon, gin, and vermouth would have sufficed for most occasions, but today the complete home bar will have a good selection of "white goods" such as vodka, rum, tequila, and, of course, white wine.

Vodka is now the single most popular liquor. To be prepared, you should stash away at least one premium variety (such as Stolichnaya, Finlandia, or Absolut) in the freezer for serving straight up or on the rocks. For mixed vodka drinks (Bloody Marys, screwdrivers, bullshots), keep some all-purpose domestic labels on hand such as Smirnoff, Popov, and Gordon's.

Bacardi remains the most popular individual brand in the country, proving that rum fanciers are very much alive and drinking well. Besides the usual white rum, aromatic dark rums (Barbancourt, Gosling) and crisp, medium-bodied gold rums (Myers, Mount Gay) are being served more frequently. Premium rums like these can be served straight up or on the rocks as an alternative to Scotch or in fresh-fruit daiquiris and other mixed drinks.

The resurgence of interest in Tex-Mex cuisine has made mastery of the Margarita a challenge for the home bartender. Tequila, the principal component, comes in three varieties: white or silver, gold, and *anejo* (aged). Premium tequilas from producers such as José Cuervo and Herradura can also be served straight up or on the rocks.

Although the fashion for gin has waned somewhat, there are still many people who prefer the traditional gin martini or a G&T —gin and tonic. Don't be caught empty-handed. Choose from such classic producers as Tanqueray, Beefeater, Bombay, and Gordon's.

Selecting a Scotch is not so simple. Basic Scotch is a blend of malted barley and neutral grain spirits. Popular labels include Johnnie Walker, Dewar's, and J&B. Premium blends benefit from containing more malt and from prolonged barrel aging (twenty-five years on the average) and cost considerably more, but can be savored like a fine cognac. Look for brands such as Chivas Royal Salute, Ballantine 30 Years, and Ambassador 25 Years.

To many whiskey aficionados, the only true Scotch is a single malt, made from 100 percent malted barley. Hailing from small independent distilleries in the Highlands, the Lowlands, Cabletown, and Islay, these Scotch whiskies provide a tour of Scotland in a glass. Glenlivet, Glenfiddich, Glenmorangie, Balvenie, Cardhu, and Macallans are a few of the better-known labels. Aged Irish whiskey, such as Old Bushmills Black Bush, is also enjoying a comeback. In the South, bourbon has never gone out of style, thanks in part to the success of Jack Daniels' "nat-ural" advertising campaign, and limited-production bourbons such as Maker's Mark, Benchmark, and the ubiquitous Wild Turkey have become nationwide hits.

Perhaps the single most important addition to the contemporary bar is white wine. While simple jug wine (*vin ordinaire*) will do, the best recourse is to stock up on generics, varietals, and estate bottlings in order to satisfy different tastes and occasions. Bone-dry domestic Chardonnay and Sauvignon Blanc and imported counterparts such as Macon Blanc, Sancerre, and Bordeaux Blanc (France) and fruity Pinot Grigios and Soave (Italy) can provide the foundation of a white wine cellar.

More and more Americans are savoring a fine *digestif* after a meal, perhaps a cognac, a liqueur, an exotic fruit brandy, or port. *Brandy* is a diminutive of the word *brandywine*, which means distilled (technically "burned") wine. For a brandy to be called cognac in France, it must have been produced in departments of Charente and Charente-Maritime (the capital of the region happens to be the town of Cognac).

By French law, no vintage dating of cognac is allowed. Since most cognacs are a blend of brandies of varying ages produced from the delimited districts (the best hail from the Grande or Petite Champagne regions), a system of stars and letters indicates the *minimum age* of the *youngest component* involved.

All three-star, VS (Very Superior), and VSP (Very Superior Pale) cognacs sold in America are no less than three years old and average up to five years of age. They may contain much older cognac. VO (Very Old), VSOP (Very Superior Old Pale) and Reserve cognacs have all been aged a minimum of four years. In practice, they average between ten and fifteen years old.

Special terms such as Vielle Réserve, Napoleon, Triomphe, Paradis, and XO (Extra Old) merely mean that the minimum age of the cognac is six years. In fact, such premium cognacs average twenty years and may contain cognac that is fifty or even one hundred years old. Some of the better-known cognac houses are Courvoisier, Delamain, Hennessy, Hine, Martell, and Rémy Martin.

Other prominent members of the brandy family are Calvados, Armagnac, and eaux-de-vie. Calvados is an apple-based brandy made in Normandy. Armagnac is a wine distillate produced in the southwest of France in a manner similar to cognac. It can be earthier and more aromatic in flavor. Vintage dating is allowed in Armagnac. Look for such producers as De Montal, Seme, and Samalens. Like cognac, Armagnac should ideally be served in a snifter at room temperature—warmed by the palm, never by a flame.

Eaux-de-vie, literally "waters of life," are colorless, fruit-infused brandies. Almost any fruit—pears, cherries, plums, raspberries—can be distilled into an eau-de-vie. They are expensive because it takes thirty pounds of cherries, for instance, to make one 750 ml bottle of kirsch. Serve well-chilled in a snifter. Look for labels from Brana, Jean Danflou, Schladerer, and Trimbach.

Port is a rich, long-lived, fortified wine produced in the Douro region of Portugal and then aged by established shippers in the town of Oporto. The best port from special vintages is bottled after two years in the barrel and aged for twenty years or more. Renowned producers include Taylor, Graham, Sandeman, and Ware.

The term *liqueur*, the shortened form of *liqueur de dessert*, has come to mean a cordial served after a meal. In theory a liqueur is a sweetened fruit- or herb-flavored spirit; in practice, the term is used to encompass any after-dinner drink.

Cream-based liqueurs, one of the latest additions to the cordial tray, made their appearance about a decade ago. They are made with fresh dairy cream and spirits. Bailey's Original Irish Cream launched the category. Other flavors of cream-based liqueurs include almond, chocolate, vanilla, and coffee.

## The Complete Bar

### Equipment

Bottle opener
Coasters
Corkscrew (easy-to-use model such as a Screwpull)
Champagne pliers (for stubborn corks)
Funnel
Ice bucket
Ice tongs
Knife and cutting board
Large mixing pitcher
Lemon/lime squeezer
Long-handled spoon
Measuring cup
Mixing glass
Napkins
Serving trays
Shaker/strainer
Trash can for empties
A good bartender's guide with drink recipes such as *Old Mr. Boston Bartender's Guide, The Indispensable Drinks Book,* or Lionel Braun's *Drink Directory*

### Optional

Ice pick
Ice cracker/crusher
Martini pitcher
Silver champagne bucket
Silver jiggers
Zester

### Aperitifs

1 case dry white wine (such as Mondavi Table Wine, Monterey Classic White, Sterling Sauvignon Blanc, Simi Chardonnay, Macon Blanc, Cavit Pinot Grigio)
6 bottles red wine (such as Beaujolais Duboeuf, Antinori Chianti, Marques de Caceros Rioja, Fetzer, or Sutter Home Zinfandel)
2 bottles sparkling wine (such as Korbel, Frexeinet, Perrier Jouet Brut Sauvage). Keep chilled in the refrigerator.

### Liquors and Other Wines

Vodka: 1 domestic, 1 premium
Rum: 1 light, 1 amber or dark
Tequila: 1 white, 1 aged (optional)
Gin: 1 imported
Whiskey: 1 Scotch (blended), 1 premium or single malt, 1 bourbon or Tennessee
Vermouth: 1 dry, 1 sweet
Sherry: 1 dry

### Mixers

Bottled water: Evian, Artesia (still), and Perrier or San Pelegrino (sparkling)
Soda/seltzer/tonic
Soft drinks
Fruit juices

### Liqueurs

| Type | Flavor |
|---|---|
| Amaretto | Almond |
| Anisette | Licorice |
| Benedictine | Cognac base |
| B&B | Benedictine and brandy |
| Chartreuse | Herbal |

| | | | | Parfait D'Amour | Violet/vanilla |
|---|---|---|---|---|---|

| | | | | |
|---|---|---|---|---|

Cassis — Blackcurrant
Cointreau — Intense orange
Curacao — Bitter orange
Crème de Menthe — Peppermint
Drambuie — Scotch base
Frangelico — Hazelnut/brandy
Glen Mist — Herbal/honey Scotch base

Grand Marnier — Orange/cognac
Jagemeister — Herbal
Kahlua — Coffee/cane spirit
Kummel — Caraway seed
Mandarine Napoleon — Tangerine/cognac
Nassau Royale — Spicy herbal
Ouzo — Anise

Parfait D'Amour — Violet/vanilla
Peter Heering — Cherry
Sambuca — Anise
Southern Comfort — Peach/bourbon
Strega — Herbal
Tia Maria — Coffee
Triple Sec — Orange

There are dozens of labels, both domestic and imported, to choose from. Some of the better known are Arrow, Bols, Jean Danflou, DeKuyper, Hiram Walker Leroux, Marie Brizard, Marnier-Lapostolle, Massenez, Regnier, and Zwack.

## Rules of Thumb for a Long Party

*Liquor.* A fifth of liquor (750 ml or 25.4 ounces) will make about 17 drinks using 1½ ounces per drink. But to be sure you won't run out, allow one bottle for every four drinkers.

*Wine.* A standard 750 ml bottle contains roughly four 6-ounce servings. Allow one bottle for every two guests who drink wine.

*Champagne.* Count on four 6-ounce glasses to the bottle. When served as an aperitif, allow one bottle for every two guests; after dinner, one bottle for every four guests.

*Liqueurs.* One bottle for every ten people.

# THE ADEPT BARTENDER

## Setting Up

Ice prepared in your home freezer can easily pick up odors from food. Commercially prepared ice cubes are generally crystal clear, odor free, and a good investment for a drink. You might want to buy enough ice to also chill the wine and champagne.

Place the ice and bottles in a washtub, utility sink, or lined garbage can. Remember to add cold water to speed up the cooling process. It usually takes less than an hour to chill wine and champagne on ice. (For small groups, you can cool a bottle of wine or champagne by placing it in the freezer for an hour.)

Many bartenders like to keep cocktails cold by chilling the glasses beforehand. The simplest way to chill a glass is to place it in the refrigerator for thirty minutes or in the freezer for five minutes (ten minutes if you want the glass itself to frost). You can also fill the glasses with ice cubes or cracked ice while you mix the drinks and discard the ice when you are ready to pour.

To sugar-frost a glass for a daiquiri, chill it and then rub the inside and top of the rim with a strip of lime peel. Dip the moistened rim into a bowl of superfine sugar, then lift the glass out and tap it gently to shake off the excess sugar. When making a Margarita, rub the rim with lime peel and dip into salt.

Whenever possible, use fresh fruits for drinks that call for fruit flavors. An orange, lemon, or lime may be softened by pressing down and rolling it on a hard surface such as a cutting board. This helps to break down the fibers and release the juice. In cutting lemon or lime peel, never include the white membrane; shave off only the colored surface in sections about 1 inch by ½ inch. Most important, squeeze only as much fresh juice as you need. Within an hour, juices can separate from the pulp and start to ferment.

## Storing and Serving Wines

Ideally, wine should be stored on its side in a temperature-controlled environment (55 degrees Fahrenheit at 40 percent humidity) to prevent premature aging and the spoilage that occurs when a cork dries out and oxygen seeps into the bottle. If you can't afford the luxury of a wine cellar, here are some com-monsense tips to prevent sour experiences: Keep wine away from all extremes of temperature and vibration, such as the stove, refrigerator, radiators, and air conditioners. A dark closet is a good bet.

White wines and champagnes should be served chilled—between 45 and 55 degrees. (The cooler the wine, the less obvious the taste. So if you're serving a nondescript jug wine, be sure it is very well chilled!) Light red wines such as Beaujolais also benefit from chilling to about 55 degrees. Robust reds require room temperature, European style, which means about 70, not 80 degrees. So in warm weather, refresh a fine red by placing it in the fridge for 40 minutes before serving.

Decanting wine—pouring it from the original bottle into another container before serving it—is generally recommended for two reasons: to remove cloudy sediment that precipitates as red wine matures; and to improve the bouquet and soften the taste of a young red wine. White wine rarely throws a deposit and almost never needs decanting.

Prior to decanting, the bottle should be

placed upright for at least two hours, preferably a day, to let the sediment settle. First uncork the bottle without disturbing the sediment. Remove the foil from the neck and wipe off any dust or deposit from the inner or outer rim. Place a flashlight or candle beneath the bottle as you start to pour in order to see the sediment as it approaches the neck. Be sure to hold the bottle firmly (label side up) and pour slowly in a continuous motion until the dark sediment reaches the neck or just a little remains in the bottle. Stop!

### Serving Beer

Beer should not be drunk directly from the bottle because its natural carbonation can be released directly into the stomach, causing bloating and general discomfort.

For the best results, beer should be served at about 42 degrees—not icy cold, because cooler temperatures will dull the taste buds. If it is stored over 80 degrees, a beer's natural ingredients begin to break down. (Unlike red wine, which can benefit from years of aging, the shelf life for most beers is about six months.) Overexposure to bright light will sour the hops and create an unpleasant odor. Beer should be poured directly into the center of a glass (not at an angle). This releases the carbonation, facilitates a fresh aroma and flavor, and allows the head to form properly.

### Opening and Serving Champagne

First remove the foil and untwist the loop of wire on the side of the cork so that you can remove the entire wire cage. (If the contents are too warm, or the champagne was bottled under too high an internal pressure, the cork and cage can fly off. So be careful to point the bottle away from you at all times.)

Now hold the bottle at an angle with the bottom toward your chest and the neck pointing away from your face, your guests, and any breakable objects. Grasp the cork with one hand and twist the bottle—*not the cork*—with the other hand. Gently ease out the cork so that it releases with a sigh, not a bang. As added insurance, hold a napkin over the cork. The effervescence, common to all good sparkling wine, will help expel the cork.

If the champagne begins to spew out, simply place the bowl of a spoon over the mouth of the bottle; never use your thumb. After

pouring each glass, turn the neck of the bottle to prevent drops from falling.

A word on correct champagne glasses. The saucer-bowled variety, popular at weddings and large receptions, tends to spill easily and, worse still, inhibits the flow of bubbles. Champagne devotees favor the flute, whose tulip-shaped bowl enhances the sparkling effervescence.

### Storing Leftovers

Spirits have a virtually unlimited shelf life, thanks to the distillation process and high alcohol content. Do recap your bottles to prevent the alcohol from evaporating. Port, although fortified, holds its own for only about two to three weeks when in a stoppered decanter.

Still wines start to deteriorate the moment they are uncorked and interact with the oxygen in the air. To retard the aging process, recork and place any half-full bottle—red or white—in the refrigerator. When dealing with a truly fine wine, decant leftovers into a smaller container to further minimize oxidation. This way, you can get an extra day or two's grace—and taste—out of your remnants.

An inexpensive little device known as a champagne recorker can be clamped down on the neck of an unfinished bottle of champagne to preserve the bubbles for an extra day's enjoyment. Be sure to refrigerate the champagne and plan to use it (perhaps in mimosas) within a day or two.

# PROVISIONS

## Equipment for a Cocktail Buffet for 75

### Bar

200 12-ounce all-purpose wine glasses (allow at least 2 glasses per person) *or* 100 8-ounce highball glasses and 100 12-ounce all-purpose goblets
2 ice tubs (to chill wine and champagne) per bar
1 plastic runner (to protect floor behind bar)
4 ice buckets (display champagne in one, ice drinks in the second)
4 bar pitchers
2 6-inch bowls per bar (for bar garnishes)

### Tables

2 8' x 2½' tables (to set up buffets)
1 6' x 1½' table (to set up bar)
6 24" round tables (cocktail tables for terrace)
24 white folding chairs (around cocktail tables)

### Cloths

84" round tablecloths (for cocktail tables)
8 72" x 120" tablecloths (2 per large table)
12 matching napkins (for bartender)

### Serving Trays and Equipment

16 14" round trays
2 large-handled trays
150 plates
100 napkins
100 knives and forks
Chafing dishes and Sterno
Trivets for hot dishes
1 trash can per bar

### Miscellaneous

2 large trash cans (keep in kitchen)
24 glass ashtrays
2 coat racks

## Liquor and Mixers for Cocktails for 75

4 liters Scotch
3 liters vodka
2 liters gin
1 liter rum
1 liter bourbon
1 750 ml vermouth
1 750 ml sherry
1 750 ml Dubonnet or Lillet
1 liter tequila (optional)
1 750 ml rye (optional)
2 cases dry white wine
6 bottles dry red wine
12 bottles beer
24 bottles sparkling water
1 case tonic
3 large cases club soda or seltzer
24 bottles mixers (ginger ale, Coca-Cola, 7-Up)
12 limes
12 lemons
Pitcher of ice water
Ice (1 pound per person)

### Notes:

1. Don't serve champagne unless you have enough (3 cases) for everyone.

2. In regions where wine is less popular, increase the quotient of vodka, Scotch, and rum. If your guests are largely wine drinkers, decrease the alcohol quotient and allow half a bottle of wine per person.

3. In the South, be sure to triple the amount of bourbon.

4. In summer months, double the amount of beer.

5. For more innovative cocktails, supply orange juice, Rose's lime juice, and tomato juice.

## Liquor and Mixers for a Blowout for 200

10 liters vodka
10 liters Scotch
6 liters gin
3 liters rum
3 liters bourbon
1 liter tequila
1 liter sherry
1 liter vermouth
1 750 ml Dubonnet or Lillet
1 750 ml rye
6 cases dry white wine
1 case dry red wine
48 bottles beer
5 cases sparkling water (5-ounce bottles)
5 large cases soda
2 cases tonic
48 bottles mixers (ginger ale, Coca-Cola, 7-Up, diet soda)
16 limes
16 lemons
Pitcher of ice water
Ice (1 pound per person)

## Help for a Crowd for Cocktails

| No. of Guests | Bartenders | Servers to Pass | Help for Buffet |
|---|---|---|---|
| 75 | 2 | 2 | 3 |
| 200 | 4 | 6–8 | 5 |
| 300 | 6 | 8–10 | 6 |
| 400 | 8 | 10–12 | 8 |

# THE INDISPENSABLE FLOWER PRIMER

## *FLOWERS AT A GLANCE*

*Key*

$ - Inexpensive

$$ - Moderately expensive

$$$ - Expensive

(F) - Fragrant

(P) - Poisonous

(O) - Unpleasant odor

### *Drying Methods*

H—*Hanging Method:* Cut the most perfect flowers prior to full bloom, tie them loosely in bunches, and hang them upside down in a warm, dry, dark area.

B—*Borax Method:* Fill an empty box with a mixture of ten parts white cornmeal to three parts borax, or three-fourths borax to one-fourth sand, and surround and fully cover the flower heads with the mixture. Stems are left exposed and upright. Dry for two to three weeks.

Silica gel may also be used. It is a chemical compound that helps flowers retain their bright color. This method is somewhat expensive, and any flower that can be dried with the borax method can be preserved with the silica gel.

G—*Glycerine:* Used for preserving foliage. Cut branches with leaves in the best condition. Hammer the stems and put in a solution of one-third glycerine to two-thirds water for about three weeks. Do not allow solution to touch leaves.

Selecting the right flowers is often as much of an art as arranging them. A trip to even the most exclusive florist need not be daunting once you're armed with the information you need. In many areas of the country flowers are available for sale on street corners, at gas stations, and in grocery stores. While the accessibility of flowers is greater than it has ever been before, the shopper must also have a sense of his or her needs in order to buy wisely. If you are having weekend guests, look for flowers that will last for at least three days. If you will be hosting several parties back to back, choose flowers that can easily be recycled.

*First Aid for Plant Poisonings*

If a plant part is swallowed or chewed:

1. Give one to two glasses of milk or water right away (unless the person cannot swallow, is in a coma, or is having a convulsion).
2. Then call the local Poison Information Center.
3. Have on hand at home syrup of Ipecac (ask your pharmacist for it) and Epsom salts. DO NOT USE either of these unless instructed to do so by the Poison Information Center.*

*Source: Poison Information Center, Children's Hospital, Birmingham, Alabama.

| Name | Color | Lasts (Days) | Months Available | Size | Conditioning | Cost |
|---|---|---|---|---|---|---|
| Acacia | Yellow | 3–5 | Nov.–May | Tiny pufflike flowers in clusters 8″–9″ long by 4″–5″ wide w/airy green leaves | Slice/split stems Dry: B | $$ |
| Agapanthus | Blue, white | 3–5 | Jun.–Oct. | 20″–30″ spidery clusters of 10–12 flowers at top of stem | Slice on diagonal | $$ |
| Allium | Purple, white | 10 | May–Nov. | 20″–30″ puffed ball. 7″ across at top of stem (giganticum to small white) | Slice on diagonal Dry: H | $$$ |
| Alstroemeria | Brick, white, pink, salmon, purple, yellow | 8 | Year round | Tall, slim stalk, 3–4 flowers 1″ in diameter, 3″–4″ across at top of stem | Slice on diagonal | $$ |
| Amaryllis | Red, variegated, pink | 8–10 | Sep.–Apr. | 20″–30″ tall, large, lily-like flower 5″–6″ across | Slice on diagonal | $$$ |
| Amaryllis (Belladonna Lily) (F) | Pink | 7–10 | Apr.–May Aug.–Nov. | 10″–14″ long with bent stems, 3–5 flowers, 3″ across at top of stem | Slice on diagonal | $$ |
| Anemone | Red, blue, magenta, white | 3–5 | Jan.–Aug. | 2½″ daisylike flower on short stem | Slice on diagonal | $ |
| Anthurium | Red, pink | 8–10 | Year round | Mini: 2½″ heart-shaped flowers; regular: 4″–5″ heart-shaped flowers | Slice on diagonal | $$ |
| Anthurium (Obaki) | White, variegated | 8–10 | Year round | 8″–10″ heart-shaped flowers | Slice on diagonal | $$$ |
| Artichoke (Globe)* | Blue | Up to 14 | Jun.–Oct. | 10″–18″ tall, 2″–4″ across, artichokelike base, puff flower | Slice on diagonal | $$ |
| Aster | Pink, purple, magenta, white | 8–10 | Jun.–Oct. | 10″–15″ tall, 2″ flower, 10–15 buds/flowers along stem | Hammer ends or split stems | $ |
| Azalea (P) | White, pink, magenta, red | 2–3 | Mar.–Apr. | Branches with several flowers 2″–5″ in diameter all over | Break stems, hammer ends | $$$ |
| Baby's Breath | White | 5–7 | Feb.–Oct. | Branches 12″–18″ long, many tiny flowers 1/16″–¼″ across | Slice on diagonal, keep bunched together Dry: H | $ |
| Bird of Paradise | Orange with touches of purple, yellow | 10–14 | Year round | 20″–30″ long, wide flower at top of stem resembles bird's head, 3″–4″ high by 8″–9″ wide | Slice on diagonal | $$ |
| Black-Eyed Susan | Yellow with black | 3–5 | Jun.–Aug. | Small, daisylike flower 1″ in diameter on slim 12″–36″ stem | Slice on diagonal Dry: B | $ |
| Bouvardia | White, pink | 3–5 | Year round | 10″–20″ stems with 3″–4″ cluster of flowers at top of stem | Slice on diagonal | $$ |

| Name | Color | Lasts (Days) | Months Available | Size | Conditioning | Cost |
|---|---|---|---|---|---|---|
| Calendula | Yellow, orange | 5–7 | Apr.–Aug. | Daisylike flowers 2″ in diameter on 6″–10″ stems | Slice on diagonal | $ |
| Calla Lily | White, pink, yellow | 5–7 | Apr.–Jun. Jul.–Nov. | Trumpetlike flower 3″–5″ high, 3″–4″ across, on 10″–15″ stem | Slice on diagonal | $ |
| Camellia | White, pink, red, variegated | 3–5 | Feb.–Mar. | Flower 2″–4″ diameter on short stems | Break and hammer stems Dry: B | $$$ |
| Campanula (Bell-flower) | Blue, white | 2–3 | Late summer | Profusions of 5-pointed flowers shaped like bell on stem with broad green leaves | Slice on diagonal. Remove all faded flowers and each bud should open out. | $ |
| Candy Tuft | White | 5–7 | Jun.–Aug. | 8″–12″ high with lots of small white flowers and green stems | Slice on diagonal | $ |
| Carnation | White, pink, red, yellow, salmon, variegated | 7–14 | Year round | Flowers 2″–3″ across on wiry stems 18″–24″ long | Slice on diagonal | $ |
| Carnation, Mini | Red, brick, white, pink, peach, lavender, salmon, purple, variegated | 7–9 | Year round | Sprays of 2–4 flowers 1½″ across on wiry stems 12″–18″ long | Slice on diagonal | $ |
| Cattail | Brown/wheat (green stem and leaves when growing) | 14 | Aug.–Sep. | 5′–8′ tall, long, sword-like 1″-wide leaves and brown cylindrical club at top of stem (½″ wide by 6″–8″ long) | Slice; spray tops with hairspray or lacquer to prevent bursting Dry: H | $$ |
| Chinese Lantern | Orange | 14 | Sep.–Dec. | Tall stems 14″–20″ high with pods ½″ across | Slice, split stem Dry: G | $$$ |
| Chrysanthemum | White, yellow, gold, purple, lavender, bronze | 10 | Year round | 3–7 flowers per stem, 1″–2½″ across, 18″–36″ long | Snap stems | $ |
| Cock's Comb | Red, pink, magenta, yellow | 7–10 | Jun.–Sep./ Oct | Short stem 8″–12″ high with flower 4″ across, undulating | Slice on diagonal Dry: H | $ |
| Cornflower | Blue, pink | 8–10 | Jun.–Aug. | Several daisylike flowers ½″ across on slender, delicate green stems | Slice on diagonal Dry: B | $ |
| Curly Willow | Natural, brown, bleached white | Indefinitely | Year round | 5′–9′ tall; sculptural bare branches | None Dry: H | $$$ |
| Daffodil (P) | Yellow, white, variegated | 2–3 | Jan.–May | 2″–3″ across on slender stems 10″–18″ high | Slice on diagonal Dry: B | $ |

| Name | Color | Lasts (Days) | Months Available | Size | Conditioning | Cost |
|---|---|---|---|---|---|---|
| Dahlia | Red, yellow, pink, white | 7–10 | Jul.–Oct. | Flowers 1½″–3″ across on 6″–10″ stems | Slice on diagonal Dry: B | $$ |
| Daisy (Shasta, Marguerite) | White | 5–8 | Apr.–Jul. | Flowers 2″–3″ in diameter on stems about 10″–16″ high | Slice or hammer | $ |
| Delphinium | White, blue, purple | 3–5 | Jun.–Aug. | Long spikes 18″–36″ with small flowers covering stem | Slice on diagonal Dry: B | $$ |
| Dogwood* | White | 2–3 | Mar.–Apr. | 5′–6′ tall ornamental branches; small flowers clustered in center of four large white bracts 1½″–3″ wide | Hammer stems | $$$ |
| Eremurus (Foxtail Lily) | Yellow, white | 4–5 | May–Sep. | 20″–30″ tall spike flowers opening 7″–10″ from top | Slice on diagonal | $$$ |
| Euphorbia | Yellow, white, orange | 3–4 | Jan.–Jun. | Many tiny flowers ¼″–½″ across along spray with green foliage 10″–14″ long | Slice on diagonal | $$$ |
| Forsythia | Yellow | 14 | Nov.–May | Branches 5′–6′ tall with tiny yellow flowers ½″ across, all over in clusters | Hammer stems | $$$ |
| Freesia (F) | Yellow, white, brick, pink, mauve, lavender | 3–4 | Year round | Stems 10″–18″ high, single and double blooms 3″–4″ across | Slice on diagonal | $$ |
| Gardenia (F) | White | 2–3 | Jun.–Sep. | Blooms 1½″–4″ across | Mist with water once cut | $$$ |
| Gerbera Daisy | Pink, white, red, salmon, yellow | 7 | Year round | Daisylike flower 2½″–3″ in diameter | Slice on diagonal | $$ |
| Ginger | Deep red | 10 | Tropical; almost year round | Tall spikes 22″–25″ high | Slice on diagonal | $$ |
| Gladiolus | White, pink, yellow, orange, red, salmon, purple, mauve, variegated | 5–7 | Year round | Spikes 3′–4′ tall with 1½″–2″ flowers all along | Slice on diagonal about 2″–3″ from bottom. Remove wilted blooms and others will replace them. | $ |
| Gladiolus, Mini | All colors, mostly variegated | 5–7 | Year round | 22″–25″ spikes with flowers all along stem | As above | $ |
| Gloriosa Lily | Red/yellow | 5–7 | Year round | Flowers 2″–3″ across, 2–3 on a stem | Slice on diagonal | $$$ |

* This is on the Garden Club of America's endangered species list, and therefore cuttings must come from your own garden.

| Name | Color | Lasts (Days) | Months Available | Size | Conditioning | Cost |
|---|---|---|---|---|---|---|
| Heather | Mauve | 10–14 | Apr.–Jul. | One type short stems with spiked flowers; other branched with tiny flowers | Slice on diagonal | $ |
| Holly Berry (P) | Red | 14–21 | Oct.–Dec. | 5"–15" branches with bright red berries and green leaves | Slice and split stems | $$ |
| Hyacinth (F) (P) | White, blue | 5–7 | Jan.–Apr. Nov.–Dec. | 4"–10" spikes with ½" flowers 3"–5" at top of stem | Slice on diagonal | $$$ |
| Hycinth, Grape | As above but miniatures | | | | | |
| Hydrangea (P) | Pink, blue, white | 3–5 | Jan.–Sep. | 7"–15" stem with huge pompomlike flowers 7"–9" diameter, made up of ½" blooms | Slice on diagonal Dry: H | $$ |
| Iris (P) | White, yellow, dark blue, light blue, purple | 3–5 | Year round | Open flower 4"–5" across, stems 20"–30" | Slice on diagonal | $ |
| Kangaroo Paw | Yellow/brown | 14 | Sep.–Feb. | 20"–30" branchy stems with brown and yellow flowers resembling paws | Slice on diagonal | $$$ |
| Larkspur | Violet, pink, blue | 3–5 | Jun.–Aug. | Medium spikes 9"–16" high with small, delicate flowers covering the stem (in the delphinium family) | Slice on diagonal Dry: B | $$ |
| Liatris | Purple | 7–10 | May–Dec. | 2'–3' spikes with tight spidery flowers at top | Slice on diagonal Dry: H | $$ |
| Lily | White, lavender | 7–10 | Nov.–May | Slim 20"–30" branches with flowers clustered in large 5"–7" spray at top | Slice and split | $$$ |
| Lily | * | 5–7 | Year round | 3"–7" flowers and buds topping a 15"–20" stem | Slice on diagonal | $$$ |
| Lily, Nerine | Red, pink, white | 7–10 | Jun.–Mar. | 15"–25" stems with clusters of 7–9 1" flowers 3"–5" across | Slice on diagonal | $$$ |
| Lily of the Valley (F) (P) | White | 2–3 | Feb.–Dec. | Short stems with cluster of small flowers at top | Usually in see-through bags; spray with water | $$ |
| Marigold | Yellow, orange | 5–7 | Jun.–Sep. | 3" blooms on 10"–13" stem | Hammer stems Dry: B | $ |
| Montebretia | Orange | 3–5 | Jun.–Oct. | 15"–20" stems, cluster of lilylike flowers at top | Slice on diagonal | $$ |

* Yellow (Connecticut King), orange (Enchantment), orange (Firecracker), white (Auratum), pink (Rubrum).

| Name | Color | Lasts (Days) | Months Available | Size | Conditioning | Cost |
|------|-------|--------------|------------------|------|--------------|------|
| Narcissus (Paperwhite) (F) | White/yellow | 3–4 | Dec.–Apr. | 7″–12″ stems, clusters of small flowers at top | Slice on diagonal Dry: B | $ |
| Nasturtium | Yellow, orange, red | 2–3 | Apr.–Jul. | 1″–1½″ flowers with rounded green leaves | Slice on diagonal | $ |
| Orchid (various) | * | 5–7 | Year round | Up to 10 1½″–2″ diameter blossoms on 10″–15″ bending stem | Slice on diagonal | $$– $$$ |
| Peach Blossom | Pink | 10–14 | Mar.–Apr. | 3′–5′ branches with ½″–1″ flowers all over | Hammer stems | $$$ |
| Pear Blossom (O) | White | 10–14 | Mar.–Apr. | Tall branches with 1″ flowers up and down stems | Hammer ends | $$$ |
| Peony | White, pink, magenta | 5–7 | Mar.–Jun. | Tight bud can be 1½″–2″, fullblown flower 5″–6″ on 8″–15″ stems, pods along stem | Slice on diagonal | $$ |
| Pepper (Ornamental) | Yellow, orange, red | 14–21 | Sep.–Dec. | 7″–15″ stems with pepperlike 1½″–2″ bloom | Slice on diagonal Dry: H | $$$ |
| Pineapple | Yellow/brown with pink and greenish leaves | 14–21 | Dec.–Mar. | 5″–9″ high pineapple on stalk | Slice on diagonal Dry: H | $$$ |
| Poinsettia (P) | Red, pink, white, variegated | 7–10 | Nov.–Dec. | 7″–10″ across spread of leaves | Slice on diagonal | $– $$$ |
| Poppy | Almost every color | 2–4 | May–Jun. | Varies in height (12″–24″ tall); single flower with 5 petals (3″ to 5″ in diameter) on a single stem; feathery leaves | Burn stem, plunge in water | $$ |
| Protea | Pinkish, gray/pink, brown | 10–14 | Year round | 6″–15″ high, flower 2″–3″ in diameter; large protea 8″–10″ in diameter | Slice on diagonal Dry: H | $$$ |
| Pussy Willow | Brown/silver gray | 14–21 | Year round | 3′–6′ branches with tiny velvety puffs up and down stem | Hammer stems Dry: H | $$$ |
| Queen Anne's Lace | White | 3–5 | Jun.–Aug. | Lacy flowers on 10″–20″ wiry stems; cluster of flowers 2″–3″ across | Slice on diagonal Dry: B | $ |
| Quince (Flowering) | Red, white | 10–14 | Jan.–May | 3′–4′ branches; 1″–1½″ flowers all over | Hammer stems | $$$ |

* Brick, (*Cymbidium*), green (*Cymbidium*), white and lavender (*Phalenopsis*), purple (*Dendrobian*), yellow (*Oncidium*), pink (*Cattleya*), white (*Dendrobian*).

| Name | Color | Lasts (Days) | Months Available | Size | Conditioning | Cost |
|------|-------|--------------|------------------|------|--------------|------|
| Ranunculus (Buttercup) | White, yellow, pink | 3–5 | Year round | 7″–12″ undulating stems with feathery leaves; flowers about 1½″ in diameter | Slice on diagonal | $$ |
| Rose | * | 3–7 | Year round | 12″–30″ stems, 1½″–2″ flowers; also medium, small, and sweetheart | Slice on diagonal, remove thorns and lower leaves Dry: H or B | $$ |
| Safflower | Orange/yellow | 10–14 | Jun.–Sep. | 20″–30″ stems with orange and yellow puffs of flowers at tip | Hammer stems Dry: H | $ |
| Snapdragon | Yellow, pink, salmon, brick, white, red | 3–5 | Jun.–Sep. | 20″–30″ stems with 1″–1½″ flowers along stalk | Slice on diagonal | $$ |
| Star of Bethlehem (P) | White | 10–14 | Jun.–Dec. | Tiny starlike flowers forming inverted cone; stems 8″–12″ long | Slice on diagonal | $ |
| Statice | Blue, purple, white, yellow | 14–21 | Summer | Tiny flowering clusters on 12″–18″ stem | Slice on diagonal Dry: H | $ |
| Stock (F) | White, purple, yellow, pink | 3–4 | Feb.–Aug. | 12″–18″ stems with 5″–6″ spikes of 1″ florets | Slice and crush stems | $$ |
| Sunflower | Yellow/brown center | 14–21 | Aug.–Oct. | Flower 5″–20″ across, stems 10″–6′ tall | Cut and hammer stems | $$$ |
| Sweet William | Mixed colors from red to white | 10–14 | Apr.–Jul. | 8″–14″ high stems with cluster of 15–20 flowers at top of stem | Slice on diagonal | $ |
| Torch Lily (P) | Red/yellow, orange/yellow, blue | 10–14 | May–Oct. | 10″–30″ stems with conelike flower | Slice on diagonal | $$$ |
| Tuberose (F) | White | 7–10 | Dec.–Aug. | 7″–12″ stems with 2″ high tight flowers | Slice on diagonal | $$ |
| Tulip | Red, pink, yellow, purple, lavender, white, orange, apricot, variegated | 3–5 | Nov.–May | 12″–24″ stems with 1″–3″ diameter bell-shaped flower | Slice on diagonal | $$ |
| Yarrow | White, yellow | 10–14 | May–Dec. | Tall, thin stalk with single 2″–4″ flowers | Hammer stem Dry: H | $ |
| Zinnia | Red, white, yellow, pink, purple, shades in between | 3–5 | Apr.–Aug. | 1″–4″ daisylike flowers on 5″–12″ stem | Slice on diagonal Dry: B | $ |

* Red (*Baccara*), pink (*Carina*), white (White Masterpiece), yellow (Diana), lavender (Sterling Silver).

# FLOWERS BY THE SHADE

## Blue

Agapanthus
Anemone
Artichoke (Globe)
Cornflower
Delphinium
Hyacinth
Hydrangea
Iris
Statice

## Brick

Alstroemeria
Carnation
Chrysanthemum
Cock's comb (Celosia)
Cymbidium orchid
Freesia
Snapdragon

## Brown

Cattail
Curly willow
Kangaroo paw
Pineapple with pink and green
Pussy willow with silver gray

## Green

Bells of Ireland
Cymbidium orchid
Gladiolus
Hydrangea

## Lavender

Allium
Carnation
Cattleya orchid
Chrysanthemum
Cymbidium orchid
Delphinium
Freesia

Gladiolus
Heather
Phalaenopsis orchid
Poppy
Rose
Slipper orchid
Stock
Tulip

## Magenta

Anemone
Aster
Azalea
Carnation
Cock's comb (Celosia)
Dendrobium orchid
Gerbera daisy
Peach blossom
Peony (light and dark)
Poppy
Tulip
Zinnia

## Orange

Bird of paradise
Calendula
Chinese lantern
Enchantment lily
Euphorbia
Firecracker lily
Gerbera daisy
Gladiolus
Marigold
Monbretia
Nasturtium
Ornamental pepper
Poppy
Rose
Safflower
Torch lily
Tulip
Zinnia

## Peach

Gerbera daisy*
Lily
Poppy
Protea
Rose

## Pink

Alstroemeria
Amaryllis
Amaryllis belladonna
Anthurium
Azalea
Bouvardia
Calla lily
Camellia
Cattleya orchid
Carnation
Cornflower
Dahlia
Flowering quince
Freesia
Gerbera daisy
Gladiolus
Hyacinth
Hydrangea
Nerine lily
Peach blossom
Poinsettia
Poppy
Protea
Ranunculus
Rose
Rubrum lily
Snapdragon
Stock
Tulip
Zinnia

*Gerbera comes in all shades. Take along a swatch of your wallpaper or a paint chip to see which matches or blends best.

## Purple

Alstroemeria
Anemone
Aster
Chinaberry
Delphinium
Dendrobium orchid
Gladiolus
Iris
Liatris
Lilac
Poppy
Statice
Stock
Tulip
Zinnia

## Red

Amaryllis
Anemone
Anthurium
Camellia
Carnation
Cock's comb (Celosia)
Dahlia
Freesia
Gerbera daisy
Ginger
Gladiolus
Gloriosa lily
Holly berry
Nerine lily
Poppy
Quince (flowering)
Rose
Sweet William (red, pink, white, all variations)
Tulip
Zinnia

**Tomato Red**

Anthurium
Azalea
Bouvardia
Camellia
Carnation
Gerbera daisy
Gladiolus
Gloriosa lily
Holly berry
Nasturtium
Ornamental pepper
Poinsettia
Poppy
Rose
Tulip
Zinnia

**White**

Agapanthus
Alstroemeria
Amaryllis
Anemone
Anthurium
Aster
Auratum lily
Baby's breath
Bouvardia
Calla lily
Camellia
Candy tuft
Carnation
Cattleya orchid
Chrysanthemum
Curly willow (bleached)
Dahlia
Daisy
Delphinium
Dogwood
Erasmus
Euphorbia
Freesia
Gardenia
Gerbera daisy
Gladiolus
Grape hyacinth
Hyacinth
Hydrangea
Lilac
Lily of the valley
Marguerite daisy
Narcissus
Queen Anne's lace
Quince
Pear blossom
Peony
Poinsettia
Poppy
Ranunculus
Rose
Snapdragon
Star of Bethlehem
Statice
Stock
Tuberose
Tulip
Yarrow
Zinnia

**Yellow**

Acacia
Alstroemeria
Anemone
Black-eyed Susan
Calendula
Calla lily
Chrysanthemum
Cock's comb (Celosia)
Connecticut king lily
Daffodil
Dahlia
Eremerus
Euphorbia
Forsythia
Freesia
Gerbera daisy
Gladiolus
Iris
Marigold
Narcissus
Oncidium orchid
Ornamental pepper
Poppy
Ranunculus
Rose
Snapdragon
Statice
Stock
Sunflower
Tulip
Yarrow
Zinnia

## FLOWER-ARRANGING TOOLS

*Basket, old suitcase,* fishing tackle box, or doctor's bag to hold the equipment.

*3 very sharp knives* kept on a magnetic knife bar. The two small knives are used to cut flowers on an angle; the large knife is used for cutting woody stems (such as forsythia and peach) and oasis (see below).

*Hammer and small cutting board* to smash woody stems so they will accept water.

*Clippers*—sharp, strong, and well oiled— for cutting greens and stems.

*Oasis,* which comes in block form, is invaluable for holding plant materials. It can be cut to any desired shape and size with a knife. Light green oasis absorbs water instantly and is used for smaller arrangements. The dark green variety requires several hours of soaking but will hold heavier materials. It must be secured in the container with stickum or adhesive florist's tape. Before it goes into the container, be sure it will fit the vase properly.

*Adhesive florist's tape* holds the oasis in the container. Cut into strips and stretch from one side of the container to the other, over the oasis.

*Stickum* is a strong adhesive used at the base of the container. Put long strips at the bottom of the container, then the oasis, and press down. It can also be used to hold greens to the sides of objects, such as votive candles.

*Glue* (Elmer's is fine) is used to stick leaves and ribbon to plastic containers.

*Wire* can be obtained in various sizes from fine to heavy.

*Florist's tape,* available in brown or green, is used to cover wire, stakes, and tubes.

*Raffia* can be used to tie flowers together. This palm fiber looks a little like straw and comes in long, thin strands.

*Water vials* are used to give each flower its own source of water. They are small, tapered plastic containers with rubber caps forming watertight seals around the stems. They can be disguised by covering with moss and tying with raffia.

*Frogs* (pinholders) come in all sizes. Use stickum to attach them to the vase.

*Spray bottle* or atomizer is needed to spray arrangement with water to preserve it.

*Small bottle of bleach.* Mix 1 teaspoon in a quart of clear water to keep the water clean by arresting the growth of bacteria. This will lengthen the life of the flowers. Bleach should be put in small vases with an eye dropper.

*Small bottle of ammonia* and various sizes of brushes are invaluable tools for cleaning out vases.

*Large buckets* or a deep sink for arranging the flowers. Have lots of plastic liners available to fit into your good vases to hold the water.

### Accessories

An assortment of smooth river rocks, colored and clear marbles, or seashells to anchor flowers in the bottom of clear vases. Wooden stands to elevate the vases.

Rolls of ribbon in all colors and textures for making bows on baskets, for tying around napkins, and for party favors.

Fabrics in solids, prints, and geometric designs, such as leftover drapery or upholstery material, can be wrapped around vases for an accent, used as a runner, or cut in shapes as place mats.

Mosses—sphagnum and Spanish—are great for covering up the mechanics of an arrangement.

Curly willow (bleached or natural) in several heights. The nine-foot variety can be used to make fantasy trees; the two-foot length will add a new dimension to plain arrangements.

Plastic foam can be cut into shapes such as hearts and letters and used as a base for a dried-flower arrangement.

## PRESERVING AND HARDENING PLANT MATERIALS

1. Pick flowers with the longest possible stems.
2. In the garden, always use sharp, clean clippers or scissors and make a clean cut.
3. Have a bucket of water into which you can immediately plunge your freshly cut stems.
4. Cut in the early morning or in the evening and let the flowers stand in water for several hours before arranging them.
5. Before arranging, cut the stems with a sharp knife under water, at an angle, to prevent air from getting into the stem. Water will fill the stem and seal the end. For stems with a milky fluid (dahlias, poppies), seal their ends with a candle flame and then dip the ends into boiling water. Woody stems need to be split four ways with clippers or a knife and smashed with a hammer.
6. Remove the bottom leaves from the stems.
7. Add drops of bleach or clear mouthwash to the water to kill any bacteria that might be in it. This will also keep the water from discoloring.
8. Always replenish the water in arrangements daily because the flowers will absorb a lot in the first few days.

Always check with a reliable gardening authority (perhaps a landscape architect or local nursery owner) in your part of the country before planting. He or she can tell you how to prepare the soil and how to maintain the plants you've chosen, as well as where to position plants so they look the most interesting. Betsy Bloomingdale, noted bi-coastal hostess, lecturer, and patron of the arts, says her greatest joy is growing, picking, and arranging flowers from her own carefully planned garden so that she can make the setting as beautiful as possible for her guests —truly a personal statement. Beverly White has designed her Palm Beach entertaining spaces around an outdoor terraced dance floor and an English formal garden.

Your local U.S. Department of Agriculture Extension Service is also a valuable resource and has many free brochures specifically for plants in your area. Make your garden work for you and remember that shape, color, and texture are very important. Be sure to choose colors that will work in your home's color scheme. Personal taste is the key here— choose what you like best and feel comfortable arranging. If you have only a small space, you can grow a variety of greens— fern, coleus, eucalyptus, ivy, philodendron —then add some flowering plants like begonia, geranium, and gerbera daisy, which all have interesting green leaves you can use whether the plant is in bloom or not. To complete the arrangement, you can add flowers from the florist.

Be sure to leave space for plants to develop and allow for adding colorful annuals, biennials, and bulbs so you'll have variety and the longest flowering period.

The following lists are suggestions for plants, both indoor and outdoor, that are particularly useful in flower arrangements.

## Greens for Your Cutting Garden

Aspidistra
Boxwood
Caladium
Camellia leaf
Coleus
Eucalyptus
Ferns, especially Boston and maidenhair
Galax
Gerbera daisy leaf
Holly
Ivy
Japanese yew
Magnolia leaf
Palm frond
Pittesporum
Rhododendron
Scotch broom

## Foliage House Plants

Asparagus fern: *Plumosus* with ferny fronds; *sprengeri* with pine-needle type leaves.
Aspidistra: Glossy, spear-shaped, broad leaves, green or striped with whitish lines.
Begonia: Large heart-shaped leaves with irregular edges; patterns with purple, red, or white.
Croton (*Codiaeum*): Glossy broad or narrow leaves; patterned, striped, or flecked with yellow, orange, or combination of both.
Coleus: Heart-shaped leaves splashed with yellow, green, red, purple, brown, or black; toothed edges.
Dieffenbachia: Large paddlelike leaves, mottled with green and white.
Ficus: *Ficus elastica* (rubber plant) with broad, pointed, glossy leaves on central stem; *Ficus pumila* (weeping fig) with heart-shaped leaves.

English ivy (*Hedera helix:*) Glossy, dark green, pointed leaves on a trailing stem; poisonous.
Philodendron: Large glossy leaves with different shapes.
Sansevieria (Mother-in-law's tongue): Sword-shaped; variegated, striped, or spattered leaves.
Wandering Jew (*Tradescantia*): *Fluminensis* with silver and green striped leaves; *blossfeldiana* with boat-shaped leaves, dark purple underneath.

## Ferns

*Adiantum* (maidenhair fern)
*Asplenium* (bird's nest fern)
*Nephrolepsis* (bladder fern)
*Pteris* (ribbon fern)

## Flowering House Plants

African violet
Azalea (poisonous)
Begonia
Bromeliad
Cactus
Christmas cherry
Chrysanthemum
Cyclamen (poisonous)
Exacum
Geranium
Gloxinia
Hydrangea (poisonous)
Impatiens
Kalanchoe
Orchid
Pepper plant (Capsicum)
Shrimp plant
Any of the bulbs, such as
narcissus, freesia, and tulips.

# *Appendix C*
# CARING FOR YOUR FAVORITE THINGS

There are those people who spend their lives with their linens packed away, their best china gathering dust in the cupboard, their silver locked in a safe, and whole rooms of their houses locked up —never to be used for fear that something might get soiled or broken.

Relax and enjoy what you have. Be sensible—don't use damask napkins at a barbecue, but do treat your guests to your lovely things. After all, entertaining is sharing those things you love best.

By following a few careful instructions, you can use your best things with ease. There are plenty of fine linens in use today that have been around for a hundred years or more, and they were preserved without the benefit of the knowledge and products of today.

## Fabrics and Linens
Bryce Reveley, noted fabric conservator and owner of the New Orleans textile conservation firm Gentle Arts, cautions: "Fine fabrics are not redeemable, so never take chances. It is better to do nothing to the fabric than to do the wrong thing. When in doubt, consult a professional textile conservator who can offer advice about treat-ment." If you don't know of a textile conservator in your area, contact a local museum, a historical society, or the Smithsonian Institution in Washington, D.C., for the names of persons you could consult.

*Never try to remove any stain until you have tested the fabric to be certain that it is colorfast.* If possible, rinse all colored cotton table linens in salt in the washing machine before you use them to keep them from running and fading when washed. This particularly applies to linens from India. Rather than ruin a piece of linen by improper or overzealous spot removal, put it aside and use it at your place at the table.

If you use heirloom linens, try not to serve red wine, gravy, or foods with tomato sauces, which can irreversibly stain. Try to keep smokers away from fine linens too. If a tablecloth does have a burn hole in it, arrange the plates or centerpiece to hide the problem.

Never store heirloom linens in cedar chests, plastic bags, tissue paper, cardboard boxes, or wooden drawers because the acid in these products causes spotting. Use old natural-fiber sheets and pillowcases or washed, unbleached muslin. Then the linens can be stored in boxes but not in the attic.

## STAIN REMOVAL

### Fabrics

| Stain | Treatment |
|---|---|
| Beer | Sponge with soap and water. |
| Blood | Wash in cold water (never warm) or hydrogen peroxide. |
| Butter/margarine | Wet the fabric thoroughly. Gently rub a scouring cleanser, such as Comet or Ajax (which contain bleach), into the stain. Let it set until the stains are gone. For colored fabrics, use a small amount of cleaning fluid and wash with detergent. |
| Candle wax | Scrape off the wax with a dull knife. Put the cloth between two white paper napkins or clean brown grocery bags and press with a warm iron. Sponge off the spot with a grease solvent. If the fabric is sturdy, stretch it over a pan and pour boiling water on the spot from a great distance. Then wash with detergent. |

322

| | |
|---|---|
| Catsup/tomato sauce | Sponge with cool water. Let stand for several hours. Use a detergent and work the spot in the same direction. Sponge with cold water and rinse. |
| Chewing gum | Put the fabric in a plastic bag and put in the freezer. Once frozen, the gum can be chipped off. Or rub the gum with Energine (mineral spirits). |
| Chocolate | Apply glycerine to the spot and rub gently. Wash with plain, cool water. |
| Coffee | Soak in one part vinegar to four parts water. Hang the fabric in the sun. |
| Fingernail polish | Sponge the stain with acetate, amyl acetate, or fingernail polish remover. |
| Grass | Make a paste of water and powdered detergent. Rub the stain and rinse. If this doesn't work, try alcohol. |
| Grease and oil | Make a paste of water and powdered detergent. Rinse in hot water. If that doesn't work, make a paste of unscented talcum powder and cleaning fluid. Put it on the spot and let it dry. Brush off and wash in hot water. |
| Ink (water soluble) | Soak in a mixture of detergent and water. |
| Ink (ballpoint) | Apply warmed (not hot) glycerine with a cotton swab. The stain can also be removed with amyl acetate or acetone. (Don't do this if the fabric contains Dynel, acetate, or Arnel.) |
| Lipstick | Rub with glycerine and set aside. Wash with detergent or use alcohol or hydrogen peroxide and wash. |
| Mildew | If the fabric is durable, use X-14 commercial mildew remover. Or rub salt and lemon juice into the stain and place the fabric in the sun. |
| Mud | Allow the mud to dry. Brush off as much as you can. Soak in cold water, then wash in detergent. |
| Mustard | Rub glycerine into the spot. Wash in detergent or make a paste of detergent and water and leave overnight. |
| Red wine | If the fabric is sturdy and washable, stretch it over a pot and carefully pour boiling water through it from a great height, or douse the fabric with club soda. Alternatively, apply hydrogen peroxide or bleach to the stain with a dropper. |
| Scorch | Pour club soda on the stain immediately. If this is not available, sponge the fabric with one part vinegar to two parts water. |
| Tea | Soak the fabric in one teaspoon of borax to one cup of water. Rinse in boiling water. Hydrogen peroxide may also work. |
| Tobacco | Apply rubbing alcohol with a piece of cotton. Wash with detergent and water. |

## Wood

| | |
|---|---|
| White spot caused by alcohol, water, or hot objects | Apply mayonnaise and rub it in hard. Apply more mayonnaise and let stand for one hour. Wipe clean. |
| Candle wax | Let it sit overnight. Put a piece of aluminum foil over the wax. Dip a cloth in very hot water, then lay it on top of the foil for a few minutes. After the wax is soft, just lift off the foil. Then rub the area with a facial tissue to remove the rest of the wax. Or, if the furniture is not veneered, apply a piece of brown paper and iron with a warm iron. The paper will blot up the wax. |
| Crayon marks | Put paste wax on a cloth and rub; wipe off. For crayon on woodwork, soak a soft cloth with kerosene and rub. |

## Crystal Goblets and Vases

| | |
|---|---|
| Calcium buildup | Put crystal in sink in 2 cups of bleach mixed with ¾ cup of water. Let sit overnight; rinse well. |

| | |
|---|---|
| Dishwasher film | Put a bowl containing 1 cup of bleach in the bottom of the dishwasher. Run through wash cycle but do not dry. Refill the bowl with 1 cup vinegar and let run through whole cycle. This removes film from both dishes and dishwasher. *Do not use on silver, brass, or aluminum dishes.* |

### Formica and Micarta

| | |
|---|---|
| Spots | Pour rubbing alcohol on surface, spread evenly, and let sit for one minute. Add bleach to alcohol, spread, and let sit one more minute. Rinse with water. Or mix one part water and one part vinegar, spread all over, and let sit one minute. Rinse with water. |

### Sinks

| | |
|---|---|
| Stains | Mix scouring powder and water into a thick paste. Spread over area, rub, leave overnight. Rinse with water. |

### Toilets

| | |
|---|---|
| Rings | Rings result from a buildup of mineral deposits. Use a liquid rust remover after lowering the water line. Or lower the water line and use a fine grade of sandpaper to remove ring. (Try dampening the sandpaper.) |

### Carpets

| | |
|---|---|
| Cigarette hole | Camouflage it. Cut away the burned fibers, then cut a few fibers from a hidden part of the carpet. Glue them to the spot with white household glue. Use tweezers to make the fibers stand up. Let dry. |
| Red wine | Soak it up immediately. Apply club soda or shaving cream; let stand for a few minutes, then wipe up and rinse with plenty of water. |

### Marble

| | |
|---|---|
| Stains—tea, coffee, and soft drinks not containing citric acid | Wash with clear water. (Sometimes a little ammonia helps.) Bleach with a poultice of hydrogen peroxide and a few drops of ammonia. |
| Etchings—iodine, beer, fruit juices, vinegar, tomato juice, catsup, horseradish, mustard, wine, Worcestershire sauce | Wash, sand if necessary, and polish with putty powder. |
| Stain and etch—ink, grape juice, vinegar (sometimes), soft drinks containing citric acid | Wash, bleach, sand if necessary, and polish. |
| Oil stains—hand creams, salad, oil, milk, cream, butter, margarine, peanut butter | Wipe stain with cloth dampened with ammonia. Apply poultice with equal parts amyl acetate and acetone. Follow with a poultice of hydrogen peroxide and ammonia. |
| Oil and etch—salad dressings | Same as oil stains. After stain is removed, polish with putty powder. |

# Appendix D
# NAPKIN FOLDS WITH FLAIR

A pretty table setting can make any meal an occasion. For that added pizzazz, buy a dozen cotton napkins in complementary colors and use them to brighten an informal meal.

Start with a clean, freshly pressed, lightly starched napkin. (Keep your napkins folded in half when storing.) If all else fails, tie a piece of ribbon around the napkin or stick a flower in it.

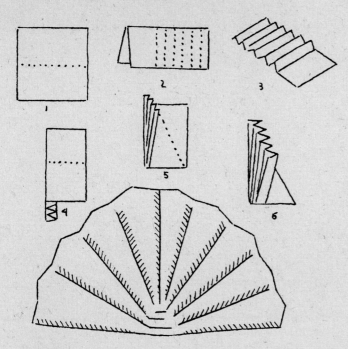

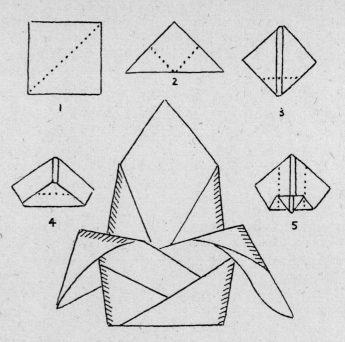

### Fan Fold
1. Halve napkin.
2. Accordion-pleat three-quarters of the length, creasing well.
3. End folds so that all pleats are on the bottom.
4. With the unpleated section on your right, back-fold napkin in half with gathered pleats on the outside and pointing up.
5. Fold unpleated section diagonally and tuck into pleats to form a stand.
6. Set on plate and spread fan.

### Scandia Fold
1. Halve napkin diagonally.
2. Front-fold two bottom points to meet top point.
3. Front-fold resulting bottom point to one inch below top point.
4. Reverse-fold bottom point down to meet bottom edge of napkin.
5. Back-fold, tucking sides into one another to form a circle.
6. Stand napkin up, adjusting two front points as shown.

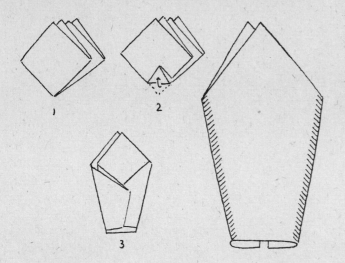

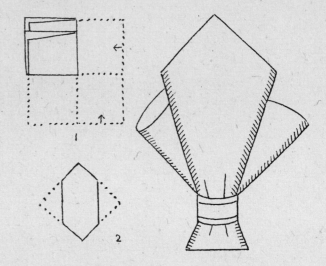

## Folded Napkin

1. Fold the napkin into quarters.
2. Turn up the bottom corner.
3. Fold into thirds.
4. Turn the napkin over and lay it flat.

## The Lily

1. With right side down, fold into quarters.
2. Turn over with ornamented point up.
3. Fold back left and right corners.
4. Pleat softly and even folds to shape.
5. Slip on napkin ring.

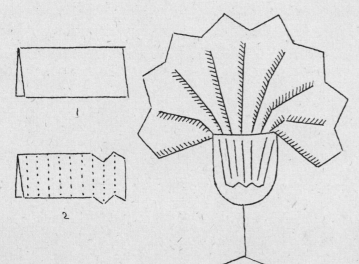

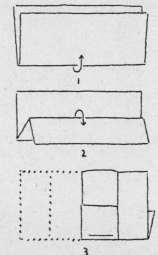

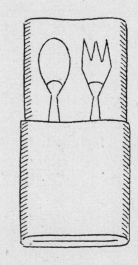

## Fan in Goblet

1. Fold the napkin in half.
2. Pleat in one-inch accordion pleats all the way to the top.
3. Slip one end into a glass and allow the other to open up.

## Cutlery Holder

1. Fold the napkin in half.
2. Fold the top flap back one half.
3. Turn the napkin over, fold it into quarters, and insert utensils.

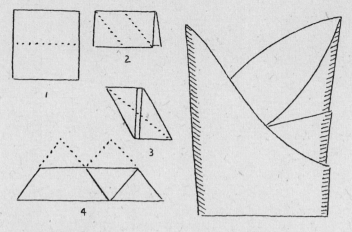

## Double-Peak Fold

1. Halve napkin.
2. Front-fold lower left corner and upper right corner toward center.
3. Pick up napkin and back-fold in half along the longest dimension. Crease fold well.
4. Pull up peaks, one in front and one in back.
5. Tuck ends into one another.

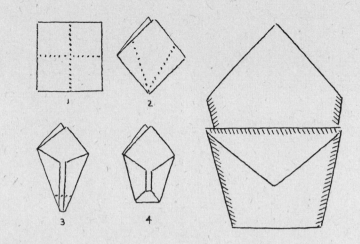

## Basket Fold

1. Quarter napkin.
2. Front-fold outer points to form a cone.
3. Front-fold tip of cone.
4. Turn napkin over and place on plate.
5. Turn down two points to form pocket for flowers, breadsticks, or silverware.

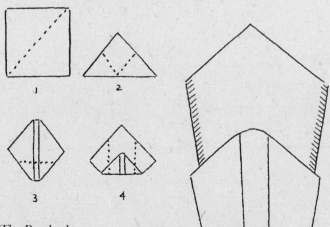

## The Rosebud

1. Halve napkin diagonally.
2. Front-fold bottom points to meet top point.
3. Back-fold bottom point of napkin as indicated.
4. Turn napkin over, tucking side points into each other to form a stand.

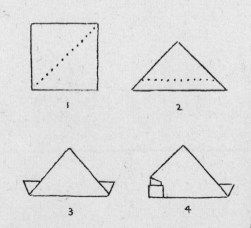

## Candle Fold

1. Halve napkin diagonally.
2. Back-fold bottom of napkin two inches or more to get a candle that is not too tall.
3. Starting at one end, roll napkin fairly tight.
4. Tuck remaining flap into bottom fold.

# Appendix E

# WEDDING AND BIRTHDAY GIFTS

The old adage that to give is more blessed than to receive has obviously been promoted by those with the imagination, the intuition, and the means to give just the right gift every time. Big occasions seem to cry out for memorable gifts, yet your thoughtful offering often misses its mark and ends up in the attic.

Keep gifts simple. If you want to give monogrammed towels, give the towels first and let the recipient choose the color and the style of the monogram. Jacqueline Onassis once gave a friend a 60 by 40 inch Venetian, hand-painted book filled with blank pages. It is the perfect guest book. Another couple gave their best friends a blank canvas and a frame and offered to retain their favorite artist to paint anything the couple requested.

## Wedding Anniversary Gifts

| | | |
|---|---|---|
| First | Paper | Stationery, book, picture album, nice fat check—or have a star named after the couple. |
| Second | Cotton | Table linens, sheets, towels, cotton rug, place mats, napkins, a new set of tennis sweaters, a specially designed T-shirt. |
| Third | Leather | Desk set with blotter, leather writing case, briefcase, jacket, coat. |
| Fourth | Fruit | Subscription to Fruit of the Month Club, fruit tree for the garden, Steuben fruit. |
| Fifth | Wood | Carved box, lap desk, chopping block, redwood lumber to make a deck, antique furniture. |
| Sixth | Iron | Fireplace accessories, someone to come and do the ironing, black iron skillet. |
| Seventh | Copper | Pot, tray, bowl for beating egg whites, weathervane. |
| Eighth | Bronze | Trip to the beach to turn that color, a favorite object bronzed, sculpture. |
| Ninth | Pottery | Ceramic serving piece, mug, sculpture for the garden. |
| Tenth | Tin | Waste basket, tea caddy, Mexican tin ornaments. |
| Eleventh | Steel | Set of flatware, gourmet knives, cookware, antique sword. |
| Twelfth | Silk | Tie, scarf, genuine Chinese silkscreen, framed designer scarf. |
| Thirteenth | Lace | Linens trimmed in lace, antique doilies, framed antique lace collar. |
| Fourteenth | Ivory | Decorative box, ivory-handled serving pieces. |

| | | | | | | |
|---|---|---|---|---|---|---|
| Fifteenth | Crystal | Vase, dessert plate, glasses, objet d'art. | | Fortieth | Rubies | Rose bush, red roses—anything ruby red. |
| Twentieth | China | Set of buffet plates, antique platter, demitasse cups, dessert plates. | | Forty-fifth | Sapphire | Anything in the color. |
| | | | | Fiftieth | Gold | Money tree (tie rolled up bills or checks on a branch, add ribbons, flowers), a clock, gold satin sheets. |
| Twenty-fifth | Silver | Picture frame, antique serving piece. | | | | |
| Thirtieth | Pearls | Mother-of-pearl handled fish server, mother-of-pearl inlaid box. | | Fifty-fifth | Emeralds | Trip to Ireland, anything in the color. |
| Thirty-fifth | Coral | Piece of coral on a stand or in a case, anything coral colored, trip to a beach resort to find coral. | | Sixtieth | Diamonds | After this long, they deserve the real thing! Also anything diamond shaped, diamond-cut crystal. |

## Birthstones and Flowers by the Month

| | | | | | | |
|---|---|---|---|---|---|---|
| January | Garnet | Carnations | | July | Ruby | Larkspur |
| February | Amethyst | Violet | | August | Peridot | Gladiolus |
| March | Aquamarine | Jonquil | | September | Sapphire | Aster |
| April | Diamond | Sweet Pea | | October | Opal/tourmaline | Calendula |
| May | Emerald | Lily of the Valley | | November | Topaz | Chrysanthemum |
| June | Pearl/moonstone | Rose | | December | Turquoise | Narcissus |

## Signs, Symbols, and Colors of the Zodiac

| | | | | | | |
|---|---|---|---|---|---|---|
| Capricorn (Dec.21– Jan. 19) | Goat | Blue, green, red | | Cancer (June 21– Jul. 20) | Crab | Any blend of color |
| Aquarius (Jan. 20– Feb. 18) | Water Carrier | Deep scarlet | | Leo (Jul. 21– Aug. 21) | Lion | Red, blue |
| Pisces (Feb. 19– Mar. 20) | Fish | Purple | | Virgo (Aug. 22– Sep. 22) | Virgin | Brown, green, yellow, red |
| Aries (Mar. 21– Apr. 20) | Ram | Red, green | | Libra (Sep. 23– Oct. 22) | Scales | Blue-green |
| Taurus (Apr. 21– May 20) | Bull | Blue | | Scorpio (Oct. 23– Nov. 22) | Scorpion | Any blend of color |
| Gemini (May 21– June 20) | Twins | Green | | Sagittarius (Nov. 23– Dec. 20) | Archer | Gold |

# RECOMMENDED READING

Asher, Jane. *Jane Asher's Fancy Dress*. Salem, N.C.: Salem House, 1984.

Beadle, Ernst, Ronoldo Maja, and Denise Otis. *Decorating with Flowers*. New York: Harry N. Abrams, 1978.

Beldon, Louise Conway. *The Festive Tradition: Table Decorations and Desserts in America, 1650–1900*. London: W. W. Norton, 1983.

Bride's Magazine. *Bride's Book of Etiquette*. New York: Putnam, 1985.

Chiles, Fran. *Parties, Parties*. Houston: Gulf Publishing, 1984.

Dariaux, Genevieve Antoine. *Entertaining with Elegance*. New York: Doubleday, 1965.

Eisenberg, Arlene, Heidi, and Sandee. *The Special Guest Cookbook*. New York: Beaufort Books, 1982.

Guest, Cornelia. *The Debutante's Guide to Life*. New York: Ballantine Books, 1986.

Healey, Deryck. *The New Art of Flower Design*. New York: Random House, 1986.

Hetzer, Linda. *Fancy Folds*. New York: Hearst Books, 1987.

Loring, John, and Henry B. Platt. *The New Tiffany Table Setting*. Garden City, New York: Doubleday, 1981.

McCafree, Mary Jane; and Pauline Innis. *Protocol: The Complete Handbook of Diplomatic, Official, and Social Usage*. Washington, D.C.: Devon Publishing Company, 1985.

MacQueen, Sheila. *Sheila MacQueen's Complete Flower Arranging*. New York: Times Books, 1980.

Martin, Judith. *Miss Manners' Guide to Excruciatingly Correct Behavior*. New York: Warner Books, 1983.

———. *Miss Manners' Guide to Rearing Perfect Children*. New York: Warner Books, 1983.

Olney, Judith. *Judith Olney's Entertainment*. New York: Barron's Educational Series, 1981.

Reed, Marjorie, and Kalia Lulow. *Entertaining Year Round*. New York: Ballantine Books, 1983.

Ruffin, Lisa. *Leonard Tharp . . . An American Style of Flower Arrangement*. Dallas: Taylor Publishing, 1986.

Sage, Jeremy. *Jeremy's Birthday Party Book*. New York: Clarkson N. Potter, 1987.

Schinz, Marina. *Visions of Paradise*. New York: Stewart, Tabori & Chang, 1985.

Scoggin, Mary Irene, Genevieve Trimble, and Lynne White. *How to Grow Better Day by Day*. New Orleans: Garden Study Club of New Orleans and New Orleans Town Gardeners, 1987.

Spencer, Andrea. *Table Decoration*. New York: St. Martin's, 1985.

Stewart, Martha. *Entertaining*. New York: Clarkson N. Potter, 1982.

———. *Weddings*. New York: Clarkson N. Potter, 1987.

Weston, Carol. *How to Honeymoon*. New York: Harper & Row, 1986.

Wolfman, Peri, and Charles Gold. *The Perfect Setting*. New York: Harry N. Abrams, 1985.

Wyman, Donald. *Wyman's Gardening Encyclopedia*. New York: Macmillan, 1971.

# ACKNOWLEDGMENTS

There would be no book if it had not been for the vision and faith of our dear friend Lena Tabori; the perseverance of Mark Magowan, Reg Kahney, Deborah Sloan, Nancy Fish, Dana Cole, and Ginny Croft; the creative guidance of our brilliant art director, Jim Wageman; the unique eye on entertaining of our illustrator, Philippe Weisbecker; the artistic spark of our sensational principal photographer, Lizzie Himmel; the creative skills of our in-house etiquette expert, Ron Misiur; Peter Meltzer, our consultant for wine and spirits; our innovative New York flower stylist, Paul Bott of Twigs; and our fabulous New York photo stylists, Maura McEvoy and Stephen Earle; the backing of our publisher, Bob Abrams; the resourcefulness of our picture researchers, Deborah Bull and Mary Z. Jenkins of Photosearch, Inc., New York; our research director/microcomputer applications expert, Hilary Brookes; Anne Strachan Crounse of Lucullus for her invaluable antiquarian expertise and flower arranging; Lydia Schloring for her dedicated caption research; Carol Vogel of *New York Times Magazine* and Jordan Schaps of *New York Magazine* for their creative input; and Lynne White for her valuable expertise in the area of children's parties.

Unending gratitude is due the two most wonderful mothers-in-law in the world, Kay Church and Jeanne Bultman, who have loved us like their own.

We offer our special heartfelt thanks to all of the people whose names and homes appear within these pages. It is their spirit and personality that have brought this book to life. We give our deep appreciation to our friends, old and new ones, who provided the glorious locations for photography: Ellis Bultman, Judi and David Burrus, Kent and Charles Davis, Patrick Dunn, Dr. Larry Hill, the Heumann family, Rosie and Pierre Levai, Mary Lou and John Ochsner, Sandra and Arthur Pulitzer, Caroline and Stephen Sontheimer, Denise and Louis Vallon, and the Windsor Court Hotel. We are indebted to all of these friends who gave of their time, ideas, and hospitality so that this book could be a reality.

To those gracious friends who acted as assistants, researchers, advisers, and sounding boards to us, we want you to know how deeply we appreciate all you gave so generously: Rebecca Atwater, Debby and Dennis Barek, Lee Barnes, Sally Belk, Bill Bell, Princess Yashodhara Scindia Bhansali, Robert D. Bjork, Sue Blair, Bill Blass, Mario Buatta, Anthony Bultman, Alma Campbell, Emery Clarke, Dathel Coleman, Al Copeland, Sharon Donovan Dodd, Karl R. Ewald III, Judy Feagin, John Funt of Tiffany, Greenleaf Wholesale Florist, the Heumann's of Rohm's Floral Design, John Jay, Peggy Kennedy, Elaine Lehman, Judith Martin, Rose Monroe, Bo Niles, Warren Platner, Karen Radkai, Ann Scharffenberger, M. I. Scoggin, Elizabeth Swanson, and Marybeth Weston.

To those whose names do not appear within these pages but who have shared their ideas, talents, and thoughts on entertaining with us—and to whom we especially dedicate this book—thank you so much, we couldn't have done it without you: Mimi and Herschel Abbott, Ervin Aden, Barbara and Wayne Amedee, Diane Amos, Stacy D. Anderson, Anichini Linea Casa, Sparky and Jay Arceneaux, Eve Arnold, Nancy and Albert Aschaffenburg, the Avant Garde Club, Emmylou Badger, Suzanne and Ben Bagert, Noel and Elaine Bailey, Pamela P. Bardo, Audrey Barnett, Carolyn Bartell, JoAnn Barwick, Wilma Bass, Fred Bates, Dorian Bennett, Lewis Bergman, Bernard and Eric Bernard, Marilyn Bethany, Darlene and Cappy Bisso, Heidi and Gretchen Bjork, Helen Boehm, Marilyn and Varujan Boghosian, Betty Boote, John and Priscilla Bosman, Victoria Legg Bourke, Lynn Bowker, Manny Bryan, Miffy Walton Bright, Ann Britain, Louisette Brown, Tom Buckholtz, Marguerite Butler, Dick Campbell, Jacquee Carvin, John and Diane Cashman, Ladd Chandler, Vickie Chandler, Chris and Joan Church, Frank Cina, Beverly Clark, Ed Clark, Peter Claverie, Mrs. Ralph Clement, Betty Coleman, Marti and Peter Coleman, Shirley Trusty Corey, Cowboy, Crescent City Depression Glass Society, Emily and Bob Cronin, Suzie Cronin of Suzo, Marilyn and Bob Crowley, Edgar Cullman of General Cigars, Margie and Walker Davis, Claudia Demien, Pat Denechaud, Gilbert Denman, Alice Depass, George DeVille, Peter Doodeheefren, Dr. Peter Dorsett, Bitsy Duggins, Mimi and Charles DuPre, Jacques Durand, Patricia Egan, America and Ed Ellinghausen, Mary Elliott, Charles Engelhart, Lynne Farwell, Kit Favrot, Sybil Favrot, Barbara Feldberg, Bee Fitzpatrick, Jessica Fitzpatrick, Peter Flanagan, Mey Fleming, Pete Fountain, David Gaillard, Pat Gallagher, Pat Galloway, Kathy Gandolfo, Mary Lynn and Gavin Garrett, Jacqueline Gonnet, Cynthia Goodman, Robert Gordy, Lois Gore, Adele and "B" Graham, Kaaren Parker Gray, Elaine Greene, G. G. and Mary Madison Griswold, Lou Gropp, Tommy Guidry, Foster Guillory, Jr., Bernard Guste, Mimi and Roy Guste, Miki Gutman, Dr. Stephen Hales, Lily Harmon, Debbie Harris of Corey's, Barbara Hawkins, Louise Heebe, Mark Higgins, John Hodge, Ann Holden, Budd Hopkins, Vicki Hrivnak, Brian Huber, The Human Performance Center at Southern Baptist Hospital, Carol Hoyt, Alixe Carpenter Hugret, Richard Jackson, Dabney Jacob, Zully Jiminez, Samantha Jones, Lin Jordan, Virginia and Ingersoll Jordan, Jan Katz, Danny Kaye, Kell Kelly, Barry Kern, Blaine Kern, Jr., Joe Kernke, Robert E. Kerrigan, Rose Lee King, April Kingsley, Kinko's, Krön Chocolatier, La Casa, Janice Lachman, Yvonne LaFleur, Carole Lalli, Ronnie LaMarque, Jule Lang, Ruth Latta, Chip LaGrange, Gay Le Breton, Joanie Lehmann, Barbara and Thomas Lemann, Roz Lewy, Little Rickie, Ann Logan, Dib and Skipper Logan, Sammi Lott, Irene Lutkewitte, Alice Lynch, Russell MacMasters, Duncan Maginnis, Archie and Olivia Manning, Robert and Suzie Marcus, Lea Marten, Rose Martinez, Kay and John Maybank, Charlotte Mayerson, Gay Noe McClendon, McIntyre Services, Inc., Shawn McKenna, Amy McMichael, Tom McWilliams, Donald Meyer, Schafer Mickal, Marsha Mitchell, Kerry Moody, Bobbie Miller, Maddie Mix, Gus Mijalis, Irene Morrah, Robert Motherwell, Marianne and Alan Mumford, Marilyn Munson, Vance Muse, Kevin Myrick, May Najola, Paul Newman, Robert Newman, Lisa Newsom of *Veranda,* Nell Nolan, Nancy O'Connell, Marguerite and David Oestricher, Dodie and Frederick Oppenheimer, Denise Otis, Connie Parker, Jean Percy, Hunter Pierson, Sidney Pierson, Debbie and Eads Poitevent, James Polster, Barbara Portsch, Kris Pottharst, Carol and Wilmer Poynor, Carol Pulitzer, Ian Quimby of Winterthur, Elizabeth Rack, Bill and Em Ralke, Joanne Ranger, Wayne Ray, William Rayner, Byrne Reese, Archie Reeves, Wendy and Boatner Reilly, Renny Reynolds, Page Rhinebeck, Betty Richards, Margaret Weese Riley, Suzie and John Ringer, Suzanne Stamps Rheinstein, Jim Roberts, Bud and Judy Robinson, Leota Robinson, Evelyn Clark Rogers, Charles and Glenna Roper, Hayne Rudolf, Marilyn and Basil Rusovich, Pam Ryan, Andree Samson, Judith and Chuck Sanders, Wilmer Sarrazin, Bronson Saunders, Nell and Gordon Saussy, Claire Schelli of Esto Photographics, Ken Schiff of D. F. Sanders Hardware, John and Melinda Schwegmann, Babs Simpson, Lea Sinclair, Marion Simpson, Debbie Slimp, Debbie Smallpage, Snowmass Resort Association, Nora Speyer, Myron Stout, Geraldine Stansbury, Duncan Strachan, Rose Strachan, Curt and Fleur Strand, Harold and Mathilde Stream, The Sun Porch, Clarke Swanson, Harold Tani, Emma Tanner, Carol Taylor, Phyllis and Patrick Taylor, Caroline and Jim Theus, Roxanne Thomas, Guy Thompson, Claire Steinart Thorn, Joe Ann Thurman, Mervyn and Edie Trail, Ann and Britton Trice, Rivers Trussell, Gina Vernaci, Jim Vial, Martha and Foster Walker, Andy Warhol, Steven and Jeanie Waters, Meade Wenzel, Gayle Wertz, Carol Weston, Sue Whitmore, Ann Wilkinson, Mrs. Chauvin Wilkinson, Ruth Wilkinson, Nina Williams, Susan Williams, Dian Winingder, Trevor Wisdom, Kit Wohl, Wendy Wolfe, Susan Woolhandler, Chiqui Woolworth, Suzanne E. Wren of Drucilla Handy Company, John Yuhasz, and Cynthia Zarin.

We owe the rich character of our photographs to all of those party planners, antiques shops, floral designers, creative consultants, and interior designers who have offered us their advice, the loan of their objects, and their willingness to share their expertise. In New Orleans: Adler's, Amistad Research Center at Tulane University, Antoine's Restaurant, Ballunacy, Nathan Bering Agency, Pontchartrain Hotel, Bremermann Designs, Confetti Corner, Davis Gallery, Happi Names, Holden and Dupuy, Hotel Dieu, Junior League of New Orleans, La Marquise Bakery, Jule Lang, Les Rubans, Louisiana Archives and Trade Labels, Lucullus, J. Allen Murphy, New Orleans Jazz and Heritage Foundation, Panache, Mike Posey Photography, Rohm's Floral Designs, Sculptures Inc., Storyland at City Park, Morrell Taggart, Temple Sinai Gift Shop, Tender Lovin' Chocolates, Tilden Foley Gallery, Mario Villa Gallery, Windsor Court Hotel.

In New York: Didier Aaron, Anichini, Arcadia, Baccarat, Bardith, Gretchen Bellinger Inc., Bernadaud, Helen Boehm, Buccellati, Clodagh Ross & Williams, Cullman & Kravis, Pierre Deux, Fitz and Floyd, Gear, General Cigars, The Ghiordian Knot, Glorious Food, Yves Gonnet, James II Galleries, Kentshire Galleries, Little Rickie, Marlo Flowers Ltd., Charlotte Moss & Co., Naga Antiques, Noguchi, Platypus, Primavera, James Robinson, D. F. Sanders Hardware, Thaxton & Company, Tiffany, Alexandra Troy Catering, Twigs, Villeroy and Boch, Wolfman Gold & Good, Yale Burge Antiques, Inc., Zézé.

*Photographers*
A debt of gratitude is due our team of photographers who have shared with us their magnificent portrayals of American entertaining. Their last names appear following the captions to their work: Peter Aaron/Esto, Jaime Ardiles-Arce, Ernst Beadle, Glade Bilby II, G. Andrew Boyd, Emerick Bronson, Karen Bussolini, Candice Cutrone, Nancy A. Davis Productions, Carlos Domenech, Daniel Eifert, Phillip Ennis, Tina Freeman, Nadine Froger, Alexander Georges, Joshua Greene, Tom Grosscup, Brian Hagiwara, Drucilla Handy Company, Ted Hardin, Elizabeth Heyert, Lizzie Himmel, Richard Jeffery, Peter J. Kaplan, Ronnie Kaufman/The Stock Market, Margaret LeCorgne, Liza-Nina, Helaine Messer, J. Barry O'Rourke/The Stock Market, Randy O'Rourke/The Stock Market, Bo Parker, Kimberly Parsons, Tim Proctor/Tatum, Toomey & Whicker, Louis Psihoyos, Rod Salazar, Marina Schinz, Keith Simms/Tatum, Toomey & Whicker, Michael Skott, Ezra Stoller/Esto, Erika Stone, Peter Vitale, and Burton Whicker/Tatum, Toomey & Whicker.

*Stylists*
Betty Blau: 263; Bethany Ewald Bultman: 18, 19, 30, 49, 50, 82, 102, 109, 110, 118, 119, 131–38, 135, 136, 141, 155, 163, 169, 171, 176, 184, 219, 242, 262, 264, 265, 275, 297; Terese Carpenter: 19, 51; John Chuck and Louis Mawcintt of TVI (party design/stylists): 298; Beverly Reese Church: 30, 31, 88, 102, 172, 190, 210, 212, 213, 215, 239, 241, 253, 265; Confetti Corner, Inc.: 240; Patsy Corbin: 138, 139, 145; John Daly: 114–15; Kent Davis: 124; Claudia Demien: 29; Anna de Ravel: 4–5, 158; Stephen Earle: 182; Peter Flanagan: 41, 101, 106; Kim Freeman: cover, 15, 147; Patrick Gallagher: 69, 73, 131; Glorious Food (party design and food): 18; Jimmy Hernandez (flower stylist): 182, 188; Karen Kleber: 152; Chip La Grange: 147; Penny Wisner Link (food stylist): 182; Yoshiko Loomis (food stylist): 182; Gerald Lowe: 272; Becky McDermott: 9, 13, 202–3; Maura McEvoy: 104, 113, 119, 120, 124, 132, 151, 178, 199, 201, 204, 205, 216, 239, 259, 261, 270; Kerry Moody: 15, 175; Dana Mumro: 144; Dennis O'Brien: 79; Mary Lou Ochsner: 76, 88; Donna Paitchel of Summit Productions (party design): 220, 286; Marlo Phillips of Marlo Flowers Ltd. (flower stylist): 18, 104, 112, 113; Tom Pierce (flower stylist): 286, 298; Kris Pottharst: 241; Dennis W. Sangster: 75, 83; Craig Santa: 238; Jordan Schaps (creative consultant/art director): 81, 179, 250; Sally Schneider (food stylist): 263; Marion Simpson: 184; Caroline Wogan Sontheimer: 44; Martha Stewart: 26, 223; Sarah Truslow: 46; Anita Walker: 110; Donald Bruce White (food stylist): 208.

# INDEX